THE 'OVERLAND' TO CHINA

ARCHIBALD R. COLQUHOUN

THE 'OVERLAND' TO CHINA

ARCHIBALD R. COLQUHOUN

WITH FRONTISPIECE, ILLUSTRATIONS, AND MAPS

ISBN : 978-93-5324-551-1 (HB)

First Published, London, 1900

Published, 2020

Published by

Facsimile Publisher
12 Pragati Market
Ashok Vihar, Ph-2
Delhi-110052
E-mail: books@facsimilepublisher.com

Printed at: G. Print Process, Delhi.

Ceylon in the Juilee Year

Author: John Ferguson

THE 'OVERLAND' TO CHINA

BY

ARCHIBALD R. COLQUHOUN

GOLD MEDALLIST ROYAL GEOGRAPHICAL SOCIETY; FORMERLY DEPUTY COMMISSIONER, BURMA;
ADMINISTRATOR OF MASHONALAND, SOUTH AFRICA;
AND SPECIAL CORRESPONDENT OF THE 'TIMES' IN THE FAR EAST;
AUTHOR OF 'CHINA IN TRANSFORMATION,' ETC.

WITH FRONTISPIECE, ILLUSTRATIONS, AND MAPS

LONDON AND NEW YORK
HARPER & BROTHERS
45, ALBEMARLE STREET, W.
1900

CONTENTS

ILLUSTRATIONS

ILLUSTRATIONS

MAPS

NOTE.—Many of the illustrations are reproduced by the permission of M. Hachette and Messrs. Virtue, from the *Géographie Universelle* of E. Réclus.

INTRODUCTION

The completion of the Trans-Siberian Railway, connecting in one unbroken line the Baltic and the China sea, will mark in a fitting manner the commencement of a new century.

The enthusiasm of the Russian government and people for this grand enterprise is not without reason, for since the discovery of the Cape route to the Indies by Vasco da Gama, almost since the discovery of America by Columbus, no human achievement has been so pregnant with consequences to mankind at large.

Intimately related to other phenomena in the Far East—the wonderful evolution of Japan, the no less amazing collapse of the Chinese Empire, the sudden appearance of the United States as a colonizing power in the Western Pacific, and other like changes —the Siberian Railway possesses an importance far beyond its merely industrial, commercial, or even strategical uses, immense as these are, *beyond* the territory of Russia itself. For with it is interwoven the whole chain of causes destined to entirely revolutionize the Far East.

These considerations induced the writer in 1898–99 to visit Siberia and the border-lands of China on the north, and to pass across the latter country from north to south. He made the journey from European Russia to the temporary terminus of the Trans-Siberian Railway at Lake Baikal, and thence by the Gobi Desert, in Eastern Mongolia, to Peking—a possible railway route which may yet connect the Chinese capital by a short cut with the administrative and commercial centre of Eastern Siberia. Journeying subsequently through that portion of China which is now of most interest to the British and American peoples, he ascended the Yangtsze River as far as its navigation-limit, and from Szechuan proceeded southward by way of the two southwestern provinces, Kweichau and Yunnan, to the Red River, completing the journey at Haiphong.

Some seven thousand miles were traversed, chiefly overland, the journey being accomplished by means of rail and tarantass, camel, camel-cart, and mule-litter, native Chinese boat and saddle pony, mule, and sedan-chair. The variety in the modes of travel was equalled by the diversity of races encountered on the way—European Russians and Siberians, Buriats and Mongols, Manchus and the Chinese of North and of Southwest China, the interesting aboriginal tribes of Yunnan and Kweichau, and, finally, the Tongkingese under French rule.

The fact that such a journey—from the Baltic to the Gulf of Tongking—was made, allowing for various sojourns *en route*, within a period of seven months, affords a striking proof of the changes which are in progress and of the rate at which distances are being annihilated in Asia. So rapid, indeed, are these changes that in the near future—when, by means of the railway, the whole journey from Europe, *via* Peking, to Central China will be accomplished in fifteen days—the magnitude of the Asiatic continent will have become a mere tradition among travellers.

The writer had made many journeys in China, north and south, during the past twenty years: had explored the southwest provinces and their borderlands towards India; served through the French campaign in Tongking as correspondent of the *Times;* and, as recently as 1896–97, made a careful study on the spot of the political and financial changes in progress in the Chinese capital, visiting also Japan. But the questions arising are both diverse and unexpected, while the general problems coming up for solution are so complex and so grave that even personal knowledge becomes obsolete, and it is impossible for the most earnest student of newspapers and books to follow intelligently the progress of events without frequently renewing and extending his studies from the life.

The present work is the result of such fresh observations, and an attempt to interest the general reader and give him an idea of the ground by presenting, without elaboration, a series of impressions of the conditions, physical and political, under which the Trans-Siberian Railway will shortly become an accomplished fact. Much of the information is drawn from original sources, and the whole is connected by a thread of the writer's personal experiences.

SIBERIA

OVERLAND TO CHINA

CHAPTER I

SIBERIA: THE CONQUEST

UNTIL quite recently "Siberia," to the idle consideration of the "man in the street," represented merely a vast, untraversable waste, vaguely attached to the outskirts of Russia; a gray wilderness of snow-weighted fir-trees, at "the back of beyond," where the few hours of struggling light in the twenty-four but served to deepen the numb despair of the succeeding darkness, and a gleam of filtered warmth in August represented all of summer the inhabitants were ever to know; a region where there were "mines," and therefore must be mineral wealth; eternal snow and ice, and therefore "furs." But chiefly, perhaps, he would picture it as the horrible *oubliette* where the few free spirits who dared to express the general thought in Russia might be dropped out of the world—to languish until death brought the merciful ukase of release.

But a new era is upon us, and even the average member of the general public, amid the eternal re-echo of other "questions of the day," begins to realize that Siberia is being transformed into as essential a part of Russia as is St. Petersburg: a huge limb, hitherto inert, but to which, even now, muscle and nerve are being supplied, and which, when the last section of the great Siberian Railway is laid, will be ready to strike out with the lusty vigor of youth.

It is curious how invariably these Slavonic achievements have come as a surprise to the world. For years, even for centuries, Russia pursues her way by parallel routes to many goals, unheard and out of sight. The world, unsuspicious and indifferent, at most vaguely supposes that "Russia is busy at something" in Central Asia, or "intriguing again" towards the East; until the day when, after the accomplished fact, she emerges, smiling benevolently at the world's simplicity, on the frontiers of Afghanistan and the shores of the Pacific, with Herat and Teheran, Port Arthur and Peking alike in the hollow of her hand. In the very year, for instance, that the world's attention was focussed on Sevastopol, and the British people were fondly imagining that Russian power lay stunned at their feet, two of the most pregnant achievements in Asian history were consummated — the defiant seizure by Russia of the Amur River, and the occupation of the Zailüsk Altai slopes — giving, on the one hand, access to the open sea, and, on the other, complete command of Central Asia. Bloodless and unapplauded victories these, but further reaching in their probable influence on the world's history than ten campaigns of

Inkermans and Almas. This faculty of ours for chronic surprise is in itself astonishing, for Russian aims and methods are neither new, disguised, difficult of comprehension, nor liable to change. They follow in infallible sequence.

Even now, while the average man in the States and in Europe, in his efforts to be "up to date," is bit by bit digesting the situation — Russia on the Pacific; Russia practically mistress at Constantinople, Teheran, and Peking; Russia overhanging Afghanistan, and with Kashgaria at her mercy — that situation is changing as he muses. Siberia, to take one instance — and Russians make no secret of it — has already fulfilled her *raison d'être*, in opening the way to the ocean; and from the rich valleys of Manchuria it is no longer towards the Amur that Russians now look, but towards the British sphere, the Yangtsze. The Siberian stage lasted three hundred years and terminated at Port Arthur; the stage now commencing will last how long? will end where?

Never in the history of the world were such areas as those of Siberia brought under an empire's rule at so ridiculously small a cost. Of men and treasure, at least, the Russian expenditure has been insignificant; practically, time and patience—two essentially Eastern qualities — have been the factors employed. And what an empire it is that has been thus quietly and unostentatiously subjugated! Magnificent enough, if itself the crown and summit of a country's ambition; but how significant when regarded as merely a stage on the road to greater ends; as but an antechamber, a desert threshold to the promised land of Russian "destiny"—the Golden South!

The term "Siberia" covers, in its broadest sense, the whole of Russia's Asiatic dominions except Trans-Caucasia, the Trans-Caspian territory, and Russian Turkistan, though in its narrowest sense limited to the Original Siberia, which included only the governments of Tobolsk and Tomsk (Western Siberia), and those of Yenisseisk and Irkutsk (Eastern Siberia).

Administratively it is divided into five regions, corresponding roughly to the basins of the five great rivers, Obi, Yenisei, Lena, Amur, and Ili. These regions are, (1 and 2) the Western and Eastern Siberia already referred to; (3) the Yakutsk, (4) the Amur and coast, and (5) the Steppe regions. The Amur and coast region is subdivided into three territories—Trans-Baikalia, the Amur, and the Littorale—and the Steppe region into the Akmolinsk, Semipalatinsk, and Semirechensk provinces.

With the acquisition of Manchuria a readjustment of the Eastern administrative divisions will, of course, be necessitated. Siberia, as thus so far defined, occupies an area twenty-five times greater than that of Germany, and one-fourteenth at least of this vast expanse is suited for agriculture. Consequently, whether regarded as a mere stage on the road which Russia has for generations been instinctively pursuing towards the warmth and light, the open seas, and the fertile wealth of the Sunny South; or whether its intrinsic value as a possession be alone taken into account, Siberia can in no case be dismissed as a *quantité négligéable*. The conquest of this vast dominion three centuries ago marked, indeed, a scarcely more important epoch than will be reached when to-morrow sees communications by rail and steamer opened up throughout its area, and the imperfectly known, but at any rate colossal, potentialities thrown wide open to the world. The twentieth century will provide no more vital problem than the readjustments necessitated when East and West are thus for the first time brought border to border.

From the point of view of our superior information, it seems astonishing that territories such as these—well-watered, inexhaustibly rich in minerals, timber, pasture, corn-lands, and fisheries—should, until even quite recently, have remained unknown for anything but an untraversable wilderness, banishment to which was held a greater penalty than death. But the old impression was to some extent justified. The natural difficulties of "the coldest country of the Old World" are so immense as to be, in a sense, insurmountable. The climate can nowhere be called a "white man's climate," five months of vegetation being the most that can be reckoned on even in the agricultural zone. North of this comparatively narrow belt running east and west through the country are thousands and thousands of square miles of tangled forest and morass, into which the boldest trapper dare not penetrate, and avoided, it is said, even by wild animals. Beyond this, again, lie vast tracks of polar *tundra* country, where nothing grows but mosses and lichens; where the earth is stiff with frost the whole year round, and—if reindeer and dogs be excepted—no domestic animal can live. A region abandoned to starving tribes of Samoyeds and Yakuts, and doomed, it would seem forever, to Arctic desolation.

There was, in the beginning, no premeditated or carefully considered policy. The conquest of Siberia resulted rather from a natural overflow of population than from prescient statecraft. Dominion grew rather than was built up, though, since the time of Peter the Great, Russian statesmen have been zealous to assist the crystallizing process, both in its expansions and consolidations.

The question next most vital to that of climate is the one of means of communication over the vast distances involved—a problem that is now on the point of solution. The chief waterways of Siberia, with the marked exception of the Amur, run northward, at right angles to the trend of traffic, and discharge into ice-bound seas which cannot be regarded as open to navigation. But the Siberian Railway will, to a great extent, remedy this drawback, and will bind and connect the present rather straggling centres of population, running, as it were, a nervous backbone through the land. If the real conquest of Siberia dated, as the Russians say, from the falling of the first grain of corn into the conquered soil, her final elevation to civilized rank must be held to commence from the day when the first train from Europe rushes through to the Pacific.

As early as the twelfth century the Russians of Novgorod already knew of the Ural Mountain Tartars and their wealth in peltry, and occasionally raided them. But it was not till four centuries later, under Ivan IV., that definite relations grew up. The Russians, having made themselves masters of the Volga basin, gradually extended towards the Urals, and at the epoch mentioned had reached their western slopes. This chain, marking the Eurasian frontier, offers no abrupt and rocky barrier to progress eastward, but is a gently undulating line of hills, bearing the character rather of a connection than a division. Only by contrast with the plains of European Russia could the Urals be regarded as "mountains."

Thus far had the Volga pioneers penetrated by the middle of the sixteenth century. They were principally outlaws, fur-traders, and trappers, with very little to distinguish them, outwardly at least, from the Tartar horsemen with whom they came into contact. Wrapped in furs, mounted on small shaggy horses, armed with lances and scimitars, of more or less Kalmuck cast of feature, it was but the *idea* of allegiance to a European over-lord that gave them cohesion against the wandering tribes who owned no common chief. The advance to the Urals was, doubtless, not accomplished in one journey, but, from camping-ground to camping-ground, over a period of months and even years. We can picture the first party of Cossacks sighting the Urals after traversing the monotonous and almost interminable plains that stretch from the Volga. At break of day, perhaps—the sun sending back their shadows in giant patches along the road they had come—they pulled up their wiry little horses, and, standing in their stirrups while they shaded their eyes, saw for the first time, across the rose-tinted desert, those hills which marked the *omne ignotum* of their magnificent dreams. The refraction of the sun's morning rays on vast sandy steppes tends, it is well known, to magnify objects. Thus may the Urals, indeed, have appeared to them mountains when viewed from afar.

On reaching the western slopes of the Urals, there was nothing to prevent these early pioneers from crossing into the then unknown Siberia, and commencing a barter-trade with the wandering Tartars of the other side—a barter which was probably not always in favor of the simple native; for a Russian proverb, with what appears a touch of unconscious admiration, still says, "Honest as a Tartar." Occasionally these pioneers are said to have levied "yassak"—a tax on furs—from the tribes they encountered. This "yassak" collection was indeed to be, later on, the usual form by which the Cossack introduced himself. One can, however, hardly imagine that this could be effected without at any rate a display of force; and the earliest Russian pioneers can have had no visible power or prestige at their back. Moreover, they are believed to have re-

YAKUTS (AMUR) STARTING ON JOURNEY WITH PACK DEER

mained, until the conquest, on fairly good terms with the natives beyond the Urals. As a matter of fact, they were probably received more or less on sufferance, as were the Russian merchants in parts of Central Asia till the other day—content, for the sake of a small profit, to endure indignities from the natives whom their countrymen were ultimately destined to absorb. More Asiatic than European, the Russian is at once in sympathy with Yakut, Kirghiz, or Tunguz; and, while in the wilds, is very content to do as the wild man does. He preserves, however, though dissembled for the time, his national traits, and has, throughout his occupation of Siberia, been known to degenerate only in the Yakutsk region, under the brutalizing effect of extreme cold.

The most prominent feature in the history of the Siberian conquest is the extraordinary vigor of private enterprise shown. Many of the most important advances—among them the first organized expedition across the Urals—were due to individual initiative, so much so that the story of early Siberia resolves itself into the history of the Stroganovs, Yermaks, Khabarovs, Demidovs, and—most illustrious name of all—Mouraviev Amursky. These led the way and carved out whole empires. Government then approved, confirmed, and developed. Scientific expeditions set the final seal. This sequence, in its general lines the same as that followed by the Anglo-Saxon—in contradistinction to the French and German methods, where official protection usually long precedes any interests that may subsequently grow up to be protected — has now been replaced in Russia by one in which the scientific expedition leads the way.

The Stroganovs, to whom the first armed expedition into Siberia was due, were an immensely rich family flourishing in the reign of Ivan IV. The Tsar had originally granted them large tracts of land in European Russia, along the Kama River, on condition that they should build towns, develop industries, raise troops, and defend the region from the incursions of "barbarian hordes," as the Russians called the Tartars (and the Tartars called them). They may, in fact, be considered the Slav equivalent of their contemporaries, the East India Company, and the prototype of the chartered company of modern days. That the country beyond the Urals was not entirely a *terra incognita* to them is proved by the fact that the course of the Obi and the site of a town called Tiumen are marked on a map dating from before the armed conquest of the region. The commercial agents of the Stroganovs had, in fact, frequently visited the kingdom of Kuchum Khan, and were received as friends where the Russians, a year or two later, were to take possession as masters. The first Stroganov settlements along the Kama succeeded to such an extent that their domains were extended by the Emperor, and permission given for offensive as well as defensive operations—and beyond the Urals!

About this time—*i. e.*, towards the end of the sixteenth century, in the reign of Ivan, surnamed "The

Terrible"—many peasants had fled their homes and sought liberty and space in the vast tracts beyond the Volga. From these coigns of vantage, however, they frequently harried the Tsar's settled territories, and became, in consequence, outlawed. Such a band of Don Cossacks, who had, under their leader Yermak, made themselves conspicuous by their free-booting exploits, eluded the pursuit of the imperial troops on one occasion by retreating up the river Kama, and so reaching the Stroganov possessions. Here they were a welcome addition to the forces, and were at once offered service.

The Stroganovs, profiting by the Tsar's permission, in 1579 organized and equipped an armed expedition for the country beyond the Urals. The nucleus of this little army of eight hundred men was Yermak's troop, and he was given the command of the expedition. Setting out in the next spring, he met and defeated the Tartar prince Yepancha on the banks of the river Tura. Continuing his advance while the summer lasted, he took up his quarters when winter set in on the site of the present town of Tiumen. The following year he marched on "Isker," or "Sibir," the capital of Kuchum Khan, the most powerful of the Tartar princes and a direct descendant of Genghis Khan. When at last he reached the town, late in the year, his force was reduced one-half, but he must attack or perish. After desperate fighting—the Tartars, being armed solely with bows and arrows, lances and swords—the town was carried by assault.

How this success was possible against a vastly superior number it is difficult to imagine. Cannon of a clumsy type may have been used by the Cossacks, though it was a long distance to have dragged them, but neither side had probably the advantage of small fire-arms. Against sword and lance, the bows and arrows of the defenders, fighting behind ramparts, could not but prove effective; and, man to man, the bronzed Tartar must have been nearly a match for even the war-seasoned Cossack. The Tartars, moreover, were a warlike race, fighting—for very existence—on their own ground. Whereas the Cossacks were attacking in an unknown country, and were separated from their base by such distances that half their number had succumbed on the way, in battle or from fatigue. They were, it is true, also fighting for dear life, anything short of victory meaning, on either side, extermination; and they had the prestige of the huge power behind them, of that "Great White Tsar" of whom even the Tartars must have heard.

Thus, on the 25th of October, 1581, the robber outlaw Yermak was able to report to the Tsar—"Lord Ivan Vasilevich"—the conquest of a new "Siberian kingdom," while, at the same time, suing for pardon. This was readily granted, and the messenger was handed by his Majesty a cloak and a medal, as rewards for the victorious Cossack. In a *bilina* upon the conquest, well known in Russian popular poetry, Yermak exclaims:

ASIA

Showing successive advances of Russia.

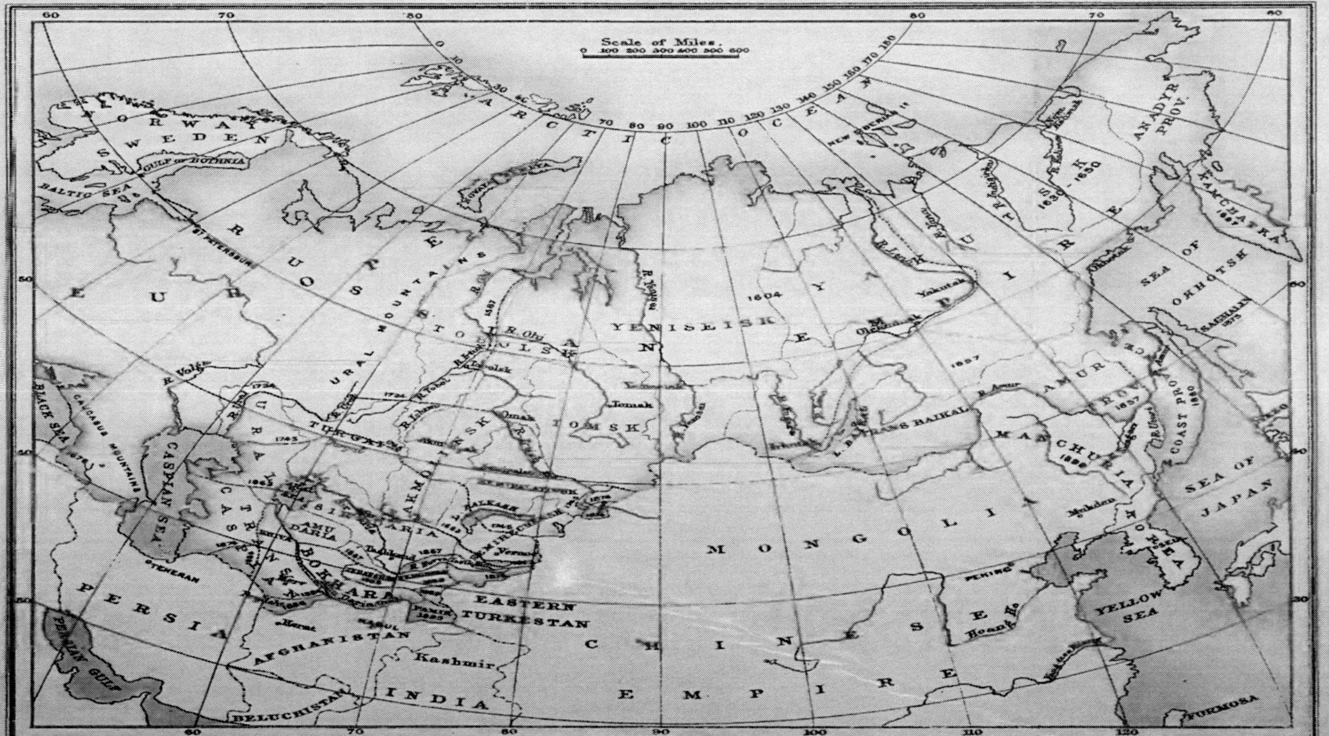

London & New York, Harper & Brothers, 45 Albemarle Street, W.

F. S. Weller, F.R.G.S. lith.

COSSACK SENTINEL

"I am the robber Hetman of the Don.
'Twas I went over the blue sea, the Caspian;
And I it was who destroyed the ships:
And now, our hope, our Orthodox Tsar,
I bring you my traitorous head.
And with it I bring the Empire of Siberia.
And the Orthodox Tsar will speak,
He will speak, the terrible Ivan Vasilevich.
'Ha! thou art Yermak, the son of Timofei,
Thou art the Hetman of the warriors of the Don.
I pardon thee and thy band,
I pardon thee for thy trusty service,
And I give thee the glorious gentle Don as an inheritance!'"

Some five years later, three hundred regulars were sent from Moscow to Yermak's aid, supplemented soon after by other five hundred. They built the towns of Tiumen and Tobolsk, and other smaller ones, the town of Tobolsk standing, as it does to-day, on the site of the former capital of Kuchum. Ostrogs, or forts, were erected at the confluence of all the rivers.

In the meanwhile, however, in 1584, Yermak had fallen. Enticed too far from his base by Tartar cunning, he perished, with the whole of his band, on the banks of the Irtysh — an instance of "catching a Tartar" vouched for by history.

Russian power, thus introduced, quickly extended over the basins of the giant rivers Obi, Yenisei, and Lena. The usual *yassak* was collected, and a great trade in furs sprang up. In the founding of Russian sovereignty in these vast tracts of country complete occupation was, of course, out of the question. But control was effected through the establishment by the Cossacks of lines of fortified posts—at the junctions of rivers, the entrances of mountain passes, and at other strategic points. Between 1630 and 1640, small bands of Cossacks penetrated the country to its extreme limits—the Arctic Ocean and the Sea of Okhotsk. They discovered the minor Arctic rivers Indighirka, Yana, and Kolyma, as well as the volcano-girt peninsula of Kamchatka. The latter was explored afresh, and finally taken possession of in 1697.

The whole story of these and a hundred other Cossack expeditions is flavored with romance and desperate adventure. The early pioneers were men of absolute hardihood and courage. On their journey northeast, they had, first, to traverse thousands of square miles of birch woods and pasture-land; then still vaster tracts of tangled forest and swamp; and, finally, the polar *tundra* border of the frozen ocean, a wilderness rigid with eternal frost, barren and doomed.

Through such successive wastes these handfuls of Cossacks worked their way into the unknown beyond. Their original means of transport must have been almost *nil*, but doubtless they pressed into their service the tribes they vanquished in their wanderings, using them as porters, forcibly borrowing their *nartas*, or sledges—drawn in the forest zones by men or horses, in the polar *tundras* by reindeer or dogs—and, where the course of a river trended in

OSTIAK MAN AND WOMAN, TYPES AND COSTUMES

the required direction, forcing them to build rafts from the profusion of timber always available.

Half savage themselves, they would be able to subsist, with the Ostiak, on fox-flesh, eaten raw, intestines first; dig with the Buriat for roots stored in the prairie-dog's burrow; or, again with the Samoyed, feast on the half-digested green stuff taken from the reindeer's stomach. They would array themselves, with the Vogul, in thick furs and hoods adorned with the ears of animals, or, with the Yakuts, in coats of fishskin. They would share, with the Tunguz, the shelter of caves in hollow tree-trunks. And thus from day to day, levying food and clothing from the very wilderness, these intrepid pioneers made their way over snow-covered wastes and through hundreds of miles of silent forest, down broad, pine-fringed rivers and across bare, schist-strewn mountains, supporting the extremes of hunger, thirst, and cold.

When, finally, having fought their way through *taiga* and *tundra* and faced the dangers of bear and elk hunts, with the alternative of starvation, they emerged upon a human habitat, it was but to engage in a still deadlier struggle with superior forces of hostile nomads. Silent Samoyed and dull Buriat, gentle Tunguz and brutal Ostiak, alike fought hard against the invader. But it was the Koriats, inhabiting Kamchatka and the adjoining coast, who proved the most formidable, because fanatical, foe. When so hard-pressed by a better-armed enemy that victory was impossible, it was the Koriat mode to kill off women and children. Then the whaleskin-cuirassed warriors, having taken oath to "lose the sun" and "make a bargain with Death," rushed into the thick of their enemies and fell, each man fighting to the last.

In spite of these and many less obvious difficulties, the astonishing fact remains that mere handfuls of Cossacks did, in the first part of the seventeenth century, succeed in establishing Russian power along the shores of the Arctic Ocean and Sea of Okhotsk, an achievement which, considering the obstacles to be overcome and the means at their disposal, appears little short of miraculous.

A simultaneous advance was being made in a southeasterly direction, initiated by another hero, famous in Siberian story—Khabarov. Originally a farmer of Yakutsk, and afterwards a salt-boiler, this man volunteered to fit out at his own expense, and personally lead, an expedition to the distant Amur—the "Black Dragon River" of the Manchus. Leaving Yakutsk in 1649, Khabarov made his way down the river Olekma, and reached the Amur the following year. He destroyed a few Daur encampments, and then returned to Yakutsk to make report on the broad, deep river that he had discovered running through fertile valleys. His glowing description fired one hundred and fifty volunteers to join the venture, and at the head of these, and with three cannon provided by the authorities, Khabarov in 1651 again reached the Amur. There, at the junction of the Emuri (from which some authorities consider the name Amur to be derived), he built the station of Albazin, and went into winter-quarters. This was but a wooden, stockaded fort, but during two years Khabarov, making it his base, occupied—or, rather, commanded—the course of the Amur, and this in spite of repeated efforts of the Manchus to dislodge him.

News of this El Dorado having reached the Tsar's ears, in 1654 Khabarov was ordered to Moscow to report in person. He did not reappear on the scene, but, as the first conqueror of the virgin Amur, has given his name to the modern town of Khabarovka, the seat of the governor-generalship of the region. His successors, Stepanov, Pashkov, and others met with more indifferent success, the first being killed in fight with the Manchus, and the second finding it impossible to effect much with the diminished remnants of Khabarov's band left at his disposal. But a year later a body of fugitive criminals, anxious to win pardon, re-established Russian rule on the Amur, rebuilt the ruined station of Albazin, and for twenty years maintained their position in peace. During that time other forts or stockades were built, and the collection of *yassak* from the former tributaries, the Tunguzes, was recommended.

After this period of tranquillity, in 1685, a powerful army of fifteen thousand Manchus invested Albazin, and the garrison of five hundred men was compelled to abandon the post, which was then burned to the ground. Some were taken prisoners and were carried to Peking, where they founded the Russian Mission, which, with its teachers and priests, has lasted down to the present day. The Russians, however, returned with reinforcements in the same year, and rebuilt the fort, replacing the wooden stockade by earthworks. Again, in 1686, the Manchus laid siege, but a year later utter exhaustion obliged them to raise it. A period of negotiation followed, in which Chinese diplomacy redeemed the defeat of Chinese arms, and in 1689 the treaty of Nerchinsk confirmed the Amur to China. This diplomatic achievement remained effective for one hundred and sixty years—until the coming of Mouraviev Amursky.

From the end of the seventeenth century permanent colonization became gradually established in the other conquered territories; forts, cities, and "yamas" (post-stations) sprang up in that order; immigration was fostered and river communication opened. Perm, on the European side of the Urals, became the government base. Commerce was introduced—under such difficulties, however, that communication between the pioneer merchants and their Moscow correspondents could only be effected once a year. But, when once established, the merchant was amply rewarded by a monopoly of the trade, the chief articles of which were cloth, glass, porcelain, groceries, and spirituous liquors.

To unsupported private enterprise, again, was due the beginning of the mining industry, which has since become so important a factor in Siberian life and progress. A merchant named Demidov discovered, in 1723, the first mines in the Altai (or "Golden")

Mountains. He opened and worked them at his own expense until they were taken over by the crown in 1747, when they became, as they are now, the private property of the Emperor.

During the more troublous times of the Russian Empire "secret colonization" also aided in the absorption of the newly acquired territory of Siberia. Criminals and political refugees, outcasts and dissenters, forming companionships in adversity, established secret settlements hidden far away in the depths of the dense forest. Here many of them lived their lives through, undiscovered and unmolested, hunting, trapping, and fishing, gathering cedar-nuts, and sowing a little corn. The sable, fox, and squirrel supplied them with wearing apparel; the birch-woods provided building logs, bark for roofing, material for implements, and fuel. A happy, peaceful life, far "out of the hurly-burly" of Russian civilization and beyond the ken of penal codes. When chanced upon by government officials, these secret settlements were at first merely taxed, no questions being asked as to possible misdemeanors in the world they had retired from. But latterly this kind of irregular colonizing became so popular and assumed such dimensions that the government found themselves forced to interfere.

At this stage of the conquest expeditions of discovery and scientific surveys followed in rapid succession. The most famous among many remarkable sea-voyages—the tonnage of the craft, absence of all charts, and dangerous character of the ice-churned seas duly considered — was undoubtedly that of Vitus Berend (Bering), a Danish sailor in the service of Peter the Great. He commanded an expedition fitted out by that monarch with the express purpose of determining whether or not a strait divided the north of America from the northeastern region of Asia. Sailing from St. Petersburg in 1728 — the year of Peter the Great's death — he eventually emerged into the open sea beyond Bering Strait, in August, 1728, thereby effecting the object of his voyage. This daring navigator commanded a second expedition in 1741, and reached the American coast. Returning, weary and battered, he was shipwrecked on the island now called after him, was landed by his comrades, and died soon after on that lonely beach.

Bering's observations led to the gradual discovery and occupation by Russia of Alaska and other parts of the North American continent, ceded to the United States in 1867. Many heroic explorers followed in Bering's track, of whom the best known, perhaps, are Pribylov and Nordenskjöld.

It is worthy of note that British sailors made, as early as the sixteenth century, repeated, though more or less unsuccessful, attempts to discover the Arctic shores of the Old World, recently circumnavigated in their entirety by Nordenskjöld. The early attempts of Willoughby, Chancellor, and Burrough failed even to reach the Siberian coast, while Ket and Jackman, in 1580, did not get beyond the Kara Sea. Their objective was, laughably enough,

China, or "Kathay," which, trusting to the maps of the period, they hoped to reach by ascending the Obi to "Lake Kathay," from which it was supposed to spring. The Dutch, too, made several as little successful voyages. The last attempt on the part of navigators from Western Europe was the famous voyage of Hudson, in 1608, for about 1616 navigation of those seas was forbidden, even to Russian subjects, on pain of death, lest foreigners should discover the way to the Siberian shores.

The exploration of the Siberian coasts was thus long left to the Siberians themselves; and they undertook many voyages in locally built craft, intended originally for river navigation. Thus, in 1648, the Cossack Dezhniev sailed with a flotilla of seven vessels, ten men to each, from the mouth of the Arctic river Kolyma. He succeeded in weathering the northeast extremity of Asia and reaching Kamchatka, thereby solving the question which Bering, some seventy-seven years later, set out to determine, unaware that he had been forestalled. After many adventures of shipwrecks and land fights with the Chukchis, a branch of the gallant Koriats referred to above, and after founding the extreme northern station of Anadyr, with the help of but twenty-five survivors of the crews he had sailed with five years previously, Dezhniev returned safe and sound to the Kolyma in 1653.

The final eastward stage of the conquest of Siberia may be regarded as the crown and completion of all the rest, marking, as it did, an epoch in the history of Asia. It was no less than the seizure of the whole course of the Amur — a magnificent waterway, running for hundreds of miles along the modern frontier of Manchuria, and affording the communication with the Pacific so essential to the development of Siberia. A vast tract of fertile virgin country was, moreover, gained for Russian agriculture, the value of which was much enhanced by the means of transport at its very door. Politically, command of the Amur assured to Russia eventual control of the rich province of Manchuria —the cradle of the reigning dynasty of China—and enabled her, by a blow at the nerve-centres, to paralyze at her pleasure the huge organism known as the Chinese Empire.

All this was the work of one man, Mouraviev, and never was title better earned than his—"Amursky." No doubt the Russian instinct towards the open sea must sooner or later have ended in the same way, but Mouraviev Amursky anticipated fate — he cut a path direct to the ever-desired goal.

Immediately on his appointment as governor-general of Eastern Siberia, this statesman realized that the value of the vast region he ruled over for the Tsar depended almost as much on free communication with the Pacific, as the welfare of Egypt on the Nile. Mouraviev's first step was to send a Petropavlovsk transport to discover the mouth of the Amur. In doing this he had only the very half-hearted permission of his government to go upon, and was hampered by conditions and limitations.

But such a chief usually finds or inspires lieutenants worthy of him, and Mouraviev's ideas found an enthusiastic executor in Captain Nevelskoy. In the transport *Baikal*, the latter circumnavigated Sakhalin, till then not known to be an island. Sakhalin blocks the mouth of the Amur, whose stream divides, passing to north and south of it; and Nevelskoy soon discovered the estuary. But after no less than forty-five attempts he was still unable to enter the river itself.

Partially convinced, in spite of themselves, by Mouraviev's urgent and persistent representations, the Russian Government, in 1850, fitted out the "Amur Expedition," Nevelskoy being given the command. This officer fulfilled the promise of his previous voyage by planting the Russian military flag for the first time on the bank of the Amur, bringing the Giliak tribe under Russian protection, and founding the station of Nicolaevsk, on the Amur, sixteen miles from the sea. During 1851–53, other posts were established.

While the world was still deafened by the cannonading at Sevastopol, Mouraviev, after many appeals, received the imperial authority to "navigate the Amur." He immediately sent a notification of this intention to the Chinese, but, *without waiting for an answer*, set sail with a small though powerful flotilla on the 18th of May, 1854. Proceeding down the river Shilka, as the Cossack pioneers had done, he entered the Amur, and reached the Mariinsk anchorage a month after starting. There he joined hands with the land expedition of 1853; and morally, as well as actually, the whole course of the Amur —from the Russian upper reaches to the newly founded posts at its mouth—was thus, at one stroke, brought under the sovereignty of the Tsar. The suitability of the Amur basin for colonizing purposes was demonstrated at the same time as the utter impotence of the Chinese to defend it. Under General Korsakov, Mouraviev's successor, no time was lost in colonizing the river-banks. This continued at high pressure for several years, in spite of the passive dissatisfaction of the Chinese officials.

On the 16th of May, 1857, Mouraviev Amursky's self-appointed task was crowned by the treaty of Aigun—practically a Chinese cession to Russia of the whole of the north, or left, bank of the river. In the next year Russia commenced the "compulsory" colonization of the Amur province; and within two years' time twelve thousand colonists and sixty-one Cossack posts, or *stanitzas*, were established in it. Finally, in the year 1860, while in China French and English were winning, by force of arms and at great cost, bare treaty rights to be as barely observed, Count Ignatiev, alone and unsupported save for Russian prestige, concluded the treaty of Peking, giving into Russian rule the whole of the Amur and Ussuri basins forever.

Simultaneously with her advance towards the Pacific, and many other achievements above hinted at, Russia had been extending her Siberian conquest southwest — slowly but surely driving a wedge

C

KIRGHIZ HORSEMEN ON THE STEPPE

through the very heart of Asia. The methods employed were distinguished by a predominance of official over private enterprise, marking the importance of political as compared with industrial interests, of strategic over trading lines of advance. In a great measure, of course, these interests coincided, and the establishment of Russian rule was synonymous with the planting of Russian colonies. But in the main the arid steppes and salt, treeless marshes of Central Asia, though vitally important politically—as an *étape* in the Russian southward extension scheme—could offer but small inducement to the settler.

It was in the year 1731 that Russia commenced her advance into the steppes sparsely inhabited by the nomad Kirghiz race. From that date she moved forward step by step, sometimes halting but never retiring from a position once taken up. Tribe after tribe, weighed upon by her advance, and threatened on flank and rear by other tribes, who were seldom helpful against the common enemy, gave up the struggle and sought Russian protection. Such were received with effusive kindness, and *les petits cadeaux qui entretiennent l'amitié*, which Russia knows so well how to use in flattering a barbaric people. Decorations, rank, positions were bestowed on the chiefs, who quickly developed pride in their allegiance to the Great White Tsar.

The years 1824–34 saw the first settlements on the Kirghiz steppes; 1836–47 a ten years' delay, due to the resistance of an unusually patriotic and devoted Khan. The fertile lands of the Great Kirghiz Horde were then entered upon, and in 1854,—while defending herself at Sevastopol and inaugurating "the Kingdom of the East" on the Amur, the Titan occupied the Zailüsk Altai, and established Fort Vernoie—a centre from which she commanded the whole of Central Asia.

Fort Perovsk was built four years later on the lowlands of the Syr-Daria, and a chain of outposts established. About 1860 Russia decided on another stride forward—to complete the subjugation of the outlying Kirghiz and the lesser kingdoms of Turkestan. This object was attained within four years' time, when the fall of Tashkend brought all Turkestan practically under Russian rule; though the Khanates of Khiva and Bokhara are still, but only nominally, "vassal" to Russia. The task was completed in 1881 by the occupation of the Trans-Caspian province to the borders of Persia and Afghanistan, and by the laying of the Trans-Caspian railway.

By far the most important in this long series of acquisitions was that of the Trans-Ilian Altai and foot-hills of the Thian Shan mountains, the home of the Kirghiz. It was solely thanks to this *point d'appui* that Russia was enabled to conquer Turkestan; and its settlements, now strongly rooted in fertile country, and under a good climate, still form an invaluable connecting link between the solid Russian possessions to the north and her more vaguely defined spheres across the desert.

Far above the burning steppe the Russian settlers

have their homes, on rich soil watered from the melting snow-peaks. Above them, up the mountain, a belt of forest holds inexhaustible supplies of wood and fuel. Still higher—between eight and eleven thousand feet—are the cool Alpine pastures whither the disinherited Kirghiz, confined to certain prescribed tracks as they pass through the Russian zone, wend their way for summer grazing. A comparatively mild winter offers no hardship, a long summer necessitates no hurried husbandry—in this, the last and the best of all Russian colonies.

CHAPTER II

THE OCCUPATION

WITH the conquest stage of Siberian history passed away the picturesque figure of the early pioneer. Rough but ready, and with a leaven of idealism to redeem much crude barbarity, the Cossack explorer had fulfilled his mission when once the limits of the new empire were set, and thenceforth survived merely as an anachronism. As danger had been his element, so courage was his characteristic; enterprise and resolution had been developed in him by almost insurmountable difficulties; and it is but natural that these robust qualities should, in his successors, have disappeared with the necessity which called them forth. For the eager blood and hot imagination which nerve the adventurer to disdain hunger, thirst, and all hardship, do not necessarily furnish the other kind of energy which is required for the humdrum toil of the potato-field. Another type—in many respects inferior—is required to carry on what the pioneer has begun.

Equally natural is it that the two types should not be mutually sympathetic, and it is therefore suggestive of the homogeneity of the Slav people that the rough Cossack and his gentler successor, in spite of a difference amounting almost to antagonism, should be possessed body and soul with the one ideal —Russia, Mistress of the World!

Representatives of the original pioneer Cossacks survive, however, to the present day at the outposts of the empire,—wherever, in fact, colonization still goes armed—in *stanitzas* strewn along the successive high-water marks of Russian advance. The bitter dislike entertained for them by their non-military fellow-settlers is a natural result of the favoritism shown them as pioneers by the crown—especially in grants of choice lands—and of resentment of the arrogance with which the Cossack asserts his privileged status. A much-quoted instance of this feud is that of the Omsk railway station, placed at a considerable distance from the town. This public inconvenience is attributed to the greedy intrigues of the Cossack proprietors of the intervening land. An indirect consequence of their manœuvres is that the baffled engineers—by way of revenge, it is said—have built the bridge over the neighboring river Irtysh for the exclusive passage of rails, leaving unfortunate foot-passengers to cross, as before, by a primitive ferry.

The Siberian estimate of the Cossack much resembles Uitlander opinion of the Boer. His qualities as a pioneer are not disputed, but to the economic development of the country he is regarded as a mere hinderance—indolent, rapacious, and hating all forms of progress. Quaintly enough, this is much the opinion hitherto held by travellers of the Siberian himself.

The country inherited by the latter from his hardy forerunner covers an area twenty-five times greater than that of Germany. Of this huge dominion at least one-fourteenth is suitable for agriculture: lying in a belt traversing the country from west to east—a *ruban de terre*, as a French writer calls it—some thirty-five hundred miles long by three hundred and fifty broad. It is through this fertile zone that the Great Siberian Railway will shortly run from ocean to ocean. Roughly speaking, Siberia may be said to contain five divisions, corresponding to the basins of its four gigantic rivers—the Obi, Yenisei, Lena, and Amur, each three thousand miles long—and of that of the Central Asian Ili, which, though smaller, is even more important to the burned-up region it waters.

If the Central Asian provinces—which, consisting for the most part of sterile wildernesses, have an almost entirely strategic value—are left out of account, Siberia may be said to lie between China and the Arctic, and the Urals and Pacific Ocean. The Siberia, however, that at present is of practical concern to the world is confined to far narrower limits, and consists of the belt of country referred to, the agricultural zone, through which for three hundred years has run the great high-road to the East, now followed by the Siberian Railway, and in which is centred the immigrant population and the immediate future of the country. It is bounded on the south by the high and bleak mountain chains separating Siberia from the Chinese Empire. To the north of it stretch thousands of square miles of forest and morass, settlement in which is placed out of the question alike by the rigors of the climate and the nature of the soil. Beyond this again lies the Polar *tundra* zone, a land of eternal frost, where the pine forests gradually dwarf to bushes, and these by degrees to the lichens and mosses which are alone found when the *tundra* zone is once fairly entered.

The above divisions are purely climatic, and depend upon the average temperature during the summer months. In what has been called the "cultivated zone," the cold, though very severe for more than half the year, is succeeded by a sufficiently long interval of warmth to allow of the ripening of crops, whereas, outside it, although a comparatively high temperature is attained during one month of the year, the warm weather is of too short duration to allow of agriculture.* It is an interesting fact that the temperature marking the northern limit of this "agricultural zone" shows a consistent tendency to fall with every degree of east longitude. Thus on the Baltic Sea 60° may be called the northern limit of cultivation, while in Western Siberia it barely attains 58°, on the Yenisei it descends to 57°, and beyond Lake Baikal to 55°. Decreasing steadily

* On the whole the climate of Western Siberia shows a lower average temperature and greater severity of winter than in corresponding latitudes of European Russia; but, on the contrary, in the "cultivated zone"—which includes a greater part of Tobolsk and Tomsk, in all about six thousand square geographical miles suitable for agriculture—the richness of the soil, plentiful forests, and more numerous rivers give a great advantage to the Asiatic provinces.

in the Amur basin, the limit of cultivation, on reaching the Pacific coast in the neighborhood of Nicolaevsk, falls to 54°, although that port is in the same latitude as Hamburg.

This belt of cultivable country, thus increasingly restricted, and a mere strip when compared with the total area of Siberia, yet represents an enormous territory. The original immigration having followed in the track of conquest from west to east, it is natural that in the western section of the belt—the early settled governments of Tobolsk and Tomsk—the population should be denser and the character of the towns more industrial and more prosperous than farther eastward—a difference in density of population which the railway, however, is rapidly adjusting.

On traversing the wooded valleys of the Urals, which, as already remarked, are mountains only in name,* the traveller emerges into the vast plain of Western Siberia, and his first impression is one of disappointment. It is so hopelessly like the sad, monotonous plains of Central Russia—bright with flowers, it is true, but deadly flat and uninteresting. In this whole plain there is only one kind of tree—the birch; only one type of village—the gray black, straggling cluster of log-houses, to which the traveller in Russia has become so accustomed. This Siberia, then, one is inclined to complain, is no new and

* The entire length of the range is about seventeen hundred miles. Its highest peak does not attain to more than six thousand feet, while many parts of the range are not above two thousand feet above sea-level.

fascinating country, but a stale replica of the vast Russian plains to which one was so glad to say adieu, a landscape in a minor key, the spirit of which reflects itself in the melancholy folk-songs of the people.

This great alluvial plain, only broken in its south-eastern corner by the Altai highlands—a rich mining region eight times the size of Switzerland, the private property of the Tsar—is *par excellence* the granary of Siberia, though many fresh corn-growing lands throughout the continent are being yearly brought under cultivation. We may therefore pause here to examine in some detail the conditions of Siberian farming—which do not vary much throughout the agricultural belt—or rather the conditions, now rapidly changing, which existed prior to the advent of the railway, enabling us to appreciate more accurately the enormous stimulus which is thereby now being applied to the prosperity of the country.

The Siberian plains must indeed have appeared almost a paradise to the peasant settler escaped from the over-taxing, over-crowding, and over-surveillance of his Russian village. The climate, it is true, is slightly more rigorous than that which he was accustomed to, but, in compensation, the rich black soil awaited him in virgin strength, and the lands adapted for agriculture were often alternated in ideal proportions with well-watered pasturage and forest. The "gifts of God," as he termed them, were bestowed on him without stint, and it is perhaps but human nature that he should have used them without thought of the morrow.

The birch woods, a characteristic, as we have said, of the agricultural zone of Siberia, supply the first requirements of the newly arrived immigrant. With the help of his axe—an essential item in the small outfit dragged or carried so many weary versts—he builds himself an *isba* of rough-hewn logs, roofed with bark. Out of the birch he fashions his rudimentary implements, to last until he can purchase better from the neighboring *kustar*, a village of wood-workers, and on it he entirely depends for fuel. Once housed, he can safely await the harvesting of his first crop. The government grant he has received supplies him with a reserve of grain, and on this he can subsist, eked out, perhaps, by an occasional capercailzie potted in the cedar-trees, or a salmon netted through a hole cut in the ice of the neighboring stream. The skins of a few squirrels, shot during the long winter, suffice for the renewal of his travel-worn fur coat; or, perhaps, if unusually energetic, he may join with a neighbor in trapping foxes, should they have been seen passing up the river on one of their strange periodical migrations.

At last the frost breaks up and the snows melt. For three weeks the much-dreaded *rasputitza* renders locomotion almost impossible, for mud and slush. Then comes the spring and summer, into the five months of which the settler must concentrate a year's labor. His simple implements are finished; the seed, on the preservation of which his very life depended, stands ready in undamaged sacks; and the black, virgin soil, clear of snow, charged with fertile essences, awaits it. The true "gold of Siberia" lies at the peasant's own door. Plough-horses are the next essential, and the settler, for the equivalent of six dollars a head, obtains his pick from the nomad Kirghiz herds of the neighboring steppe. Half a dozen of these hardy little animals, a few milch cows, and some sheep purchased at the same time make up a sufficient stock to start with.

Let us imagine that the season is a good one. The cattle thrive and fatten in the lush pasture; the crops of wheat and rye are heavy; and the settler sees himself, on the approach of winter, safe from immediate want. The gathered harvest more than suffices for his household needs, as well as for the following year's sowing. The ease with which fortune has come to him suggests no misgiving for the future, and, as the winter season allows of no field work, the farmer is content to doze the long months through in his stifling *isba*, endeavoring to kill time over pipe and *vodka* bottle, for all the world like a hibernating bear.

Next year luck is again with him, and without manuring or weeding, and with a minimum of labor, he once more harvests heavy crops. His cattle and horses have multiplied, and he is now able to invest in some draught-horses from Tomsk, slower than those of Kirghiz strain, but of more power. His large surplus of grain he manages this year to convey in sledges to the nearest fair—to be thence distributed to Russia, to distant mining or non-agricultural districts, to the spirit distillers, or for the supply of the great Siberian track, the highway to the East. In the course of a very few such prosperous years the settler becomes well-to-do. The virgin lands surrounding him will yield, without rest or manure, and perhaps with only a change from wheat to less-exhausting barley, and from rye to oats, heavy crops for another twenty years. Indeed, there exist lands in the south of Tobolsk which have been incessantly tilled for a hundred years. The settler is able to pay off the government grant and to increase his land. His foals at foot, gambolling in the snow-fed pasture, promise good increase of draught-horses. The cows and goats give more milk than he can now consume, and, after supplying his family, he is able to send his first lot of butter to market. With the proceeds of the sale he purchases from the Kirghiz a few of their special breed of "Kurdiuk," or fat-tailed sheep—an improvement on the light-fleeced Tobolsk breed with which he has hitherto had to be content.

His style of living, however, does not keep pace with the improvement in his financial position. The log-house is by this time blackened with weather and smoke, but still suffices for his simple tastes. A little white paint on the window-frames, which then stand out in bold relief on the black background of the *isba*, is the only concession he makes to æstheticism. The same red shirt, over which his long, curling beard and tangled flaxen locks fall in wild profusion; the same battered cap, with a yellow band round it if he be a Cossack, and as such subject to special military calls; the same greasy trousers, tucked into the same clumsy, crinkled high boots; the same brown home-made *kaftan*, or summer overcoat; and the same vermin-haunted *shuba*, or sheepskin, will always suffice his not very critical taste. He needs no books, for he cannot read. Uneducated and brutalized, wealth is of no use to him; warmth, tobacco, and the *nepenthe* of intoxication alone appeal to his undeveloped instincts—though, if opportunity offers, the national passion for gambling will strike a quick response in his Russian blood.

But to return: his flaxen-haired children, playing round the farm, in orthodox red tunics, each with a medallion of St. Vladimir or St. Paul round his neck, are, one and all, plump and rosy-cheeked. Everything points to a steadily rising tide in our farmer's affairs. No imaginative anxiety as to the future troubles his Siberian phlegm. The logs, it is true, have to be brought a longer distance now than when he first settled on the spot, but the woods behind still appear inexhaustible. His fields, no doubt, are gradually losing strength, but why should he labor to manure them when, at his pleasure, they can be abandoned for new? And as for the education of the children, the settler is himself too ignorant to even appreciate the advantage of it. In the country districts of Siberia only one child in a hundred receives any schooling whatever; in the towns, less than five per cent.

The utter wastefulness of Siberian farming is its principal characteristic. The surface-soil is merely scratched by rudimentary implements, the sub-soil being left unutilized. Manuring is unknown, or, at any rate, not practised. The thin layer of surface soil, however rich, is rapidly exhausted, and, when exhausted, abandoned. After a long interval of years such land is sometimes—on the reappearance of certain weeds indicating a return of strength—placed again under cultivation, though for a much shorter period. But in few cases does the actual yield of a Siberian farm exceed a fraction of the possible production under scientific methods and judicious handling.

Suddenly, however, in full summer of the farmer's prosperity, there "comes a frost," a year positively fraught with disaster. As the cattle have hitherto managed to feed themselves throughout the winter by scratching away the snow from the herbage, the ease-loving farmer has not troubled to make provision of hay. But the usual first snowfall of autumn is, this year, followed by rain, and that again by frost; and nearly the whole of his flocks, unable to pierce the hard-caked surface, starve before his eyes. The remnants suffer further loss in an unusually severe *buran*, or blizzard, swept over precipice and into snow-drift. To add to these misfortunes, when spring comes, the farmer, in his fear of autumn hoar-frosts blighting the almost ripened ear, is a day early in sowing, and the young shoots get nipped by a late spring frost. Or, when he has imagined his crop assured, the locust of the Kirghiz steppes, the dreaded *kobylka*, discovers and devours them. And finally, in the autumn, the *chuma* gives the finishing stroke to those of his draught-horses that have survived the other plagues. Under these repeated calamities his position changes rapidly indeed. There is no system of organized credit to help him, and, although his whole district has suffered, no assistance is forthcoming from the immensely distant (though officially neighboring) government. Such is the want of means of transport, that surplus in Tomsk cannot supply deficit in Tobolsk. Nor can the ruined farmer hope for any repayment in kind of the grain he has disposed of in prosperous years; except, perhaps, from the distilleries, in the form of *vodka* to drown his troubles.

With such risks to be taken into account, it is not surprising that, until recently, many a settler turned from agriculture to the more certain, if in some years less remunerative, livelihood to be earned on the great Siberian track. This was, until the coming of steamers and railway, the great artery of traffic between East and West. It employed tens of thousands of men and hundreds of thousands of horses. If the settler opened an inn, custom was assured to him from the continuous stream of travellers, prisoners, troops, and officials passing his door. Or he might earn a good and, what was scarcely less valued by him, a lazy living as a teamster. The chief imports from Russia, varying from millinery to machinery and from buttons to bar-iron, passed that way; and he could return westward with a load of grain, hides, tallow, or skin-bound chests of China tea. The owner of a sledge and a team of five good horses often earned in the old days as much as £25 for a two-thousand-mile trip from Tomsk to Irkutsk and back, occupying two months; and, into the bargain, was found in the keep of his horses. Having pocketed, and perhaps partially converted into *vodka*, the bargain-money for the trip, he could take his seat with a light heart on the forepart of the sledge, and, muffled in warm sheepskins, give himself up to vacuous enjoyment. But with steamer and railway competition sledge freights have been cut down to nothing, and the population of the Siberian track is gradually being converted to agriculture—against its will, however, and with many an anathema on the new railway.

The manner in which land is divided among the farmers is naturally very varied—there being in some districts more than can be cultivated, while in others tillable land has to be created, by drainage or irrigation, and, again, elsewhere arable preponderates over meadow, or forest over arable. All land, however, belongs to the crown, and is only held by the peasants in usufruct; though in certain parts of the country the areas are practically limitless, and the peasants claim rights "wherever hatchet, scythe, and plough may go." In others—*e.g.*, the villages of Tobolsk—a strict thirteen acres, and no more, is the allotment to each male. The average throughout Siberia is forty-eight acres *per caput* male.

No uniform government survey exists. In some cases a general boundary has been fixed for whole *volosts* of fifteen thousand souls, leaving the peasants to use the land in common or divide it according to settlements. In other cases the government surveyors have marked out the lands of each settlement, or even of each group of villages.

In newly settled districts the *zaimka* is the form of division. Each farmer leaves the village at the commencement of spring for his own farmstead or *zaimka.* Here he lives throughout the summer, only returning to the village for winter-quarters. Around his *zaimka* he cultivates any land he chooses—the rich man perhaps two thousand acres; the poor, one hundred and fifty. But there is no opening for envy, as rich and poor alike are free to seize any additional unoccupied land, and there is plenty of room for all. Nevertheless, gradually all the good land gets taken up, and more is required by the increasing population, and the *zaimka* develops into the *volnaia* system. This is the communal system principally followed in Tomsk and Tobolsk. By it a man has right only to that land into which he puts his labor, and only for so long as he continues to cultivate it. Meadow-land grass, grown without labor, is free to the community; each peasant mows where he wills, but the hay belongs to him who cuts and makes it. Similarly, the forest is free; becoming private property only where enclosed by a ditch, cleared of dead wood, or otherwise labored upon. Pasture is free, each member being allowed to graze his cattle on the ground set apart by the community for the purpose, but none may enclose a piece for his own sole use.

Such is the agricultural aspect of "Western Siberia," a country whose development has been much retarded by the fact that the Obi, its chief waterway—a noble river, 3180 miles in length and navigable throughout—flows north at right angles to the trend of traffic, and, falling into the ice-bound gulf at its mouth, affords no practical communication with the markets of the world. But the Siberian Railway is now supplying the long-required means of communication.

CHAPTER III

THE OCCUPATION—(Continued)

Some slight hints have already been given as to the undeveloped moral state of the colonists. French travellers, in spite of the fond alliance, are particularly vivacious on the subject, and, in view of the bias which their Russian sympathies may be supposed to lend, their estimate can be quoted without suspicion of unfairness. In general, the great Napoleon's famous dictum is confirmed—"Grattez le Russe, et vous trouverez le Tartare." One modern Gallic traveller describes the Siberian race as indolent and apathetic beyond all imagination—even a French journalist's!—and in his opinion Siberian sluggishness is exceeded by only one thing—Siberian pig-headedness! The Spartan Siberian, he asserts, will forego every luxury rather than raise a finger to work for it, and he concludes by declaring that Siberia is the only country in the world where the almighty dollar becomes impotent in face of the extraordinary *vis inertiæ* of the peasantry. All foreigners whom the writer met in Siberia, and even European Russians, and all travellers, Latin and Teutonic alike, agree in further crediting the Siberian with having brought lying to the rank of a positive fine art. But it is perhaps M. Legras who most picturesquely voices the general opinion when, in the preface to his *En Sibérie*, a work enjoying a considerable popularity in France, he says: ". . . on ment avec délices, le plus souvent sans intérêt, par habitude, par désœuvrement, pour l'amour de l'art."

This does not prevent the Siberian from being, like the Boer, extremely fond of quotations from Holy Writ, when judiciously applied. As might be expected, however, the texts hanging in pious profusion from his walls usually exhort to self-denial and abstention rather than to enterprise and effort. Accordingly, a favorite verse is, "Blessed are the poor in spirit, for theirs is the Kingdom of Heaven," or, as read by the disgusted traveller through the murky fumes and greasy darkness of a wayside Siberian hostelry, "Happy are they who expect little, for verily they shall not be disappointed." These hostelries, which have been denounced in unmeasured terms, though extremely primitive, are not, however, more so than is usual in newly made colonies. If reasonable allowance be made, the accommodation is not bad, although many things which to the Western mind are absolute essentials—towels, bed-sheets, or baths—are treated as unnecessary luxuries, obtained with difficulty, and charged for egregiously. The traveller must bring his own provisions, too, for boiling water is the only thing he can rely on finding.

We have seen how the ignorant farmer beguiles the long winter hours, seated, pipe in mouth, by his

THE CATHEDRAL, IRKUTSK

fireside. His one idea of enjoyment out of doors—which he shares with all his uneducated countrymen—is to listen to a hand-organ, and, should good-fortune take him to a town, to ride on the gravitating railway, a form of amusement which was originally invented by a Russian. The pleasures of the rich mine-owner, though more expensive, are scarcely less boorish. The unique aspiration of the average magnate is the gross display of wealth, effected in true Oriental fashion. For, metaphorically as well as sartorially, the dress-coat he so much affects is no guarantee of irreproachable linen beneath it; his mansion, which costs a fortune, is comfortless; his retinues of servants dirty and inefficient; and, of a stableful of horses, none is fit for his guest to ride. The generally accepted criterion of magnificence appears to be profuse libations of champagne. A cigarette-bowl, too, hollowed from a solid gold nugget, stamps the fortunate possessor a "Corinthian" of taste. Or the man of cultured aspirations may—and, unless rumor lies, sometimes *does*—achieve refinement by having his sitting-room floor washed occasionally with Piper Heidsieck. In fact, although the subject of it be two hundred years old, Lord Macaulay's epigram is scarcely antiquated, and one can without much difficulty still imagine the Siberian grandee appearing at court "dropping pearls and vermin."

The most intelligent, progressive, and by far the best-informed section of Siberian society are the Germans, or descendants of Germans. They are found at the extreme borders of the empire, and are not merely the most enterprising traders, but provide some of the best teachers and most skilled workmen to be found in the whole country. A type of these was met by the writer at Kiachta, who, with another German friend and his daughter, was able to beguile an evening with really excellent music and most intelligent talk. It was a curious sensation, in the primitive room of a wooden house, far away from everything that means culture and refinement to a Western mind — in a half-savage town on the very borders of civilization—to listen to airs from Mozart and concertos by Beethoven, which were last heard, perhaps, in some gilded salon of Berlin or concert-room in London.

Latterly, of course—greatly owing to the educating influence of the railway — a very marked difference has come over the outward appearance, at least, of Siberian social life. In the large towns, such as Tomsk and Tobolsk in Western, and Krasnoiarsk* in Eastern Siberia, there are cathedrals, theatres, universities, museums, schools, libraries, and other means of public instruction and amusement. Many of these buildings are handsome, and one at least, the cathedral at Irkutsk, has some pretensions to architectural beauty. Tomsk, the capital of Western Siberia, the seat of government and residence of the Russian archbishop, has a very important

* The population of Tomsk is 40,000; Irkutsk, 50,000; Tobolsk, 20,000; Krasnoiarsk, 15,000.

BRIDGE AT IRKUTSK

university, with a really good library and museum. Hitherto it only possessed the faculty of medicine, but now has clinical and other lectures, and is the first of the numerous government establishments for public education. Even here, however, the streets and squares—many of them built of stone—are badly kept and out of repair. The lack of completeness and harmony is noticeable in all Siberian towns—for instance, at Irkutsk a really fine opera-house is spoiled by miserable corridors and foyer. In this large city, whose population is already over fifty thousand, there is only one indifferent public library, and the booksellers' shops contain merely a second-class collection of books, such as French novels, *Le Nu au Salon* picture-books, and equally edifying publications. It does not speak well for the civilizing mission of Russia to the "savage tribes" among whom she has planted her flag that such a state of things should exist in her great outpost cities, which ought to be centres of light and learning. The inhabitants of these cities have not yet acquired, even in the smallest degree, "the gentle art of beauty." Their clothes, bought ready-made (there are only four tailors in all Irkutsk), are ugly and unbecoming, a fact much to be regretted, especially in the case of the fair sex, who are no better in this respect than their male-folk, for the Siberian woman is not sufficiently endowed by nature to be able to dispense with artificial aids to comeliness.

It is, however, doubtful whether any efforts of an eclectic nature would have much influence at present, in raising the standard of life, for from highest to lowest the ruling passions are still gambling and drinking, while lying and all sorts of official corruption are still notoriously the rule and not the exception. Academical education is not enough. What is essential is the infusion of a new spirit from outside, consequent upon the opening up of the country to the world; new objectives and ideals, competition and rivalries, which will leave no room for the existing slothful debaucheries; new standards of morality, or, at the least, of commercial expediency, which will discredit as stupid and clumsy such a semi-civilized weapon as promiscuous lying.

The character of the country remains unchanged until the river Obi is reached. Then the birch woods, through which we have travelled for some hundreds of miles without ever noting another species of tree, commence to include an increasing proportion of pines. The plain itself becomes broken up; the horizon is no longer one flat circle, but undulates in hills. On the farther side of the Yenisei these hills develop into mountains, the advance-guards of an extensive country of forest and mountain. The road, of course, also loses its hitherto monotonous character, and now winds its way up hill and down dale, bordered on either side by a solid wall of pine forests, leaving a general impression of bare, red, straight stems and dusky foliage. The very waters of the rivers become altered, the turgid streams of Western Siberia being succeeded by the limpid waters of the noble Yenisei.

YENISEI RIVER, SCORED BY ICE

The Yenisei shares with the Obi and Lena the disadvantage of a northerly direction, at right angles to the trade routes, but its embouchure is far more accessible than theirs, thanks partly to the action of the tail-end of the Gulf Stream in clearing the ice of the Kara Sea. It was an Englishman, Captain Wiggins, of Newcastle, who, in 1874, proved that a vessel can make Yenisei Bay in late autumn and slip away again before the ice closes in, and who thereby won a bonus of £2000 offered by the explorer Sidorov.

Eastern Siberia, the second of the five great divisions, occupies, roughly speaking, the basin of the river Yenisei, and comprises an area equal to twice the combined extent of Germany, Austria, and France. In climate it is even less favored than Western Siberia, and one-twelfth only of its whole area is at all suitable for cultivation, the rest being forest, morass, and *tundra*. Agriculture has consequently given way to cattle-breeding to a great extent, and the proportion of domestic animals to man—a sure index of the industrial development of a country or the reverse—is correspondingly high. Whereas, for instance, in Great Britain and Belgium the percentage of horses to human population is only five, and in the United States and European Russia but twenty-two, in Eastern Siberia it reaches the high figure of seventy-two.

Another indication of the changing character of the country is the increased proportion of natives, who, while rarely met with in the highly cultivated districts of Tomsk, form in the Yenisseisk and Irkutsk governments twenty-three per cent. of the population. Of these the greater part are Buriats, a tribe of cattle-breeding Buddhists who migrated north in the thirteenth century, when Genghis Khan ruled supreme in Mongolia. Although subdued by the Cossacks two centuries later, after a protracted struggle, it is noteworthy that this people do not as yet show the usual native tendency to die out when in contact with the Russians.

The principal mountain chain of the region is the Sayan, separating it on the south from China. One of the valleys in this range, shut in on all sides by high mountains, was known in ancient times as the Irghana-Kon, and is celebrated as the cradle of the great Tiursk tribe, the nucleus of Central Asian peoples. In another valley of the Sayan, guarded by Mount Khamar-Daban, lies Lake Baikal, one of the largest sheets of fresh water in the world. One of its many phenomena is a species of seal. Water-fowl frequent its shores in countless numbers, and gulls in particular are so numerous that the rocks are covered with thick layers of guano, which, when the Siberian farmer is eventually compelled to manure his fields, will supply him, it is estimated, for generations. Frozen in winter, the Baikal lake then affords a route for sledges, while in summer steamers ply on it. No long interval elapses between the two, for in these latitudes the first ice-grip of autumn comes suddenly, and the story, almost true enough to be good, told in North China of the last

FISHING VILLAGE, LAKE BAIKAL, SIBERIA

Peiho steamer of the season being compelled, as she rammed her way out through the ice, to whistle a warning to the carts crossing her bow, applies to Lake Baikal, for the track across the ice is dotted

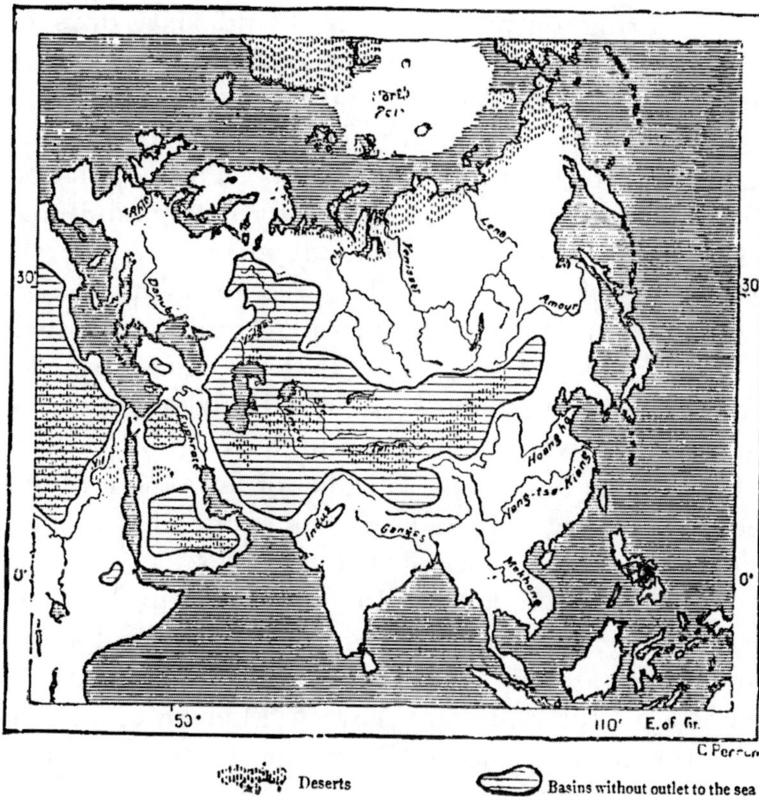

BARREN REGIONS AND BASINS WITHOUT OUTLET IN ASIA

with booths and stations, and the traffic is often cleared just as the whole surface is about to give way.

Far larger than either East or West Siberia is the Yakutsk region situated in the northeast, an inhospitable, mountainous area, 70,000 miles square, Arctic in climate, covered with impenetrable forest, morass, and polar *tundras* only fit for reindeer-breeding. Its waterway, the gigantic Lena—free of ice during only one hundred and sixty days of the year—is even less practicable for navigation than the Obi or Yenisei, falling as it does into no gulf or estuary, but winding its way to the sea through an intricate maze of delta. The population of this miserable country is mostly native, and concentrated in the forest zone at an average of six inhabitants to a square mile. In the polar *tundras* there are but six to each ten square miles. In such a region it is not surprising that the Russians, who have valiantly preserved their national characteristics even in Amur swamps and Kirghiz deserts, should have found the burden of local conditions too heavy for them, and, intermarriage aiding, have sunk to the brutish level of the natives.

Agriculture and cattle-breeding are in Yakutsk replaced by hunting, trapping, and fishing. The fur animals, gradually exterminated in the cultivated zone, are still abundant here. The white bear is sometimes carried to its shores on floating ice from its habitat in the polar islands; the brown bear and elk roam the forest; the sable is common; the fox abounds, and many other species. Commonest of all is the squirrel, of which the hunter bags, on an average, three hundred head in a season. In the pursuit of the large fur animals success is greatly a question of luck. The bear-hunter may make his hundreds of rubles in a few weeks, or he may wander through the forest the whole winter and scarcely earn the keep of his dogs.

There are no exact statistics of the fur trade, but some idea may be formed of its extent from the official figures of a few years back. These gave for the whole of Siberia a total of no less than one and a quarter million skins of eighteen varieties of animals. The rarest enumerated were four tigers, shot perhaps in the reed swamps of Lake Balkash, twenty black foxes, and forty-five white polar bears. The commonest were one million squirrels and over thirty thousand sables. The central marts of the Siberian fur trade are, curiously enough, not in Russia, but in London and Leipzig, where the industry is now firmly established.

The native hunters, as was to be expected, have, since they came in contact with the civilized world, been much exploited. On the distant coasts and islands of the northeast, foreign whalers have for years obtained quantities of furs in barter for spirit of the vilest quality and other contraband products of civilization. Other fur-hunting tribes within easier reach by land are still more systematically taken advantage of: the Kamchatkans by the Russians themselves; the Golos, or Orochs, by the Chinese; and the Tunguses by the Yakuts. The usual system is to make advances on the season's furs, and thus entangle the guileless native in debt. That accomplished, he is never allowed to escape the toils, and the furs are procured, year by year, for prices far below their real value. In other branches of trade the natives are no less shamelessly cheated, Russian officialdom offering no protection.

The fresh-water fishing industry, though carried out on a large scale, is at present of hardly more

TUNGUSE IN WINTER HUNTING COSTUME

than local importance. The fish is mostly consumed locally, Siberian salting being too roughly executed to have created much export trade. Originally the Siberian rivers abounded in fish, but the wasteful and indiscriminate methods which have characterized the fisheries during the past generation have had a visibly perceptible influence on their numbers. A conservancy department and improved processes of preparation for distant markets would, however, notwithstanding past waste, establish this industry as one of the leading auxiliary sources of revenue of the country. The same remark applies to the fur industry, which, under the present want of system, is also threatened with serious diminution, owing to the ruthless and ill-regulated slaughter of fur animals. The cheaper skins, those for example that find their way into China, are open to the criticism of being badly prepared for export.

Siberian fish include some splendid species of sturgeon and salmon. The latter especially are said to ascend the Amur in countless numbers, and Vladivostok, smoked salmon is a well-known delicacy. The spectacle of these fish, frozen stiff, and propped on their tails in rows against the counters, is extremely quaint and often remarked upon by travellers in Siberia.

Of far greater interest than the Yakutsk mainland are the "three new Siberian islands" off its coast. Traders in mammoth ivory and morse tusks reach them in sledges across the frozen sea, spend the short summer there, and return as they came when the ice sets in. These islands hold the buried record of the whole organic world, as it formerly existed in 75°–76° north latitude. The shaggy, red-haired mammoth, the rhinoceros, buffalo, musk-ox, and other extinct species have here their cemetery; and trees allied to those of the temperate zone, such as the elm and hazel, are here found fossilized.

The fur trade and minor industries cannot, however, suffice for the development of the "coldest country in the world," and the future of Yakutsk must depend, like that of the Klondike, on the development of its mineral wealth. This, unfortunately, is a more or less remote potentiality, the precious metals being, so far as is at present known, but thinly scattered over a vast surface.

The fourth great division of Siberia is the Amur littoral region, which includes the basin of the Amur and the whole coast-line from the peninsula of Kamchatka to the island of Sakhalin. Of this the Trans-Baikal province is the corn-growing centre, enjoying a powerful sun, clear air, and an almost snowless winter. Here the rhododendron of the western ranges grows, together with the oak, elm, hazel, and wild apple of the temperate zone, and the wild apricot, dog-rose, and tamarisk, peculiar to this part of Siberia.

Along the Amur and Ussuri rivers the climate is less favorable, a general excess of moisture causing in the cereals a tendency to run to straw, so that Amur crops, though heavy, are often poor in quality. Some districts have even had to be entirely abandoned on account of the "intoxicating bread" they produce, due to fungoid growths in the ears of corn. In these damper regions flourish the Manchurian cedar, the pitch-pine and the yew, peculiar to the Caucasus and indicating approach to the sea; the maple and ash, unknown elsewhere in Siberia; and a cork-tree, not met with in all Russia. The shrubs include a number of Chinese kinds.

Bordering on their own, these lands naturally attract many thousands of Corean and Chinese settlers, whose careful and intensive farming offers a contrast very unfavorable to that of their Russian neighbors. Ownership of fields may be told at a glance—the ones sown in mathematical rows, copiously manured, and scrupulously weeded; the others left to grow untended and choked with weeds. The Corean's principal crop is "buda," of which a couple of well-sown acres will support his whole family for more than a year.

Along the sea-coast north of the Amur the climate becomes execrable. The Kamchatkan peninsula is described as alternately "wrapped in fog, drenched with rain, or smothered by snow." The Sea of Okhotsk, though of the same latitude as the English Channel, is polar in its character, and is, besides, subject to "monsoons," caused by the rapid cooling and heating of land as compared with sea. These gales blow with such force across the neighboring Stanovoi range that neither men nor pack animals can stand against them. Of the stunted flora of this desolate land the most characteristic is a nettle which is rapidly ousting all other vegetation. Settled agriculture is out of the question, and the whole land is practically abandoned to the aborigines, who correspond in character to those of the north coast of West Siberia, and maintain themselves by fishing, trapping, and reindeer breeding. Of these animals they own large herds, often in the proportion of six to each member of the tribe, and the reindeer is as essential to their existence as the birch-tree is that of the settler in the southwest; while living it is invaluable as a means of transport, and when dead its skin provides clothes, its flesh food, its sinews thread, and its bones needles and knives. The natives also own numbers of sledge-dogs resembling the Esquimau breed, which are harnessed in teams, without reins or bridles. One dog, specially prized, and valued at nearly £6—a fortune to the Koriat—leads the way as guide, the others draw a load, averaging one hundred pounds per dog, at the rate of some eight miles an hour. A peculiarity of these valuable animals is that they cannot bark. How precarious is the existence of these wandering peoples is evidenced by the fact that they regard death from starvation as a natural ending, and, till comparatively recent times, practised the filial duty of stabbing an aged parent to save him from more protracted pangs.

In vivid contrast to its climatic rigors, the coast of Kamchatka is dotted with giant volcanoes, many in full eruption. The red glow of their craters on ice-pack and frozen cape; the torrents of boiling snow—if the description be allowable—which scar their sides; the silent line of huge white sentinels, standing with quenched fires guarding the Arctic seas—all serve to form an impressive picture of the warring forces of nature.

The development of land industries being hopeless, the economical future of this region centres in the vast sea industries of its coast. The Sea

DOG-SLEDGE, AMUR REGION

of Okhotsk and Bering Sea have always been a favorite feeding-ground for marine animals, abounding in fish, mollusks, crustaceans, and beds of "sea-cabbage." Specimens of the now extinct sea-cow, an animal weighing fifty thousand pounds, were last killed on Bering Island in 1780. The fast-disappearing sea-lion also frequented these waters;

SAMOYEDE PILOT

whales, dolphins, and seals are here in thousands, and cod, herring, and other fish in countless shoals. The chief spoils have, however, gone to the American whaling and sealing schooners, a contraband trade which the Russians have feebly endeavored to check by means of one or two patrolling gunboats. It is amusing to note in a Russian government report that the crews of captured vessels have been "always set at liberty without the exaction of any fine"; but the United States sealing skipper, unlike European governments, does not pay so much attention to what Russian officialdom *says*, as to what it *does*, and has a holy horror of falling into such generous hands.

The seal-fishery is a subject of international importance, owing to the conflicting interests involved, besides being the principal source of government revenue along the inhospitable coast described, and a few remarks may therefore be permitted on the subject, even though they can claim no novel interest. The seal is known in Russian as the *morskoi kotik*, or sea-cat, the common name among fishermen for a full-grown specimen being *siekach*, supposed to be a corruption of the English "sea-catch." The younger ones are called in Russian *kholostiak*, or bachelor, the equivalent term in the foreign trade being *holuschickie*. It is the latter that are principally slaughtered, between 1st of June and 15th of July, when the moulting season commences. The seals never show fight, and a couple of men can "hold" a herd of several thousand—*i. e.*, prevent their breaking back to the seashore, the seal being easily killed by a slight blow on the head with a stick. Slaughtering, skinning, salting, and packing proceed simultaneously, the seal islands being during the season the rendezvous of many different aborigines—natives of Kamchatka, of Yakutsk, of the Aleutian Islands joining with the Cossacks in the seal-skin business. Seals were first known on the Commander Islands, called after the intrepid Bering, but the fur-traders were soon convinced that the seal must have other haunts, which were eventually discovered, after a two years' voyage, in the Pribylov group, named after their discoverer; and these islands, now the property of the United States, have since been the best-known sealing resort. It was only, however, after the thirties that the seal-skin industry developed to anything like its modern dimensions. Till that time the demand for seal-skins had been for the greater part confined to Russia and China. But in the thirties a new process was discovered, the secret—that of plucking out the long hairs in the seal-skin and dyeing the down which remains—being for a long time successfully guarded. A demand sprang up in England, the fur thus artificially treated became the fashion, and the whole trade, as already said, gravitated to London and Leipzig.

CHAPTER IV

THE OCCUPATION—(Continued)

THE fifth and last administrative division of Siberia is the Kirghiz steppe region of Central Asia. As has been already observed, this vast territory, though belonging to Siberia Proper, scarcely forms part of the modern Siberia, the new industrial and commercial field in which the world is interested. In the scheme of the Russian invasion of the south, the Kirghiz steppe is of supreme value as a line of communication, but is not altogether valueless from other points of view, though lying far beyond what promises to be the beaten track between west and east. A third of the area of the Kirghiz steppe region—twenty-five thousand square miles—is mountainous, the rest barren steppe. These arid plains are totally impracticable for cultivation—salt, treeless wastes, whose chief future value lies in the development of mineral riches. Coal-fields are known to exist, of which some are now in operation, while copper, lead, and silver ores have been prospected. There is some possibility also of the region being made available as a cattle-raising country on a large scale, this being practically the only use to which the former possessors, the nomad Kirghiz, have ever been able to put it. The great want is, of course, a sufficient water supply, though there are two waterways of considerable, and even majestic, proportions. The Ili, which is a thousand miles long, and the Narym traverse the country, but the other streams are on a totally insufficient scale, and elaborate irrigation works are required before the present sterile nature of the desert can be modified. The mountain-streams run into the arid, burning wastes, to meander sluggishly through the desert — their course marked by the solitary trees to be seen in the plain—until they are sucked up by the sands or evaporate into what may be called the atmospheric ocean. The burning surfaces around are bare, except for one characteristic plant, a dwarfed and crooked shrub, on whose silvery foliage camels delight to browse. Country such as this occupies, as we have said, two-thirds of the steppe region of Siberia.

The other mountainous third has as its principal chain the Thian Shan, consisting of lines of snow-clad summits running parallel to the Chinese frontier. The passes are rugged, and attain a height of thirteen thousand feet. At the foot of these mountains and extending to the Zailüsk Altai on the north, stretches a zone of fertile soil brought down by the mountain torrents and watered from the snow-peaks. This zone, however, ceases wherever the mountains are below the snow-line, and is consequently of comparatively small extent, but it is eminently suited for colonization and represents the cream of

Siberian arable land. Lying between two thousand and five thousand feet above the burning steppe, it enjoys a climate among the best in all Russia. Gardening is here possible, as nowhere else in Siberia, and even grape-culture. Between five thousand and eight thousand feet lies the forest belt, providing a supplementary industry for Russian settlers. Above this again, until the line of eternal snow is reached at about eleven thousand feet, lie the "Sazas," or Alpine meadows—the cool summer pastures of the Kirghiz who winter on the steppe. These nomads have been partially compensated for the loss of their lands—the temperate zone at present occupied by the Russians—which they cultivated only in desultory fashion, by the ready market now provided for the disposal of their cattle.

These upland pastures are luxuriantly verdured, and are rich in flora. Among the most characteristic is the gray-leaved, yellow-on-rose-flowered "camel's-tail"; and the large yellow-petalled wild onion, from which the Thian Shan range gets its Chinese sobriquet of "Tsun Lin," or "Onion," Mountains. The fauna of this region is no less varied and numerous. On the inaccessible peaks beyond the snow-line roams the *kochgar*, a wild sheep called after the old Venetian traveller, *Ovis Poli;* the tiger of Southern Asia reaches his northern limits in the reeds of the neighboring Lake Balkash; wild boars and Himalayan bears frequent the wooded slopes; the *arkhar*, another species of mountain sheep, is common; a great concourse of wild fowl breed in the solitary lakes and rivers of the steppe; and the pelican has here his habitat. Many beautiful species of pheasants are found in the sheltered valleys of the mountains, and here was probably the original home of the hardy pheasant which, introduced into England some fifty years ago, is now the dominant species in English preserves.

It was from these fertile slopes that the Huns migrated westward two centuries before Christ, and that successive irruptions of the Central Asian populations have followed, some overflowing into the rich plains of China, while others, sweeping north or south of the Caspian, poured into Europe. Last of all came the great Mongolian wave of the thirteenth century under Genghis Khan, which deposited the Kirghiz hordes far to the southwest, and the Buriats, as we have seen, beyond the Amur. Hemmed in as is this region by lofty mountains, impassable to nomads with their herds, these migrations were only possible owing to there being three vast natural gateways available—the Ili valley, the Lake Ala-kul depression, and the plain stretching between the Tarbagatai and Altai highlands. From the establishment of the Russians on this hospitable oasis, situated between the almost Arctic expanses to the northward and the burning wastes extending to the Himalayas, virtually dated the Tsar's conquest of the heart of Asia.

The acquisition of such vast unpopulated areas as those of Siberia necessarily gave rise to the State problem to which the Russian Government has during a century given continual attention—namely, that of immigration. The impression has falsely passed into currency that the principal stock of the Siberian population is made up of the convicts and political exiles who preceded the voluntary immigrants. The numbers of prisoners sent to Siberia, however, have been too unimportant of themselves to have any marked effect on the population; and the conditions of their life precluded much likelihood of serious increase beyond their original numbers. Male exiles were often separated from their wives, or wives from their husbands; and while the Bohemian restlessness which had probably been a factor in their original offence made the prospect of a settled conjugal life distasteful to the single members of the exile communities, there was also a not unnatural prejudice on the part of the peasant settlers and other inhabitants against union with people on whose life lay a shadow if not a stain. Vice and disease, very prevalent among the convicts, also contributed to the stationary totals. Neither did the secret colonization, before referred to, probably contribute largely to the census, and legitimate immigration under government auspices may be taken to have filled by far the largest rôle in the populating of Siberia.

During the last decade intending immigrants have had to undergo a strict censorship on the part of the Russian Minister of the Interior. Only those families who by reason of numbers, health, and the possession of a certain small capital proved eligible

IN THE ALEXANDROVSKY CENTRAL PRISON, SIBERIA

were allowed to emigrate from their native provinces and to attempt to settle in the more thinly populated yet favorable districts of the Siberian governments. Government help was bestowed in the form of an advance of capital, of grants of land on extremely favorable terms, and of exemption, during certain periods, from military service and civil taxation.* Still more energetic measures were taken in those parts of the dominion where, as in the Amur region, there was urgent political necessity for knitting together the loose, newly acquired territories with industrious human fibre. Not only was immigration to these parts allowed, but the Government tried the comparatively costly experiment of importing peasant immigrants from the Black Sea—a process which has been termed "compulsory" colonization, though the persuasion used probably resembled closely that of an ordinary emigration agency. The more lately acquired, more distant, and altogether less attractive South Ussuri region was thus in three years furnished with a population of forty-five hundred colonists, brought out *via* Suez in steamers of the "volunteer fleet," and at a cost of over a million rubles. Since the opening of the railway immigrants have poured in at the rate of a quarter of a million souls a year, and what has till lately been regarded as the "cesspool" is rapidly

* Assistance has also been given to immigrant settlers in various other forms; for instance, they are conveyed at a rate of three rubles per one thousand versts, or less than one shilling per one hundred miles.

becoming the "reservoir." In Siberia the overflow of Russian life and labor can for many years to come find a prosperous outlet.

According to more than one observer before railway days, who, travelling through Siberia in quest of information, had been granted "every facility" for seeing life as it does *not* exist by the Government at St. Petersburg, the evils of the convict system have been grossly underrated. It has even been represented as almost an ideal system, which the rest of Europe might well study. By others again, in past days notably by Kennan, it has perhaps been painted in unduly black colors. However this may be, it is certainly an error to consider the Siberia of the end of the nineteenth century as merely a great convict settlement; nor would the word "Siberia," uttered in sepulchral tones, be a name of such terror to Russians in general as the usual Nihilist novel would have us suppose. Since the sixteenth century a steady stream of immigration, only at first compulsory, has been kept up, and with the acquisition by Russia of the more fertile provinces has gradually come an improvement in the convict system and a distinct voluntary movement, though gravely hindered by the fact that many unnecessary legal forms must be gone through and official formalities be complied with before a peasant can leave European Russia.

"The old order changeth"; but before we say good-bye to every method of travelling but by railway, it may be as well to refer to the various modes

TRAVEL WITH "TARANTASS," ON THE STEPPE

by which, hitherto, distance has been bridged. Most picturesque perhaps, save to the unfortunate being who is compelled to employ it, is the *tarantass*, the typical Russian conveyance, to which reference will be found elsewhere. If the traveller be sufficiently experienced to have avoided any luggage with corners to it, and to provide himself with cushions and rugs innumerable, he may hold on tight while the three loosely harnessed horses dash down a steep incline and bump the cart violently across a corduroy bridge of poles, but he will not escape without a shaking and the bruises which are the lot of the less wary. In the Kirghiz highlands, and among the Buriats in Trans-Baikatia, camel-sledges and carts are in use. The writer in his journey from Kiachta to Peking employed no less than five methods — namely, tarantass, telega, camels, camel-carts, and mule litter. As far as railway and sledge travelling is concerned, much misapprehension has hitherto existed as to the difficulties and dangers of overland journeys in Siberia. As a matter of fact, travel has for many years past been as free from risk as in Europe or the United States. Delicate ladies have made the journey from Peking to St. Petersburg, and, bathed in the elixir of steppe air, they have, notwithstanding the hardships, found "roughing it" invigorating rather than exhausting.

The public impression of the hazards of Siberian travel has, however, been unavoidably influenced by the ridiculous heroics of certain travellers seeking cheap glory rather than information. Conspicuous among these is the lively Gaul. He feels apparently obliged to play up to the photograph of himself in furs, which seemingly is the chief inducement to make the journey. Who, for instance, from this description of M. Meignan's, would imagine he was describing the common sledge route across Lake Baikal? "Between life and death, between the air we breathed and the bottom of the lake, there was only one foot of ice. . . . Who at this distance could have heard our last desperate cry of anguish, at the moment when the ice, breaking under our weight, would open and then close over us forever?"

The same author, having lost his way for a few hours in a snow-storm—not a very terrible experience in a well-covered sledge, with abundance of furs, victuals, and cognac handy!—thus (naïvely, we think) describes his feelings for the benefit of his fellow-countrymen: "We saw passing, in imagination, caravans of Kirghiz—from whom we were, in reality, not distant—and we fancied ourselves led prisoners into Tartary, in some wild, lawless territory not yet brought under subjection; we saw also—but this time it was not a vision—five or six packs of wolves prowling around our poor beasts." The Mongol, most harmless of men, is painted by this gentleman in no less vivid colors: "Armed as formidably as they appeared to be, sometimes with a bow and arrows, sometimes with a musket bristling with a spike, and always with a murderous-looking knife, these savage-looking rovers were calculated to fill one with

BURIAT CAMEL-SLEDGE

misgivings as to their pacific intentions." Another French writer of the same mettle has to walk, unarmed, a mile home to his inn after dinner, on a fine night. His Siberian host—in the sinister-sounding town of Krivochokovo, whose eleven thousand five hundred inhabitants, he assures his readers, were *all* of them the scum of Siberia—does not order out the carriage at ten o'clock at night; consequently: "What a whirl of thoughts! Rage, anger at my host, regret for my carelessness, good resolutions for the future—should I ever come out alive—then terror, and finally resignation to the worst. Must I detail my agony, my hesitation, my stumblings? . . . I reached my room drenched with sweat, shaking with fever and fatigue, and collapsed, fainting, only conscious that I had spent an hour and a half . . ."—in a badly lighted street!

Books written in this tone of heroic combating with windmills do not give much helpful information as to the real Siberia now in process of development. Neither do dusty volumes of government gazetteers, packed though they be with geographical and ethnographical statistics; nor picturesque and propagandist descriptions of exiles and Jews. The need of information is, however, urgent—of information neither too dry for assimilation nor tantalizingly frothy.

A new era is dawning for Siberia: improved mining methods; systematic conservancy of forests, fisheries, and hunting-grounds; organized credit. Good communications, with accessible markets, will soon throw her, armed at all points, into the commercial arena. The gravity of the prospect can scarcely be overrated.

The awakening to life of a whole fifth of the world's surface, long thought dead, must necessitate no slight readjustment among the other occupants. And when, with the dawn of the twentieth century, the new challenger enters the world's lists, it will not do for the Anglo-Saxon to plead that he had had no notice of the jousts!

CHAPTER V

INDUSTRIES AND PRODUCTS

Prominent among Siberian industries stands mining, and of all the mining exploitation at present carried on in the country, that of gold is the most important, Siberia ranking as a gold-producing region next after the United States, Australia, and the Transvaal. That she occupies such a position is all the more noteworthy when one considers that hitherto only the easiest and richest surface deposits have been touched, and that modern machinery, such as is now employed in all the great gold-fields of the world, has till now been dispensed with. So far as such limitations have allowed, however, gold has been exploited throughout Siberia: on the banks of the Obi, Yenisei, Lena, and Amur rivers, and on the shores of Lake Baikal. The deposits have hitherto been found chiefly below the elevation of two thousand feet, and on the western slopes of mountains connecting the Arctic Ocean with the Siberian lowlands. The prospecting has been, however, of the most rudimentary nature, and the wealth already known to exist must be considered as but an indication of the vast riches still awaiting discovery.

The deposits in the Yenisei region rank as the richest in all Russia, and as large a proportion as seven-tenths of the total Russian gold production may be said to come from Eastern Siberia, Western Siberia supplying only between five and seven per cent. The total export from Siberia to European Russia a couple of years ago had already reached an average of five millions sterling per annum. The number of miners at present employed in Western Siberia is about ten thousand, while in Eastern Siberia three times that number are at work, the ratio of production to the amount of labor employed in the respective districts being sufficient testimony to the superior richness of the Eastern Siberian deposits. There is no doubt that in Siberia, as in other parts of the world, the result of the mining industry has been to improve the condition of things generally, and especially in the matter of roads, steam navigation, and education.

One of the most noted Siberian mining districts is the Olekminsk, in the Yakutsk region, where, in 1880, a single company produced gold to the value of over a million sterling, and has even now an annual output of three-quarters of a million. Ten years ago these mines were employing two thousand three hundred horses and over two thousand reindeer for transport purposes. With the railway will certainly come more liberal legislation and improved methods, and these cannot fail to attract an ever-increasing amount of capital to Olekminsk, as well as to the mining-centres of Trans-Baikalia, the Amur, and the Lena, all very rich in auriferous deposits as yet only partially developed. It is possible, indeed, that the improved conditions may even cause a revival of the Yenisei and Altai mining industries, where the miners have hitherto, so to speak, merely scratched the surface, or, as the Russians say, picked out the eyes and then abandoned the carcass.

The system known as "placer mining" is the usual method adopted, being, in fact, almost the sole system employed so far. Apart altogether from drawbacks of climate and restrictions imposed by Government, the obstacles presented by difficulty of transport, absence of skilled labor, and want of capital wherewith to provide the necessarily costly crushing apparatus required, have tended to retard the development of quartz or veinous gold-mining, which has been hitherto almost entirely neglected. All Siberian methods are characterized by their inefficient and rudimentary character. The "heroic" period of mining, so to speak, is as yet scarcely past, the aid of modern science having but recently been evoked with the introduction of more businesslike methods and a larger amount of capital. The inhabitants are wont to plead that the backward condition of Siberia is not unnatural, and that the want of enterprise hitherto evinced on all sides has been due to the absence of communications and to the enormous distances involved. Machinery, for instance, they tell one, which had to be transported from the Ural, could only be procured at treble its original cost. But, true though this may be, Siberian inertia, due to isolation and want of education, for which *vodka* is so largely responsible, has also been to blame. Affairs will doubtless assume a very different aspect as soon as outside energy, no less needed than outside capital, shall find its way into the country, as it will inevitably do in the wake of the railway.

A more advanced state of things already obtains in the Amur region, where the mines are worked by well-capitalized companies, instead of being in the hands of private individuals, and when the railway, with its numerous branches, is in working order, it is probable that this superior condition of mining will spread through other parts of Siberia. The mineral wealth of Siberia and Manchuria is indeed considered by the Russians, and not merely by them, to have a great future before it, and, if one speaks merely of gold, the "dreams of avarice" might well be satiated by the prospect. At least that is the tune which is being played to the phlegmatic Siberians by enterprising Russian concessionaires and enthusiastic British and American mining engineers, many of whom the writer met at various stages of his journey, traversing the country in quest of adventure in their own particular line. It is chiefly on the results achieved in South Africa that are based their extremely sanguine calculations: "Beats the Rand," is what one hears on all sides, and, dull though they be, the natives are not so indifferent as to be insensible to the voice of the charmer who carries gold for his talisman; and having heard, of course in an exaggerated form, of the colossal fortunes made in mining enterpises in South Africa, they are quite ready for the early advent of a great "boom" in Siberia. Speculators in town land are on the alert, and the idea is being diligently disseminated that Irkutsk is to become the "Chicago of the Far East," and that building-plots there will ere long be sold at so many thousand rubles a foot. Allowing a reasonable discount in estimating at their real value these optimistic views, it is certain that gold in immense quantities does abound in the country. Still, much has yet to be done in the way of prospecting before it is possible for the industry to be raised to the level of the modern standard of production. As for Irkutsk itself, that city has immense advantages. There can be little doubt that its future prosperity is assured, for it has the great advantage of proximity to several of the most important waterways of Siberia, and is, in addition, admirably situated at what will be the central junction of the principal lines of railway, in the very centre of a large and promising gold-yielding region. A great obstacle to the advance of gold-mining in Siberia, and consequently to the prosperity of the whole country, has to be faced in the terrible winters that prevail. During the four or five months when the country is ice-bound, every industry is at a stand-still, and all mining operations have perforce to be carried out between May and September, when the days are bright and sunny and the nights clear and frosty. Nothing could be more favorable for work or more enjoyable than this season, but towards the end of September a complete change may be brought about within a few hours, and one may be placed without notice in the heart of winter, as the writer knows from experience, when further mining operations become of course out of the question.

Existing legislation, too, is also a serious handicap to the prosperity of gold-mining. Under the Gold Industry Law of 1870, still in force, miners on proprietary lands pay a tax on the output, those on state lands being charged a royalty in addition. Thus the Olekminsk mines pay a ten per cent. tax and about four rubles per acre ground-rent; those in the Amur region five per cent. tax and five rubles royalty; and other mines throughout the empire three per cent. tax and one ruble royalty. Worse, however, in its effects than either tax or royalty is the regulation providing that all Siberian gold must be sent to the Government smelting-houses (which are situated at Tomsk for Western, and at Irkutsk for Eastern Siberia), where the gold is smelted, assayed, and then despatched to the St. Petersburg mint, the mine-owners receiving bills payable only on arrival of the consignment in the capital. The many objections to this antiquated system are obvious. It offers a direct incentive to the merchant to engage in illicit dealings and to circumvent the Government by effecting a sale on the spot or by shipping direct to some foreign agency; for by so doing he not only saves the legal Government dues, but also avoids the official peculations which prevail, and against which he has but little redress—less redress in Siberia, it will be readily understood, than he would have in European Russia—while at the same time he does not have to remain for so long a time out of pocket. As it is, not being able to sustain the alternative of long delay, he is frequently forced to have his Government bills discounted locally, at an extortionate rate of course. The whole machinery, extremely cumbrous even from a Government point of view, necessitating as it does an armed road-escort and other precautions, must soon give way, in its turn, to some system more in consonance with the spirit of the time.

Next in importance to gold come iron and coal mining, neither of which, however, has been as yet to any extent developed, although incalculably vast deposits of both are known to exist. Such iron as was imperatively required was till recently supplied from "that metallurgical treasure-house of Russia," the Ural Mountains, geographically part of Siberia, although, strange to say, still officially classed as belonging to Europe. Until the other day, only four iron-works were in operation throughout the whole extent of Siberia, but doubtless the railway will give rise to a great change in this respect, and will lead to the development of some of the other iron-fields which abound, as well as to the opening up of the valuable coal-fields which are known to exist in every province, but which are at present only worked in the Kousnetsk basin, on the island of Sakhalin, and in the Kirghiz steppes. In the Kousnetsk region, which lies on the eastern frontier of the Altai mining region, the value of the coal deposit is much increased by its juxtaposition to inexhaustible supplies of fuel and rich deposits of magnetic iron ore. The Sakhalin coal, of a quality equal to the best Welsh coal, has for thirty years been used by Russian and other vessels frequenting the Pacific coast, the present annual output exceeding twenty-five thousand tons. The discovery of coal on the Kirghiz steppe, after a most careful and protracted search on the part of the Government, was a matter for congratulation, the steppe having otherwise no fuel, with the exception of dried dung, even for heating purposes, and much less for the development of its vast stores of silver, copper, and lead. Since the recent fortunate discovery, however, the Kirghiz highlands may be considered as fully guaranteed in this all-important respect.

The silver, lead, and copper of Siberia have as yet chiefly a potential value. In locating the mines, Russian prospectors have in some instances been aided by the discovery of certain old workings, attributed to the "Chuds" or "Wander" men, aborigines of the Stone Age. The Altai Mountains have been found to be particularly rich in the minerals mentioned, but these industries, in proportion to their possibilities, have been barely touched in recent years, although some really valuable copper-smelting works were established as early as 1726. Notwithstanding that as many as eight hundred deposits of metallic ore are known to exist in the Altai region, only eight silver and two copper mines, and those on an insignificant scale, are now in operation. In this connection it is perhaps not generally known that as long ago as 1766 a mining engineer named Polzounov is said to have erected at Barnaoul an engine worked by steam and used for the blast-furnaces, by virtue of which achievement he is claimed as a Russian precursor of Watts. Tin and mercury were early discovered and made use of by the half-savage Buriats and Yakuts, but no Siberian works of any importance have as yet been established. Graphite, first introduced to the world at the London Exhibition of 1862, the principal mine-owner helping Faber, the well-known pencil-maker, to make a large fortune by inducing him to adopt it, is found in the Kirghiz steppe and in the regions belonging to the Yenisseisk and Irkutsk governments.

Another important product of Siberia is salt, which in the western districts is obtained exclusively from the self-depositing lakes, while in the eastern portions of the country, though rock-salt abounds, the richest deposits and the best salt-springs are situated in sparsely inhabited districts, where transport is at present extremely costly. Improved means of communication will before long open up large stores of this product, and when the writer was in Siberia projects were already being discussed between sanguine concessionnaires and the local governments. The present annual production is altogether insufficient for the wants of the population, and Government assistance is therefore given at an annual expenditure of one hundred thousand rubles, salt being issued free to the Kirghiz and Cossack levies, while in the saltless regions depots have been established where the Government article can be procured at a low price. Foreign salt is allowed to pass duty free at the Siberian Pacific ports.

Precious stones and minerals are known to exist in large quantities in various parts of the country, the chief centre of these deposits being Trans-Baikalia, a subdivision, as before described, of the Amur-Littoral region. Between the rivers Onon and Onon-Borza rise the granitic mountains Admar-Chilon, celebrated for topaz, beryl, aquamarine, and other precious stones, while on the Onon, fifty miles from Nertchinsk, are found garnets of a good quality. In the Baikal Mountains lapis-lazuli, put to many artistic uses in the various imperial palaces, is abundant, as are also red garnets, mica, and asphanite. The Altai Mountains are famous for their porphyry and jasper, which are in great demand for the court at St. Petersburg, whither they are sent after passing through the Kolivan polishing works. In the Altai region there are altogether eight quarries producing porphyry, jasper, agate, topaz, and chalcedony, together with a variety of building-stone, felspar, quartz, and other more or less valuable rocks and minerals.

Next after the mineral resources of the country comes, in natural order, the forest wealth. Till quite recently this was made use of only for local needs, the most primitive methods of working being employed. Indeed, the indiscriminate and reckless felling, together with the frequently recurring forest-fires, must ere this have reduced to a low ebb even such extensive forests as these, had they been readily exhaustible. They may be said to run through Siberia in three zones, from west to east, the first of these extending between the meridian of cultivation and the Polar *tundras* in vast areas of unbroken and in many parts absolutely virgin forest. Here are found hundreds of miles of pine woods, whose lonely aisles of bare red trunks are said to be avoided even by all wild animals, and where, even if this were not the case, the most experienced trappers would scarcely trust themselves. Here, locked up for want of communication, lies a storehouse of timber representing vast future revenues. The second zone is that of the birch, which, to the exclusion of all other trees, covers the Western Siberian plains. The trees grow in *koloks*, or spinnies, which, viewed in masses from the road, present the appearance of an unbroken forest. Birchwood serves many purposes in Siberia, being employed as building material and as fuel, while it is also largely used in the manufacture of farm implements. It is being fast used up, however, and preservative measures are urgently required, especially as the railway will enormously increase the demand for fuel. The third belt of forest-land extends along the northern slopes of the almost uninterrupted chain of mountains which, under various names, connects Semirechia with Vladivostok, while dividing Siberia from China. These forests consist chiefly of conifers, but although the timber is excellent the difficulties of felling and of transport are so great that it is scarcely worth while to bring it to a market. No raftage is possible on the wild mountain torrents of this neighborhood, and the logs have sometimes to be actually transported on camel-back.

According to law, the forest was at one time free to the inhabitants, and the peasants therefore came to regard it as their own, as a "gift of God," in fact, like air and water, and to be squandered accordingly. Consequently the forests easiest of access are in a chaotic condition, and in some districts the countryside is absolutely denuded of trees. The terrible fires, too, which may be seen by the traveller as the train rushes through the country, are playing vast havoc. A "Woods and Forests" Department is urgently needed, to assume control and turn what is at present most wanton waste into an increasingly valuable source of revenue.

Among the natural resources of Siberia one ought to be able to give a foremost place to the abundance of fish in the rivers, which at one time was almost fabulous; but, as has been already said, the same lack of forethought, which is denuding some parts of the country of valuable timber, has led to a reckless waste in fishing also, and in the cultivated zone the supply now only suffices for local wants. The fishing is mostly done individually, and without any organization, being only carried on wholesale during the summer with huge drift-nets, many as much as a mile in length. In spring the fish are caught while rushing up small streams, through holes cut in the ice. If sent to market they are frozen or salted, but the process is not well carried out, which greatly hinders the development of what ought to be an important industry. The fur industry has suffered in the same way from indiscriminate slaughter, and in Western Siberia fur animals have almost disappeared, the supplies now coming mostly from due north of Eastern Siberia. The squirrel affords the most certain livelihood to the hunter, the average being three hundred head in a winter. The larger animals, bear and elk, must be carefully stalked, and much depends on luck as well as skill in the killing of them. Fire-arms are used, and traps of the most varied construction, but the natives, who are the chief hunters and traders, still adhere in some parts to the primitive bow and arrow. In Yakutsk sables are still plentiful, though hunters are few, and the Arctic fox can be trapped in large numbers during its curious migration from the sea up the rivers. During a great migration in 1860, seven thousand were caught, the rivers being fenced in at certain points. Several varieties of birds, such as the ryabtchik (the delicious *gelinotte*, or hazel-grouse), are shot for European markets, while the wild goose, duck, and black-cock are merely shot for sport.

To pass from products to industries: Owing to scanty population and to wretched communications, the Siberian manufacturing industry, like the mining, has not developed in proportion to the natural wealth of the country. Manufactures were, indeed, initiated with great difficulty, and have only succeeded where they immediately supplied a local want, or (and this not very often the case) when they produced articles of sufficient value to cover the high cost of transport. The total product of Siberian manufactures did not till recently exceed ten million rubles in yearly value, an altogether insignificant figure for such a vast territory, and one possessing, too, such illimitable resources. Oil-mills and cheese-making represented forty-five per cent. of this, naphtha of a quality resembling the Caucasian product being found in large quantities in Sakhalin; second to these come tanning and sheepskin-dressing, then tallow-making, soap-boiling, and kindred industries, the cultivation of beet-sugar occupying a not unimportant place. The distilling of spirits from grain and potatoes; the growth of a poor kind of tobacco for local consumption; the manufacture of matches, and other industries exist, but all to an insignificant degree.

The total taxes for the whole of Siberia amount to scarcely one million rubles. Of the annual turnover, woollen and cotton goods represent thirty-six per cent., groceries fifteen per cent., and liquors eleven per cent. The exports westward are principally the raw materials of agriculture and cattle-raising, and include grain, flour, flax, linseed, tow, nuts, tallow, butter, hair, wool, hides, skins, and furs. The imports (mostly Russian, although a small proportion of foreign goods also change hands) are chiefly the products of manufacturing industries, such as cloth,

RUSSIAN ASIA

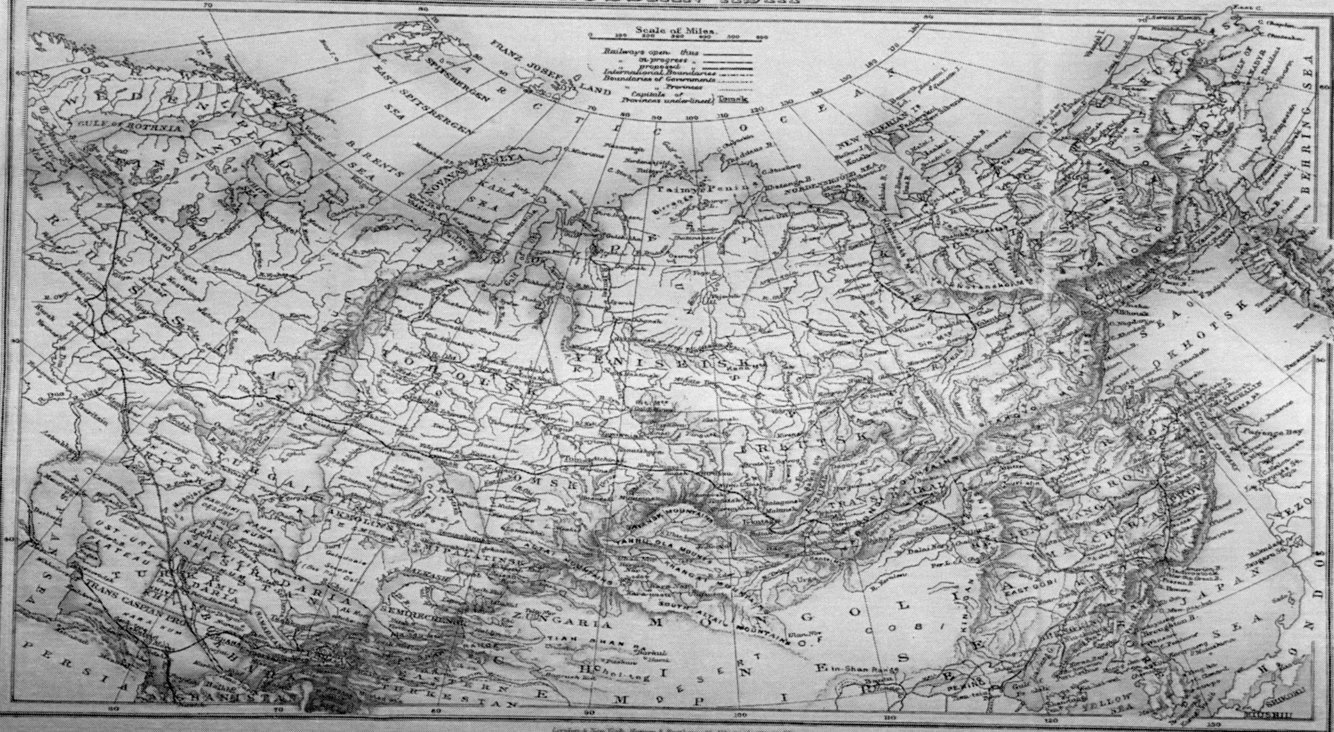

haberdashery, groceries, metals, pottery, glass, spirits, sugar, tobacco, and mineral oils. Owing to the extent to which the Siberian population is scattered—only eleven cities of over ten thousand inhabitants are to be found throughout the length and breadth of this enormous territory—monopolies and "corners" are frequent, the absence of good communications being an effective factor in their operation.

Fairs have hitherto been a prominent feature in Siberian trade, as in European Russia, the most ancient being that founded in 1643 at Irbit, in the Perm Government. During February of this year (1899) this little town accommodated no less than fifteen thousand strangers, and transacted business amounting in value to some fifty million rubles. Other fairs, often dealing with a special class of articles such as tallow, butter, hides, live cattle, or furs, are held in various parts of the dominion.

The Arctic shores of Siberia being practically closed to navigation, foreign trade is confined to the Pacific littoral and the frontier of the Chinese Empire. The development of trade relations with China is a traditional aim of Russian policy, and various commercial treaties have from time to time been made in order to further this object; but, principally owing to want of good communication, the overland trade with the south has so far shown but little tendency to increase. The most important route for trade between China and Russia, as it is also the one most frequented by travellers, is that *via* the Siberian track, Irkutsk, Kiachta, Maimachen, Urga, and Kalgan, the route which the writer followed, and which is largely used for the import trade. Two less important roads, principally used for export to China, connect Peking with the province of Semipalatinsk. The value of the Siberian exports, it may be noted, has never exceeded three million rubles, while the imports reach the amount of fifteen million rubles, of which, however, twelve millions represent tea in transit to Russia, thus leaving Siberian exports and imports about equal. The Russian trade with Mongolia is carried on chiefly from the Trans-Baikal territory. The tea trade with China has existed for over two centuries, reaching latterly the huge total of over sixty-four million puds a year, one-half being imported overland through Siberia, and the other going by sea to Odessa. The finer kinds (as, for instance, bohea), required for consumption in Russia, are sent by the latter route, but coarser varieties, made up in "bricks," and intended for consumption among the Siberians, Kirghiz, and Kalmuks, are, as a rule, despatched overland. The tariff for bohea is thirteen rubles per pud (equal to thirty-six pounds in British weight) at Irkutsk, and twenty-one rubles on the European frontier, the difference in price being due to the increased expense, risk, and delay of the land transit, which often occupies a year from Hankow to Nijni-Novgorod, thus necessitating extremely careful packing and supervision. Here again the railway will introduce a completely new factor in the development of the trade.

As to other items of foreign commerce, all imports into Siberia are duty free, with the exception of sugars and confectioneries, liquors, mineral oils, and matches, these exceptions, however, being allowed only on the route passing through Eastern Siberia. Foreign goods enter this Eastern region by four routes—Vladivostok, Nicolaevsk, Blagovechensk, and Ayan—but by none of these routes can payment of customs dues at Irkutsk be avoided.

The foreign imports may be classified as follows: From European Russia—cheap cottons, woollens, tobacco, spirits, sugar, illuminants, leather, manufactured iron, stationery, haberdashery, and *articles de luxe*. From Great Britain—cotton and woollen yarn and fabrics, iron, tin-plate. From Belgium—glass and yarn. From France—*articles de luxe*, preserves, wine. From the United States—flour and other articles of food, machinery, and agricultural implements, leather goods, and guns. From Germany—various goods, mostly of inferior quality, including furniture, sugar, wine, kitchen utensils, cottons, and woollens. From Korea—grain, vegetables, and cattle. From Japan—wheat, rice, salt, fruits, and *articles de luxe*. From China—tea.

At Vladivostok, the principal place of import, cottons and woollens represent twenty-five per cent. of the imports; grain and flour fifteen; and other provisions ten per cent. Of these, Germany provides thirty per cent., European Russia twenty-five, England thirteen, Japan thirteen, China twelve, and America five per cent. The Vladivostok trade is in the hands of foreigners, chiefly Germans and Chinese, its exports being principally confined to the products of the whaling and the horse industry—about one and a half million rubles, and furs one million. Sea-weed, timber, and sundries make up a total of some three million rubles, a truly insignificant sum for a seaport which, on the completion of the Trans-Siberian Railway, is destined perhaps to become as important as Southampton, just as Talienwan will become another Hong-Kong or Hamburg.

CHAPTER VI

THE GREAT TRANS-SIBERIAN-MANCHURIAN RAILWAY

It is a well-known fact that there are two ways of seeing Russia in general and Siberia in particular. The first is under quasi-government conduct, and all those whose object is to travel in luxury or to meet everywhere with deference, and frequently with obsequiousness, naturally seek for official introductions to high government authorities. But, like everything else, the convenience and comfort of the personally conducted system have to be paid for, and the payment in this case takes the form of general restriction of view, coupled with an obligation, enjoined by the merest courtesy, to speak nothing but what is pleasant and flattering to the country. One may, therefore, spend months under the vigilant care of Russian officials, so that not a hair of one's head shall be injured, and yet learn just as little of the country as does, for instance, a Viceroy of India, during his progress from Calcutta to Simla, of the dominions under his rule.

Those, however, who are prepared to face some amount of discomfort, or to chance the risk of detention, in order that they may be able to use their own eyes, without having the everlasting *ispravnik* (chief police official of a district) to take them by the hand at every stopping-place, will probably find that, by travelling as individuals of no consideration, they will obtain a larger amount of information than would be possible under official patronage. This, at any rate, was the plan adopted by the writer when travelling in 1898-99 by the great Siberian Railway from Moscow to Irkutsk (to which point the railway was even then in working order) on his way to China. Whenever deviation was made from the plan of action decided upon, disappointment was the result, of which the following instance is an example. It was important to shorten the journey from the Siberian frontier to Peking, owing to the lateness of the season. On arrival at Kiachta, there was some difficulty in hiring the necessary conveyance, and the writer, therefore, wired to the British Ambassador at St. Petersburg, asking him to kindly procure from the officials concerned telegraphic instructions to the commissioner of the frontier, to aid in securing horses for the continuation of the journey as far as Urga, on the edge of the Gobi Desert. That functionary, however, found himself unable to give assistance, alleging, "with much regret," that he had no instructions. A second telegram was thereupon despatched to the ambassador, who replied that orders had been sent by telegraph both to the commissioner at Kiachta and to the consul-general at Urga, by the ministers for home and foreign affairs respectively. But evidently the ambassador

EN ROUTE WITH "TARANTASS," SIBERIA

had been misled by a Russian "assurance," which, though legal tender at St. Petersburg, would not pass current on the Russo-Chinese frontier, for both the frontier commissioner and the consul-general declared that no instructions of any kind having any reference to the journey had been received. Later on, however, the writer had reason to believe that the Asiatic Department at St. Petersburg had communicated with at least Urga, concerning the matter of the journey. It may here be mentioned that the traveller who obtains Russian official assistance can cover the distance between Moscow and Peking in thirty and a half days—that is to say, by rail to Irkutsk, ten and a half days; thence to Kiachta by the post-road, four days; Kiachta to Urga by post-road, three days; thence to Kalgan over the Gobi Desert in ten days, or even less; Kalgan to Peking in three days.

Many "hints to travellers" might be given, but one in particular should be remembered by those who go to Siberia in quest of information. It is to avoid the discussion of all political questions, and especially those of the prison administration and the convict system, as one would shun the plague. An American, who when young had spent some years in Siberia as a mechanical engineer, was once relating to the writer some of his experiences, and incidentally spoke of certain advice he had received from an old hand, a fellow-countryman of his own: "Young man, let me whisper something in your ear. If you wish to stay in Russia, avoid politics and religion; above all, never allow yourself to know there is such a thing as a 'convict system.'" At the present moment, perhaps, this advice may be considered less necessary, for the first place in the mind of every one interested in Russian development is now of course occupied by consideration of the great railway scheme, of which the world has but recently taken cognizance, but which, nevertheless, is the slowly ripened fruit of nearly half a century's inspirations, suggestions, plans, and deliberations.

Whether regarded from a commercial or a political point of view, the urgent need for good communications in Siberia has been obvious to the Russian authorities for over a quarter of a century, although, it is true, this stupendous conception of a Russian-Pacific railroad was not from the beginning grasped in its entirety. The earlier plans combined rail and river communication, tramways and ferries, and it was but gradually that the idea was conceived of the unparalleled achievement to which the imperial rescript of March 17, 1891, was to give birth. That famous document, read by the present Emperor, then Tsarevitch, at Vladivostok, in May of the same year, notified the adoption in fullest measure of the much-hoped-for undertaking, and announced "the immediate construction through the entire length of Siberia." Until the year 1880 the sectional system of railways was the one favored, but eventually the Emperor took the matter in hand, and a grand unified scheme was adopted. The knot of all the technical official controversies between rival projectors was cut by him in the manner of his grandfather, who forty years previously settled the question of the route to be followed between St. Petersburg and Moscow by laying the ruler across the map and drawing with his pencil a straight line between the two termini. With what incredible energy the work —which marks, unless forecasts deceive us, a new era for the whole world—has been carried out since it was sanctioned by the Tsar is known. Outside interest, at first vaguely informed and rather languid, has increased with the approaching realization of the enterprise; and the great Siberian Railway now commands in public opinion the respect due to an almost accomplished work of such vast importance.

In course of construction the line has, however, become much changed in character. No longer a purely internal enterprise — running through unknown territories, to terminate at an obscure Russian port far away somewhere in the north—by the Manchurian alignment it has become the world's highway from West to East, a route which is to bring the vast empire of China for the first time into intimate touch with Europe. The scope of the railway has been infinitely enlarged. From being a merely domestic work, pertaining solely to internal administration, it has become a great international undertaking, and has passed into the domain of foreign affairs; from being little more than a local enterprise, it now promises to develop into one of the greatest arteries of traffic the world has yet seen, and into a political instrument whose far-reaching effects it is difficult to gauge.

How far this is the result of what would appear to be a fortuitous combination of circumstances, and how far the outcome of Russian foresight, must be largely matter for conjecture. Whichever view may be the true one—whether the result was brought about by chance or by statecraft—the fact remains that nothing could have turned out more happily for Russia. The course mapped out for the Siberian Railway, as originally announced to the world, could not possibly provoke either jealousy or hostility, whereas had the 1891 programme included, as does the present one, a short cut across a Chinese province and the extension southward to Port Arthur, with the establishment of a terminal fortified stronghold—another Sevastopol, in fact, commanding the whole Gulf of Pechihli and even Peking itself—the inevitable shock to the world must have jeopardized success. But, whether by design or accident, that shock was spared to the world, and the warnings of the few who could foresee events passed unheeded. The radical change in the character of the line has, indeed, been effected with the graduated gentleness and the assured result of a process of nature. That the railway is primarily a strategic line is beyond question, this being emphasized by the provision which has been made to keep the main line clear for through traffic in case of emergency.

Final choice of the line the railway was to take through Western Siberia lay between three much-discussed alternative points of departure—namely, Tiumen, Zlatoost, and Orenburg, at each of which points the Russian railways cut the Ural Mountains. Of these alternative lines, the one chosen was in any case to make its way to the fixed point of Nijni-Oudinsk, half-way between the Yenisei and Lake Baikal. The one *via* Zlatoost and Cheliabinsk, known as the central project, was the one selected.*

According to the imperial rescript, the total distance of line to be constructed, at a total cost of £34,700,000, was, in round numbers, 7080 versts, or over 4700 miles; and it was divided into six sections, on which work was to be commenced simultaneously. These were Cheliabinsk to the Obi, *via* Omsk, 885

* The chief features of the three routes receiving consideration, which led to the adoption of the central project, were as follows:

1. If Tiumen were made the starting-point, the distance to be traversed to Nijni-Oudinsk would be 1638 miles. But the Ural Railway, of which Tiumen is the terminus, not being connected with the Russian system, it would be necessary to first fill in a hiatus of 662 miles (between Perm and Nijni-Novgorod), making the total length of the Tiumen alternative 2300 miles.

2. By the central project, which took Zlatoost as the starting-place, 92 miles already open between that town and Cheliabinsk could be utilized; this would therefore only necessitate the construction of 1817 miles of new line. In places it would have the disadvantage of skirting the barren steppe, but, on the other hand, it would tap the great industrial centre of Omsk, and would, generally, traverse a more fertile region than that which the proposed northern line (1) would pass through.

3. The immense extent, 2319 miles, of sterile and mountainous country through which the southern or Orenburg line would have to pass put the adoption of that route out of the question, and the central project, starting from Cheliabinsk, was the one finally decided upon.

miles; the Obi to Irkutsk, *via* Krasnoiarsk, 1169; Irkutsk to Listvenitchnaya and Mysovsk, on Lake Baikal (with ice-breaker, pier, harbor, and "train-ferry" across lake), 195; Mysovsk to Stretensk (the Trans-Baikal section), 673; Stretensk to Khabarovsk (the Amur section), 1333; and Khabarovsk to Vladivostok (the Ussuri section, which is completed), 486 miles. This plan has been, however, as will be seen, considerably modified; particularly in regard to the abandonment of the permanent "train-ferry" crossing of Lake Baikal, in favor of a line to run round the southern edge of the lake, and of section five (Stretensk to Khabarovsk)—the longest and certainly not the easiest of all. Until the Amur section was reached, the railway survey followed pretty closely the natural high-road eastward, and practically the only one traversing Siberia. Each section so far had been already surveyed and was easily determined on. But in Trans-Baikalia and the Amur region it was a far different matter. In the latter, the only road was that provided by the lower slopes of the river itself, the sole traffic on the lower Amur being by steamer in summer and sledge in winter. Around the southern edge of Lake Baikal some heavy tunnelling has to be done,* and the difficulties both of survey and execution were here, but in Trans-Baikalia especially, enormously increased, and it is reasonably open to doubt whether the authorities ever seriously intended to make the main line run *via*

* At one time as much as two and a half miles of tunnel-work was anticipated, but this has been largely reduced.

the Amur. The fact that Russian engineers secretly made surveys in Manchuria even some years prior to the crisis of 1895, and the haste with which Chinese permission for the running of the line through Manchuria, with the necessary police to protect it, was then claimed—as recompense for Russian help against the Japanese — cannot be forgotten. It would therefore appear by no means improbable that a short cut across Northern Manchuria to Vladivostok had been planned many years ago, and that the inclusion of section five in the programme was merely tentative, while the project was maturing. As originally planned, the railway was to be constructed simultaneously from both ends, the line from the west to meet that from Vladivostok at Irkutsk. In the modified plan, however, the section completed from Vladivostok to Khabarovsk is not utilized, while from the other end the main line branches off at Onon, 100 miles on the west side of Stretensk, and at Nikolaevsk, 67 miles north of Vladivostok, joins the already opened section between that port and Khabarovsk. The section between Onon and Nikolaevsk is estimated at 1200 miles, of which some 900 are on Chinese and over 300 on Russian territory. This reduces the total distance between Cheliabinsk and Vladivostok to about 4000 miles, instead of 4700; but these estimates of distance are vague and probably below the mark.

The line from Onon junction will, however, be continued, as originally planned, to Stretensk, where it will be connected with steamboat traffic on the

Upper Amur, the main line running from Onon southeastward, probably past Tsitsikar, Kirin, and Mukden, to the Gulf of Pechihli at Port Arthur; while a branch line will be built from Vladivostok, or rather from the Nikolaevsk junction, to join the Manchurian Railway at some central point on the Sungari. These sections are timed to be completed in the autumn of 1902, but before this date, in 1900, Russia, it is important to note, pending the full completion of the Siberian-Manchurian Railway, will have at her disposal an uninterrupted line of rail and river communication—rail to Stretensk, thence steamer to Khabarovsk, and again rail to Vladivostok on the Pacific. As a supplementary measure, train-ferry-boats, as used in America and Denmark, are to be run across Lake Baikal from Listvenitchnaya (the harbor and pier on the west shore of Lake Baikal), to the opposite shore at Mysovsk.*

The estimate of the time required for the completion of the line to Port Arthur is based on the work already accomplished, which has all been done within the time calculated, the estimate not having been exceeded in any of the sections as yet opened. As the most extraordinary exertions are being made with the construction round the south end of Lake Baikal and from the Port Arthur ter-

* The ice-breaker to be used on Lake Baikal was constructed by Messrs. Armstrong, and shipped in sections to its destination. Built entirely of steel, two hundred and ninety feet in length, it is capable of breaking through ice several feet thick, and is to be in use during the winter months—that is, from October onward. The railway cars are to be run direct on board, and ferried across the lake.

minus, working both ways, as well as in the centre, by means of the Manchurian waterways (the Sungari, the Argun, and the Ussuri, which are being made use of for the transport of material, some special tug-boats for towing rail-laden barges having already been imported from England), it is as certain as any such calculation can be that the time-limit for the remainder of the operations, *i.e.*, 1902, will not be exceeded.

If the original financial estimates have been exceeded, that, after all, is the affair of the Russian Government. The world is only concerned in the due accomplishment of the task which will work so great a revolution. It is of some interest to make, as far as the data are known, a rough comparison with what has been previously accomplished in the way of gigantic railway construction, and for that purpose we may take the first American line between the Atlantic and the Pacific. It must, however, be remembered that in the quarter of a century which has elapsed between the execution of the two undertakings wider experience and improved knowledge have accumulated, to the great advantage of the Russian enterprise.

In sheer length the Trans-Siberian will be almost double that of the Trans-American continental railway. The maximum altitude of 3608 feet, overcome by very gentle gradients while crossing the Yablonoi or "Apple" Mountains (so called from their rounded contours), cannot, however, for a moment be compared with the giddy precipices of the Sierra Nevada, or the 6500 feet ascent of the Rocky Mountains. And although the Siberian plains are, perhaps, as scantily populated as were those of the Far West in 1860–70, they include no such waterless tracts as the Utah and Nevada wildernesses. Leaving Trans-Baikalia and Manchuria out of the question, the Siberian line was an exceptionally easy one from an engineering point of view. Beyond the Urals the rails could be laid in straight lines over immense plains. Between the Obi and the Yenisei there are but gentle undulations to be overcome. After crossing the Yenisei, a series of hills, never exceeding 2000 feet, are traversed at right angles. In the whole distance from Cheliabinsk to Irkutsk no single tunnel occurs, no gradient steeper than 17½ in 1000, no curve sharper than a 270 yards' radius. Beyond Irkutsk, however, there is really serious work to be done, and the obstacles which have had to be overcome so far may be regarded as infinitesimal when compared with those which must be surmounted. These are, (1) round the southern edge of Lake Baikal; (2) eastward, across Trans-Baikalia from the lake to the navigation limit of the Amur (at or near Stretensk); and (3) from the point where the Manchurian line, leaving the Trans-Baikal section of the Siberian Railway—whether at Onon, precisely, or some other point, has not yet been finally decided—passes across the hilly country enclosed between the Argun and the Upper Amur, skirting the lower slopes of the Yablonoi range, from the Argun continuing its route across the Khingan range *via* Hailar to Tsitsikar (or some place south of that town) on the Upper Sungari, in Manchuria. Beyond Lake Baikal there is a gradual ascent from 1300 to 3600 feet, through the valleys of the Selenga and its tributaries; then a somewhat abrupt descent to the Amur, and after that a short section of some 200 miles along the mountain spurs and across the occasional marshes in the valleys of the Ingoda and the Shilka.

Much attention has been given to the bridges, of which there are many, the Siberian waterways running in general from south to north, at right angles to the railway line. The four most important bridges, all now completed, are those over the Irtysh and Obi, each about 930 yards long; and over the Yenisei and Selenga, each about 1700 yards in length. The Obi bridge is a particularly fine structure, being at least 50 feet above the river at times of flood, while on ordinary occasions one looks down upon the waters from a height of 80 feet. The Yenisei bridge is similar in many respects, and, indeed, all the bridges are of the same type, being constructed of iron, with stone piers supporting spans which in some cases measure as much as 100 yards in length, and across which a single line is laid through girder lattice work. Most Siberian bridges are of specially difficult construction, owing to the great variation of heat and cold, the swampy, inundated, and yielding nature of the river-banks and approaches, and the unusually solid stone supports required to resist the impact of ice.

In point of actual rate of construction, the Siberian

maximum is far behind the American one, though it must be considered fast under the circumstances. Six versts, or three miles and three-quarters, per diem, is the highest ever achieved by the Russians —a poor record when compared with the ten and a half miles credited to American brain and Chinese labor on the San Francisco section of the American line. But the Americans, on the other hand, took nearly seven years to complete a distance of 1800 miles; whereas in Siberia nearly a thousand miles beyond that amount was accomplished in less than eight years. As has been shown, the difficulties of the country itself were immeasurably greater on the American line, but, as a set off, it must be remembered that the working season in Siberia lasts only six months, from April to September, at other times the ground being frozen too hard for anything to be done. As the line is single, and the rails are merely laid on notched sleepers and clamped down on the inside, the speed in construction might perhaps have been even greater. Great precautions are taken in working the line, men being stationed at very short intervals with green flags, to show their section to be clear.

On the Siberian Railway the labor question—an enormously important one, since during the greater part of the construction no less than 150,000 laborers were employed — was saved from developing into a "problem" (as it would have done in another country) by the exceptional character of the Russian peasantry, who are not averse to being moved

TYPICAL FERRY, SIBERIA

from one place to another. The population along the Siberian track proved, as had been foreseen, quite unable to provide the labor required. Neither were soldiers, as in the case of the Trans-Caspian line, available in sufficient numbers. Convict labor was tried, but, except in the neighborhood of Irkutsk, proved a failure. Fortunately, as remarked above, the Russian peasant is always willing to leave his home for two or three years, and proceed to any distance for assured employment. If possible he likes to get home-leave for the harvest-time, but in the case of the Siberian Railway, laborers had to content themselves with leave during the slack winter season. No foreigners are employed. The Siberian Railway, as described to the writer during his journey, is "a Russian railway, made by Russian engineers, for Russia."

Speaking generally, when all the difficulties are taken into due consideration, credit is due to the Russian authorities for the excellence of the main plan of the line, the good general organization, and the rapidity of the execution. The last, indeed, may be held to cover a multitude of sins. The main object was, first and foremost, speed in completion—a rapid linking of west and east—and that has been attained. Overland communication, by rail and steamer, has already been almost established between Europe and the Pacific. Trains fitted up with all modern luxuries are now actually running through the heart of the Siberian wastes. As far as Ob-Krivoschikovo (the junction for Tomsk) a *train de luxe* is available, which includes library, gymnasium, bath-rooms, lavatories, and even a piano, and thence to Irkutsk, the ordinary trains are provided with buffets and other comforts and luxuries. In view of such a brilliant result it may seem almost invidious to criticise such minor shortcomings as, until recently, the comfortless journey in cold weather across the Yenisei and Oka by ferry. The bridges over these rivers were not yet entirely completed when the writer passed, in the autumn of 1898.

There are, however, more serious shortcomings than this. In the first place, the general plan, though in itself excellent, has been badly worked out in detail. The Russian-European engineers, quite unused (be it said in their defence) to mountains, which are rarely met with in their own country, often avoided easy slopes along the hills and carried the line through marshes where solid foothold was difficult to obtain, and where the line must be continually subject to inundations. The want of solidity of the low-lying sections was, indeed, the only problem of any difficulty that the Siberian Railway engineers, until they reached Lake Baikal, had to face, and their solution of the difficulty redounds but little to their credit. In places cuttings, too, were frequently made where tunnels might well have been employed. To this fatal want of confidence in their skill in dealing with such problems, and the consequent frequency with which the line, often quite unnecessarily, is made to traverse swampy valleys, is mainly due the disasters that have hitherto occurred, such as destruction of the permanent way by inundation. In the Stretensk section the spectacle has actually been seen of three miles of rails, afloat on the sleepers, being carried down-stream. In the section beyond Baikal, now in hand, the difficulties, as before remarked, will be greatly increased, and will test the skill of the Russian engineers.

It is not only in the matter of engineering work, however, that the carrying out of the scheme is open to criticism. Many of the sections of the permanent way will have to be re-made, and most of it is insufficiently ballasted. As at present constructed, the lines would be incapable of supporting a continuous or heavy train service, and it is indeed proposed to use the rails for the construction of light branch lines for the transport of local products to favorable markets, and to lay down heavier metals in their place. Even in 1898, £10,000,000 were voted for the improvement of the permanent way in the western half of the line alone, although it was only just completed!* Bad material, too, has often, from motives

*The present intention is to re-lay the whole of the central and Trans-Baikalian sections with rails weighing 24 pounds to the foot, instead of the 18-pound rails now in use. In addition to this, 1429 wooden bridges are to be replaced by stone and iron ones. The stations, all built on sidings, are at present about 25 miles apart; a recent order provides for the construction of additional sidings every few miles, the total additions amounting to 91. Orders have also been given for the ballasting of a greater portion of the permanent way. The expenditure involved in all these improvements is to be spread over eight years, by the end of which time it is hoped that a maximum speed of 33 miles an hour for passenger-trains will have been attained.

best not inquired into, been ordered from small local contractors. There has been, and still continues to be, a large amount of what must be regarded as barbaric waste. New engines have been seen lying uncased and rusting on the ground; twisted rails strewn alongside the track; sleepers allowed to rot before the time came to use them. Neither is it without good reason that peculation and misappropriation are alleged to be common.

Again, as previously mentioned, the cost of the line will greatly exceed the original estimates, at first thirty-five and later thirty-eight millions sterling, which were in their mileage rate low as compared with that of England. According to competent authority, this is estimated at £50,000 per mile, at which rate fifty millions sterling would not have carried the Siberian Railway much beyond the Obi. But in comparing the English and Russian charges, the cheapness of labor, and the altogether insignificant cost of land—in the latter country practically *nil*—must be taken into account. The final cost of the Russian scheme promises, according to a well-disposed French critic, to rival that of any line in Europe or America, a view which must, however, be accepted with caution. But here again it must be remembered that the total is swelled by such items as Russian rails and girders employed when English or American could have been purchased at half the price—an outcome of the protectionist ideas favored in Russia. Seeing, however, that Indian railways, in spite of their enormous initial cost, pay fairly well, there is every probability that the Siberian Railway will also eventually pay as a purely commercial speculation, notwithstanding the corruption and waste which are so prevalent at present. As a Government state measure, the success of the railway is of course already assured. Additional engines and trucks, ordered in hundreds, are yet insufficient to cope with the goods traffic on the sections of the line already opened. Under special exemption from the imperial ukase which forbade the use of any but Russian rolling-stock, and as a matter of special urgency, order after order has been placed abroad, principally in the United States and France. In 1898 it was estimated that expenditure for new rolling-stock on the western section alone would reach twenty million rubles. In the autumn of 1897, freight exceeded 490,000 tons—or double the amount anticipated in the most sanguine expectations. Of these, 320,000 tons were cereals for Russia. In spite of 600 new trucks and 1600 wagons borrowed from other Russian lines, 70,000 truck-loads of grain and other produce could not be carried. The estimated freight for 1899 is 600,000 tons; and by 1901 it is expected to rise to 800,000, owing to the large immigration along the line and the rate at which land is being taken up. Opinions differ considerably as to the ultimate fate of these immigrants, the land on which they are settling being described by some as highly productive and by others being spoken of in very gloomy terms. But the fact remains that 200,000 immigrants arrived during 1897 and took up homesteads, and the same number in 1898; and this in addition to an ordinary passenger traffic of some 400,000.

Still more assured is the prosperity of the line as a great international undertaking. The saving in time would alone insure a large passenger traffic between Europe and the Far East, for, from the very outset, an average of sixteen miles an hour may confidently be expected—which, on the completion of the line, will land the traveller at Port Arthur within fifteen days of his departure from London—a journey at present occupying more than double that time. When the line has settled down into smooth working order and is more permanently ballasted, at least the same pace may be expected as is maintained on the ordinary American and Canadian trans-continental lines—*i.e.*, an average of twenty-five miles an hour. Indeed, when the heavier rails (twenty-four pounds) are laid, as much as thirty-three miles per hour is counted on by the railway authorities—a somewhat sanguine estimate. The journey from Paris to the Pacific coast will then occupy eleven days only, and that to Shanghai, at the most, fifteen, as compared with the present minimum of about one month and a half. The Siberian Railway will proportionately shorten the journey to all places in the east which are north and east of Tongking, while the saving in money will be no less marked than the saving in time. At present a first-class fare by mail-steamer to Central China (say to Shanghai), costs just over £70, whereas the expenditure for the journey overland will amount to less than half this sum, made up as follows:

	£	s.
Express from London to Russia	7	0
Rail to Port Arthur	11	10
Cost of Meals, etc.	8	0
Steamer, Port Arthur to Shanghai	6	0
Total	32	10

And when there is railway communication between Northern China and the Yangtsze valley, the above rate may possibly be still further reduced, if the Russian rates are not raised later on, a contingency which must be taken into account.

Many people, of course, who do not happen to be pressed for time, and who dread the exhausting strain of a fortnight's incessant railway travelling, will still prefer the sea-route; but there are large numbers to whom the Far East would forever remain a closed book were there to be no means of approaching it but by sea, and to whom the attraction of a journey through such novel longitudes will to some extent no doubt neutralize any possible discomfort involved. The commencement of the journey is certainly anything but interesting, passing, as it does in the Akmolinsk province, through dreary, desolate regions inhabited by a sparse population of Kirghiz nomads, who maintain a precarious existence on the borders of the far-stretching "Hunger Steppes," where the very water—what there is of it—is salt, and where clouds of sand still blow over the regions where the ruins of many buried towns are to be found. After passing Omsk, however, a more flourishing country is traversed, of which the inhabitants are chiefly fishermen and trappers, but which will probably in time become an agricultural district. Indeed, the ever-varying character of the country to be seen throughout the province of Tomsk will alone probably reconcile the traveller to the overland route, and should this not suffice, there is the striking scenery round Lake Baikal and in Trans-Baikalia.

As regards the goods traffic: the present average freight per ton from Shanghai to London may be estimated at 32*s.*; therefore, leaving out of the question the freight from Shanghai to a Siberian centre, it is evident that, in order to successfully compete with present charges, the railway freight must not exceed 32*s.*—*i.e.*, half the actual rates charged on the cheapest lines in the world for such a distance! It is practically certain, then, that no heavy through goods traffic from Central China is likely to be inaugurated; though valuable and easily damaged articles like silk and tea, as also light goods and postal packets, would probably prove exceptions, and would be sent by rail.

In the Manchurian section of the line, only Russians and Chinese are allowed to become shareholders. The president, chosen by the Chinese Government, with the supposed mission of guarding Chinese interests, is happily described by a French writer as "un président chinois de parade"—in other words, a mere figure-head. A vice-president is, theoretically, elected by the shareholders as the head of the executive, but his nomination is liable to the veto of the Russian Minister of Finance! The appointments of chief-engineer, constructor, heads of departments, and all engineers, have similarly to be ratified by the minister, and all plans and estimates have to be approved by him. In all other conditions the line is, as essentially as in the above, a Russian line. Gauge and speed are to be the same as on the Siberian line; tariffs are to correspond; mails must be franked; and all material is to be exempted from duty. On the other hand, to China is reserved, after thirty-six years from the opening of the line to traffic, the right to buy out the company — but only by paying every expense, every debt, every fraction of interest, or other liability incurred in the mean time—and what a bill that will be, prepared, too, by the hands of the Russian Government! Should this arrangement fall through, China is to enter into free possession after eighty years; but it requires no special gift of foresight to see to whom the railway—and not merely the railway — will belong before the expiration of this period — within the next few years, indeed!

Russian opinion on the subject is, as usual, more clearly indicated in deeds than in words, though even in words the Muscovite does not trouble to veil a brutal frankness. Practically, under the excuse of the necessity for protecting the railway, Russia has already overrun Manchuria with Cossacks, terrorizing the inhabitants, securing railway land either "by purchase of pike and carronade," or at purely nominal rates, and adopting generally an attitude of *væ victis!* These high-handed proceedings must bring their own retribution, in insurrections and riots; but in the mean time they clearly show—and whoever runs may read—how Russians regard the probabilities of the railway reverting to China eighty years hence!

Regarding the natural difficulties of the Manchurian section—Manchuria consists, from the engineer's point of view, of the basins of the Sungari (a tributary of the Amur) and of the Liao River, which debouches at Newchwang. There is an intermediate zone of steppe, 125 miles broad, which is the continuation of the Desert of Gobi. The railway will have to traverse: (1) 364 miles of mountainous country, with several ascents to over 3000 feet and an ultimate descent into the Argun valley (altitude 1800 feet); (2) 130 miles of uninhabited, unexplored, mountainous country, where the line will again rise to over 3000 feet; (3) 330 miles across the valley of the Sungari River; and (4) again up and down over the mountains at an average height of 2000 feet, until finally the line descends to Nikolsk, 130 feet above sea-level. Here again the mountains are not the principal obstacle, which is encountered in the yielding character of the soil. The whole plain of the Sungari is reported to be in autumn one expanse of liquid mud—with, however, a stratum of gravel at a depth of a few feet.

The Manchurian line alone is estimated to cost

sixteen millions sterling, but, as hinted before, there is in its construction, as in that of the Siberian Railway, little question of expense or of economy, of easy country or shortness of route. It is, as has been said, above everything a political and military line, passing close to the Gulf of Pechihli, and from Port Arthur, when fully fortified, commanding Peking and the Gulf of Pechihli. Russia will be able, at her pleasure, to transport large bodies of troops to advantageous points on the neighboring frontier, and to dominate Northern China, while she pushes southward her railways, by means of which she intends to conquer China bit by bit. Although the acquisition of Port Arthur (now "Dalny") and Talienwan—unlooked for, so far as one may say *what* Russia does or does not look for, when the Siberian Railway was commenced—has necessitated the construction of a line of 530 miles or so to those ports, Vladivostok is not to be abandoned. That port is not only a growing commercial centre, but a safe harbor, and open throughout the year, now that the new ice-breaker can be effectively employed, and would be of great importance in the event of a war—for instance, with Russia's neighbor, Japan.

Although not properly pertaining to the Trans-Siberian-Manchurian Railway, it is necessary here to specially note the three alternative plans for a great line in Central Asia, to be built after the completion of the Trans-Siberian, with which it is to be linked, thus joining the two great systems, the Trans-Siberian and the Trans-Caspian. These are: (1) by a line from Tashkend through Aluata, Vernoe, Semipalatinsk, Sergiopol to Barnaoul and Polotentse on the Siberian Railway, 2100 miles; (2) from Orenburg *via* Turkistan town to Tashkend, 1800 miles; and (3) from Saratov across the Uralsk steppes south of Lake Aral to Khiva-Charjui. The first is probably the line that will be constructed, as Prince Hilkoff (the Minister for Ways and Communications) is strongly in its favor, and as it will pass near important Crown coal and mineral mines at Barnaoul.

The fact to be always kept in mind with regard to this great Russian railway is, then, that it is a strategic line, which has been carried out at high pressure, from start to finish, expense being disregarded as an unimportant item when compared with the results aimed at, one of the most noteworthy features in its construction being the vast number of sidings built, in order that the single main line may be always kept open in case of emergency. The importance of a line such as this, which will pass right through from St. Petersburg to Port Arthur, being joined later by a branch from the Trans-Caspian system, is obvious. The bear's arms are closing on India.

The commercial future of Siberia cannot be regarded as difficult to foretell. All authorities agree as to the vast riches of the country, which, although at present chiefly potential, are in no wise chimerical. Siberia could, without doubt, achieve high commercial status as a corn-growing country alone; or as a cattle-raising land. Or, again, she might rely on her vast wealth in timber, on which future generations, in view of the rapid exhaustion of forest in other quarters of the globe, will be compelled to draw. As a gold-producing region Siberia, in spite of ridiculously antiquated and ineffective methods, already holds the fourth place in the world's production, while her stores of iron, coal, and copper would prove a no less valid title to a high place in the world's market. Any one of these resources would suffice—and Siberia possesses them all. The treasury is there, and but awaits the golden key.

This key is Good Communications. These cover all obstacles to Siberian progress that have ever been adduced—difficulties of transport, prohibitive wages, unscientific methods, deficient capital and organization, official maladministration. With the iron road awakening the echoes of the vast tracks of solemn forest where, three centuries ago, the Tunguz and Buriat might only note the cries of animals scarcely wilder than themselves; and bridging rivers where, till yesterday, the fisherman's birch-bark canoe alone glided through the solitary reaches, Siberia will be, indeed, conquered, and, with a steel yoke about her neck, compelled to yield her all: of grain and cattle, furs, fish, and timber; porphyry and gold; coal, lead, and mercury; silver, copper, and iron—all the wealth she has, under guard of eternal snow and ice, so long held in trust for future centuries.

Nor, once opened up to free intercourse with the civilized world, will Siberia gain advantages merely of an economic order. Intimate relations with thinking, energetic, and progressive humanity will supply the boorish moujik and the arbitrary official with an education that no mere Government schools can offer him. The method of Siberian exile, even now under process of amelioration, will be revolutionized slowly but surely, and the present crude and antiquated system will be swept away by the vivifying current from the swift streams of the outer world, and the complete transformation of the country will be effected through the moral elevation of its inhabitants.

The political future of Siberia requires no more profound power of prophetic judgment. She must benefit more and more, together with European Russia, by her position on the future world's-route to the East. Whatever the eventual destinies of China, Siberia cannot but profit by close neighborhood to the last and greatest virgin market now remaining to the world, and by the commanding position now held by Russia on the Pacific. No graft, but an actual growth of Russia, Siberia has a continental solidity which should enable her to defy all attack. There seems now no likelihood that she may prove to have outgrown her strength, and that she may split up from sheer bulk, that the Eastern (Mongolian) Siberia may throw off allegiance to the Slav. Those who hold this theory, and speak of the possibility of a Siberian Republic, do not appreciate the power of the iron road to Russianize Siberia, and have small conception of the absolute solidarity that welds all Russians, from autocrat to moujik. Whatever may be the case in European Russia, the feeling of revolt and disaffection, which many suppose to be fermenting the masses in Siberia, does not exist there. The average Russian abroad, safe in an English or American drawing-room and among sympathetic democratic companions, may inveigh against the official class, but the people speak of the expansion of Russia with hearty enthusiasm, and are, in this respect at least, in thorough sympathy with the aims of the bureaucracy. "Russia, Mistress of the World," is a motto which unites all Russians, from Archangel to Port Arthur.

Thus is Russia entering into possession in Asia, developing strength on strength in her own territories, and paralyzing the vital centres of the neighboring Chinese Empire, which her "destiny" will later on force her to absorb. Under the cloak of legitimate effort, she has again secured the world's approval, and has retained it until the matter had gone too far for other powers to do anything but review another "stricken field." The lesson is never learned, though examples may be multiplied *ad infinitum.* While the sentimentalists in Britain and the United States have scarcely dried their tears of Christian joy over Russia's magnanimous and self-imposed mission of peacemaker to the world, Russian statesmen are busy on the task of stirring up a world-wide coalition against "England the Tyrant"—which coalition, it is intended, shall pick Russia's chestnuts out of the fire, and deal a death-blow at Anglo-Saxon power and progress.

CHAPTER VII

PEKING: PAST AND PRESENT

Of the many memorable sights of China—quaint, charming, or revolting—that which leaves the deepest impression is, in the writer's opinion, one's first view of Peking. Other spectacles have, for the most part, some parallel in Western countries: cliff-darkened rivers; hills glowing in an arrested sunset of rhododendron blossom; turquoise waters gemmed with green islets; the throng and roar of busy streets; the tawdry pomp of mandarin processions—these can all be matched. Peking alone stands incomparable and apart; typifying what is, when we come to think of it, the most astounding piece of antiquity that yet survives—the Chinese Empire! In it we have no mere fossil remains, to be reconstructed and labelled for us by the archæologist: we need pore over no cuneiforms and ransack no musty libraries in order to appreciate it. The Past itself confronts us—no mere dry bones, but the breathing flesh—in the city walls, still guarded by bow and arrow and painted cannon; in the ruins, still inhabited; and in the language, literature, dress, and manners of the citizens, practically unaltered since the period when our woad-stained British forefathers yet ran naked in the woods. Until quite recently no echo from the great outer world had disturbed the quiet courts of the Middle Kingdom, and nothing had moved forward beyond the lines of that early attained civilization. Broken bridge, gaping drain, and crumbling pagoda point rather to how, during many centuries, things had retrograded.

The Nankow Pass, through which Peking is approached from the north after leaving Kalgan ("the Barrier"), is the last mountain gateway on the long road from St. Petersburg, and marks the final stage of the journey. On emerging from its rocky defile the traveller finds himself in a cultivated plain, which stretches unbroken to the Gulf of Pechihli, a hundred miles away. A day's ride out into this plain lies Peking. The blue barrier of mountains, curving northeast until it cuts the sea at Shan-Hai-Kuan, forms a fitting background to the great city of Asia. From summit to summit over the bare mountain-crests runs an offshoot of the "ten thousand li wall" —the Great Wall of China—crossing the Nankow Pass at right angles and disappearing to right and left, like some huge gray snake, over the mountain-tops. This portion of the "wall" is in reality a rampart of solid masonry, about twenty feet wide and nearly as high, with double-crenellated parapet, and watch-towers at short intervals — wonderfully little impaired by the centuries that have passed over it. The effect of this elaborate structure maintaining its imperious course without regard for natural difficulties — now assailing a rugged crest, now plunging into a valley—is not soon forgotten.

These mountains have a further historical interest as the last resting-place of Chinese sovereigns. In a secluded valley to the north of Nankow are the tombs of the emperors of the Ming dynasty. An avenue of giant stone figures guards the approach—elephants, camels, horses, and ministers of state, in pairs, alternately standing and kneeling. This weird gray line of watchers extends for fully a mile up the centre of a valley of desolation, lonely as a dried-up watercourse, silent, bowlder-strewn, and shut in by barren hills. No human habitation desecrates, no voice breaks the eternal stillness of this abode of awe and silence. The mighty dead sleep undisturbed.

At the upper end of the valley, masked by trees, are grouped the tombs—magnificent temple-like pavilions, tiled with imperial yellow, and supported by wooden pillars each hewn from a single giant trunk. The entrance gates and successive courtyards and terraces are on the usual plan of Buddhist temples. First among these tombs is that of the Emperor Yung Lo, who in 1426 transferred the court from Nanking, the "southern," to Peking, the "northern capital." Both the Great Wall and the "Ming tombs" are favorite objectives of tourists, some of whom brave a roughish trip, including the prospect of two or three nights in a native inn, apparently for the questionable satisfaction of scrawling their barbarian names over the historic stones.

When the writer passed that way in late autumn, the high crops of maize had of course been cut, leaving the plain bare. In the open country there are no hedges, walls, or fences to break the dead level of the fields. The brown expanse is, however, relieved by frequent clusters of trees, denoting hamlets, and by symmetrical pine-groves marking the private burial-grounds of the wealthy. The resulting effect is that of a fairly wooded country. The Chinese, however, take no pains to grow trees, except around villages and graves—the abodes of the living and the dead, over which the whispering branches are supposed to exercise a benign influence. Though undoubtedly possessing a feeling for the picturesque, they do not indulge it except where no sacrifice of good husbandry is involved.

Beyond Peking the plain becomes more open still, and often extends uninterruptedly to the horizon. Like the sea, however, the barest stretch of plain has surprises for us when brought under the alchemy of a brilliant sun and sapphire sky. Dull russets then become golds, saffrons, and chocolates, while the universal blue coats of the peasants seem to reflect a little of the sky itself as they move across the brown plain.

The country roads are mere loose, sandy tracks—worn, not made. Carts struggle through them with much straining and creaking, and seldom faster than at a walk; but foot-passengers and horsemen usually find an alternative path affording firmer going along the edges of the fields. Cycling would be quite out of the question. In bad weather such travelling is most depressing. The crumbling, earth-walled cottages are squalid; the roads, after snow or rain, mere quagmires; and the whole country resolves itself into mud and water. The brilliant North China sun and sparkling air are essential to the landscape; and it is fortunate that, for the greater part of the year, such perfection of weather can be reckoned on.

Some twenty miles from Nankow, on rounding an outlying mountain-spur, we strike a stone causeway which leads to the capital. Like everything else, it is in the utmost disrepair; and not much used except when the summer rains have made the by-ways impassable. The character of the road now changes. We begin to pass high walls and enclosures—private gardens and princely residences; a few shops and houses, neatly built of gray brick, spring up on either side; while through vistas of trees we occasionally catch a glimpse of the curved roof and faded vermilion walls of a temple peacefully basking in the open country beyond the road. The wooded eminences of the summer palace—known as the Wan Shou Shan, or "Hill of Ten Thousand Years of Life"—rising on the right, lead our thoughts back to 1860, when the *Yuan Ming Yuan*, standing in those same lovely gardens, was burned to the ground by the English forces, as a retribution which should fall on the Emperor himself, and not on his innocent subjects, for the treacherous murder of a party kidnapped under flag of truce. The French, who, arriving first, looted the palace in the most undisciplined manner—smashing priceless porcelain and *objets d'art* in the wantonness of destruction—held up their hands at our barbarity, and have ever since quoted what was a stern and calculated act of justice as an example of Anglo-Saxon vandalism!

Between the summer palace and Peking the causeway is irregularly bordered with venerable trees. There are, however, no signs of saplings, excepting a few waifs sown by nature, and the whole scene savors of decay—of past splendor defaced by sheer force of time and of neglect. After passing through the village of Hai Tien—a name often recurring in the annals of the war, but now only associated with good snipe-shooting—the country, except for occasional houses, temples, and enclosures, remains open, without sign of suburb. But indication of approach to the capital is sufficiently afforded by the increasing bustle and traffic of the road. We begin to meet tinkling files of donkeys, evidently fresh from town; the little beasts pattering along resignedly, though often so overtopped with Chinaman as to suggest the simile of an "improper fraction." Then a string of creaking wheelbarrows, pushed by perspiring coolies, bronzed to the waist, their glistening muscles standing out like polished metal. The barrow resembles a miniature jaunting-car on a single wheel, and is often used, especially in the south, for carrying passengers, farmer and pig sometimes balancing each other, one on each side. In the early Shanghai days, English ladies are said to have used them, in default of sedan-chairs. These wheelbarrows, employed in the north principally for goods, are occasionally seen with a rag of a calico sail set; to which Milton may have alluded when, in *Paradise Lost*, he speaks of

> "Where Chineses drive,
> With wind and sail, their caney wagons light."

The neighborhood through which we are passing being one where imperial and princely residences are frequent, there is, too, a considerable *va-et-vient* of officials and mounted messengers along the causeway. The former ride, like ourselves, in carts; mandarin and muleteer alike dressed in regulation official robe and black winter hat, these differing only in material. They pass us with an expression of freezing indifference. The grimy-faced messengers, ragged, but none the less official — witness the stiff felt hat and (once) crimson tassel — clatter past on unkempt ponies with flowing mane and tail. Most quaint apparitions! The rider is perched, knees close to chin, on a high peaked saddle, whose black leather flaps half envelop the pony's barrel; broad, dark-blue cloth reins, jingling bell, enormous chased metal stirrup-irons, and short-handled whip completing the equipment. It is noteworthy that natural horsemen —Arabs, Cossacks, Kirghiz, Mongols—all ride with these extremely short stirrups. Then from a side-road emerges a farmer's cart, filled with cabbages. The team—in this case a bullock, donkey, and pony —are roped together somehow, though quite effectively, in an apology for harness, and are driven by voice without aid of reins. This old-fashioned equipage is succeeded by a specimen of the Peking *jeunesse dorée*, who, arrayed in silks, ambles haughtily past on a very tall, sleek mule, richly caparisoned.

As we near the capital the stream of life becomes continuous. Mule-litters and sedan-chairs, though less frequent, add their touch of quaintness to the scene; and strings of solemn, silent-footed camels occasionally block the roads—each tied by a string through the nose to the tail of its foregoer. From the shaggy neck of the leader jangles a deep-toned, not unmelodious bell; and on its back a Mongol nods and sways half asleep, his purple robe and yellow sash adding a note of color to the dingy humps he bestrides. The scene is a fascinating one for the new arrival, whether from over seas or over land: the tinkle and clang of mule and camel bells; the cries of the drivers; the grunting sing-song of the barrow coolies; the strange, blue-coated, bronze-featured throng, all working out their existence unconscious of any world beyond a radius of a few *li*. And yet so civilized! To our polite "Chieh Kuang!" (Lend me your light!) they make way at once, showing no rude surprise at our sudden appearance, incongruous and travel-stained. Often the conventional "Shang na'rh?" is asked in return—a "Whither bound?" to which we are at last able to reply, not to such-and-such a village or mountain-pass, but "Chin Ch'êng!" (To town!).

This medley of new, strange life is set in as picturesque a framework: the broken causeway over whose gray flag-stones—now flecked with sunshine and a tracery of leafless branches—so many imperial pageants have passed in a bygone age; the sombre groves of pine, contrasting so artistically with the frequent vistas of country and farmsteads mellowed in the sunlight; and the keen, exhilarating air circulating through it all—reminding us to push on before the sun goes down. Although there is neither steeple nor minaret to guide us, and the country is still open, we *feel* that Peking must be close at hand. Even our weary mules seem to know instinctively that their long journey is finishing, and of their own accord quicken the pace. The excitement increases with each turn of the road, with each obscuring clump of trees; and the suspense is become so tense as to be almost unpleasant, when, quite suddenly, the huge walls stand before us. Revealed at once from base to parapet, they dwarf all else to insignificance and fill the entire landscape. In the last rays of the afternoon sun the weather-beaten masonry is suffused with rose tints, the sands glow, and the moat beyond becomes a stream of molten gold; while overhead the clear air thrills with the sweet, sad strain from the flocks of pigeons wheeling and flashing through the limpid blue.*

How far and dim the cramped architecture and feverish bustle of Europe seem, when, in the hush of sunset, we gaze on such a scene! Before us,

* A small whistle, or set of pipes, is fastened to the tail-feathers of pigeons, to frighten the hawks.

springing straight from the sand, tower the monuments of the conquering Manchu, so lofty that men are dwarfed by them to pygmies, so broad that three chariots might race abreast along their jungle-covered tops, and solid as the walls of Jericho before the trumpet blast! In that pure air the crenellated parapets stand out clear-cut, distance is practically annihilated, and the eye can follow bastion after bastion, stretching away in a long line, from which, like giant sentinels, the many-storied towers, marking the nine great gates, look out across the plain. The walls themselves are of earth faced with huge bricks, and are built at an inward slope from base to parapet. To the interstices cling many a bush and even trees, while from the gate-towers frown tier upon tier of painted representations of cannon. As our cart clatters under the echoing arch of the vast gateway the sun sets; and in a dusty stream of camels, horsemen, and strange vehicles, we enter the Middle Ages. The grooves in the flag-stones, in which we jolt, have been worn by generations of traffic; the tattered proclamations in the gateways might—both for form and matter—be a thousand years old. Under the gloomy archway and in the chill quadrangle beyond it is already night; and not without some slight uneasiness do we reflect that in a few minutes, when complete darkness has set in, the ponderous gates will be closed behind us, and we shall be prisoners till the daybreak.

CHAPTER VIII

PAST AND PRESENT—(*Continued*)

ONCE inside the gates we find ourselves in a Tartar camp, with a wilderness of mushroom houses for tents. The city occupies a square, facing the cardinal points. Each wall is three miles long and contains two gates, a mile from each corner, and, consequently, from each other. In the south wall a third gate in the very centre corresponds to the main gate of the imperial palace within. From each gate-tower a vast thoroughfare runs straight through the city to the opposite gate, making four main thoroughfares in all—running east and west, north and south. The city is thus divided into nine squares, each facing the cardinal points—an arrangement which much facilitates the finding of one's way. Roughly pardiallel with these main arteries run roads of lesser dimensions; the intervals being filled up by houses, rubbish spaces, and an infinity of tortuous lanes and alleys. Attached to the south side of the city proper, or "Tartar City," is the "Chinese City," a large walled-in suburb in which are situated most of the shops, restaurants, and theatres. Communication is absolutely closed between the two cities at sundown, except for a few minutes after midnight, when the "night gate" is opened to admit officials on their way to palace audiences at three o'clock in the morning.

Viewed from the wall in summer, the Tartar City appears a mass of foliage, with roofs peeping through here and there, a harmony of green and gray, each main thoroughfare a broad, dark track, swarming with atomies and running in long perspective to the gate-tower rising in the blue distance. In the centre of all is the "Forbidden City," enclosed in high walls of faded vermilion, and appearing from the city wall to consist mainly of a line of glittering, yellow-tiled pavilions, extending to just within the "Ch'ien Mên," or "front gate," before alluded to. No other buildings of more than one story being permitted in the city, the palace roofs stand high above the gray sea of tiles that surges all around them. Exceptions are the temples and pagodas, and the French Catholic Cathedral—the only spire in the city and a great eyesore to the Pekingese. On descending into the streets, the trees, which appeared so marked a feature from the wall, are barely noticeable; there are no boulevards, and, except in court-yards and gardens, scarcely a tree is growing. The thoroughfares on nearer examination are found to be earthen tracks, some fifty yards wide, and appearing even wider by contrast with the mushroom houses that border them. Roads they cannot be termed; at least in the sense of macadam or any sort of paving. Down the centre runs a loose earth embankment, just wide enough for a double line of wheeled traffic, while on either side a hollow separates the embankment from the houses — a waste of refuse, stagnant water, and filth, through which run the remains of an open stone drain. Foot-passengers pick their way along the shop fronts, by an uneven track beaten in the mud or dust, as the case may be. During the summer rains these thoroughfares become sloughs of unimaginable despond. Men and mules have been drowned in the cesspools which form between the houses and the embankment, and even the street in which the foreign legations are situated is not much better. Outside the Netherlands legation a few years ago a pond of this sort was appropriately named the Zuyder Zee. Fishing "waders" would form a useful adjunct to evening dress for any one rash enough to venture out on foot when the rains are at their worst. A Russian *chargé* has been known to ride out to dine with his United States colleague "pick-a-back" on a Cossack of the Escort. When cesspools, foot-path, and boundary-stones are thus submerged, only an *habitué* who remembers the bearings of every stone and every hole could make the journey to the club without risk.

A sickly odor given out by the slime as the waters evaporate under a midsummer sun is not the least objectionable feature. Then follows dry weather, during which dust, stirred by each cart, hangs in heavy canopy over the streets—transformed to a golden haze in the evening sun. The only watering is done with slops and sewage, resulting in such a stench as to make one welcome the acrid dust again. Practically there is no street lighting, which is the less missed as the majority of Chinese stay at home after dark. There are, it is true, quaint wooden stands about four feet high and with tops forming a sort of lantern cage, which rise like beacons at intervals along the edge of the embanked roadway. But the mutton-fat dips which they are intended to burn are only lighted for a few minutes in each month, while the *cortége* of the "General of the Nine Gates" (the Governor of Peking) is passing on his round of inspection! The consequent blackness of a moonless night in Peking is difficult to describe—an inky, tangible blackness, in which the paper lanterns of belated foot-passengers and carts flicker like will-o'-the-wisps. Even when armed with a lantern, caution is required to avoid leprous beggars, pariah dogs, and cesspools—all mere smudges in the general darkness. Without a lantern one might almost as well be blind.

As will already have been made clear, European life in Peking differs greatly from that in "the ports." There is, to begin with, no "concession," no municipal council, no "Victoria Gardens," no foreign houses, no macadam, no dog-carts or jinrikishas, no electric lighting! The merchant at the treaty port remembers the hour's visit he was once curious enough to make to the "filthy native city" as a sort of horrible nightmare, and is only too content to pass his remaining twenty-five years in China within the bounds of the well-ordered Settlement. In Peking, it is in the very heart of this "native city" that gentle lady and fastidious *attaché* have to be content to live. And there are, besides bad roads and odors, dust and dirt, corresponding disagreeables of a moral nature. In the treaty-port concession the foreigner is on his own ground; it is, if any one, the native who appears ridiculous and out of place. In Peking the case is reversed. It is, one feels, only the ever-present fear of bodily chastisement that restrains the populace to an attitude of sullen dislike, or, at very best, of polite indifference: their true sentiments being, however, voiced by the rowdies who, from a safe distance, shout constant abuse—obscenity of which the mildest specimen, and one incessantly heard, is not repeatable here. On the foreigner's approach, Wang calls to Sung: "Ni chiu chiu lai la!" (Here's your *maternal* uncle!) —a roundabout insult, not to the man addressed, but to the foreigner's sister!

Chinese in foreign employment do, I believe, appreciate our good qualities, and gradually become accustomed to our indecently short, tight, or *décolleté* costumes, our taillessness (as eccentric as the appearance of a bobtailed sheep-dog or Manx cat), our unshaven scalps (as if we were in mourning!), our general beardedness (though we cannot possibly be *all* forty years old), our ever-brandished stick, our curious mania for physical exercise, our cooled drinks and heated apartments, and the thousand incongruities of bearing that make the little Manchu children laugh so heartily. A "boy" has, for instance, been overheard explaining to a carter: "Wai kuo jên pu huai sa huang!" (Foreigners never tell lies!), and there is, no doubt, some slight leaven of the sort steadily at work. But the legation and other servants represent only a small fraction of the population, and evidence of theirs in our favor is considerably discounted by the stigma which attaches to a "foreign devil's slave." On the foreigner's side there are equal difficulties in the way of sympathy with the people in the street. You may be thoroughly convinced of the sterling qualities of the Chinese and sincerely well disposed towards them as a nation, and yet a brick hurled from the city wall as you ride below, or a reflection on female relatives of whom you happen to be fond, bawled in your ear, may make the most forbearing very angry. And how can one prevent disgust and loathing from getting the better of any theoretical admiration when greeted with such sights and smells as meet one in Peking on every morning stroll or afternoon excursion? The sunny side of a legation wall, at noon, within two feet of a frequented path, is by the Pekingese considered sufficiently private for any purpose. The disgusting scavenger duties which pigs, dogs, and fowls dispute with biped professionals give the finishing touch to one's rising gorge. "*This* the polished, the civilized, the exemplary Chinese people! Why, they are worse than brutes!" one exclaims, in one's first hot indignation.

Fortunately this is but the *revers de la médaille*, and the epigram of a late German plenipotentiary is no less true for being witty: "You approach Peking in tears, but you leave it weeping!" The factor mainly responsible for such a miracle is the quality of the air—in winter dry and sparkling, the very champagne of atmospheric vintages; in spring and autumn a delicious blending of frost and sun. Life is then one continual exhilaration; the floods of light pour a tonic into the blood, the keen air braces the nerves until mere movement is a joy. After the summer heats and steamy downpours, who shall describe the first crisp blow from the north—the whispered message of autumn from the steppes? Or who forget the sweet Æolian melody of the wheeling pigeons; the almost motionless wings of the great brown hawks, poised against the blue; the sparkling, frosted hills when snow has fallen and every outline shines clear in the luminous air; the tinkle of distant camel-bells; or, indeed, any of the hundred nothings that make up the unique and indescribable Peking atmosphere?

But it is not only the health and physical enjoyment of their sojourn that people remember wistfully in after-years. Peking society—at any rate, till quite recently—had also its special charm. The capital not being "open to trade," the community practically consisted of the diplomatic corps and the inspectorate-general of Chinese maritime customs, amounting in all to about a hundred, of whom about fifteen were ladies. The social atmosphere was as genial as it was refined. Old friends met again who had last known each other in Rome or Washington, Vienna or The Hague. Outside his *chancellerie*, no one was Russian or British or Spanish, but only one of a little band of foreigners isolated in a semi-hostile country. Every function bore a cosmopolitan character, and the geniality of good-fellowship was agreeably controlled within tactful diplomatic forms. A minister's assured position, which no one disregarded, did not prevent his being *bon enfant;* nor, on the other hand, did mere rank, as such, monopolize attentions. A talented student might be, for the time, a greater personage in the *salon* than a dull plenipotentiary, and a brilliant cotillon leader eclipse even a *chambellan de l'Empereur* (but gouty) while the music lasted. Neither was there any incentive to vain display where ranks and incomes were so clearly defined. If any stranger were in doubt as to his exact status, it was only necessary to send for the old Peking barber and see what position he was assigned in that artist's rigid scale of charges: hair cutting, $1 for a plenipotentiary and envoy extraordinary, 80 cents for a *chargé d'affaires*, 30 for an *attaché*, 20 cents for a student, and 10 for a missionary, with all intermediate and subtle graduations—customs commissioner, secretary of legation, and so forth.

In those days the tone was set by the British legation, whether in diplomatic or social matters. The preponderance of British trade—over eighty per cent. of the whole—was too indisputable to be competed with; the exquisite old-school courtesy and the profuse hospitality of the British minister equally admitted of no successful rivalry. Stiff but friendly German, official Frenchman, genial American, smiling Japanese, and suave Russian followed with good grace where the *Ying Kuo Fu** led. The smaller fry—Italians, Belgians, Spaniards, and Dutchmen—were even more glad to benefit by the British ice-breaker, although, to be precise, ice-breaking was rarely needed. If we except the pretensions of France to control Roman Catholicism—of whatever nationality—*in partibus infidelium*, there may be said to have been no conflicting interests; negotiations with China in those golden days being practically confined to the audience, transit pass, and missionary questions (including the settlement of perennial claims), questions all so long outstanding as to have become chronic. The legations, when action was necessary, made common cause, the victory of one being hailed as a gain to all, and the initiative being usually intrusted to H. B. M.'s representative. It is, however, open to doubt whether the honorable and considerate tone that then prevailed was appreciated as fully by the Chinese as it would be now. They have experienced other treatment since with which to compare it.

Relations with the Chinese were, however, very limited. Visits to the Tsungli Yamên were in those days of rare occurrence, being held to mean merely a fruitless half-hour in a chilly, stone-floored outhouse, sitting round a table nibbling melon-seeds and sipping green tea with the quorum of heavily befurred ministers, whose dexterity in passing the

* British legation

ball before being collared would have done credit to a Rugby forward, and successfully prevented a discussion from ever being brought to a definite issue.

A running fire of correspondence was also kept up: red-enveloped despatches written in Chinese, and for the most part threshing out the same old chaff so often threshed before; or perhaps announcing that the Emperor was to pass along a certain route at a certain hour, and inviting each minister to keep his nationals out of the way, "lest there might be a disturbance"—whether caused by the said nationals or not being left in polite ambiguity. All this insured a moderate amount of routine work for the highly qualified Chinese secretaries, but left the diplomatic birds of passage, the secretaries of legation, with superabundance of leisure for manifold duties as honorary *aides-de-camp* to the minister's wife—in organizing picnics and cotillons, drawing up invitation lists, and, on occasion, acting as M. C. As the British legation roll includes such names as Malet, Goschen, Howard, Greville, and Beauclerk, it seems as though there must inevitably have been great waste of force. A plenipotentiary, first and second secretaries, Chinese secretaries, an accountant, two consular "assistants," a physician, a chaplain, and half a dozen student interpreters, appearing indeed ponderous machinery for cracking such an egg as the audience question—and only to find it addled.

The introduction-call of a newly appointed minister would be returned by the members of the Yamên at his legation; and at New-year the Chinese ministers came in a body to offer the compliments of the season, to be returned by the diplomatic corps at China New-year (which comes later). But beyond these formalities there was absolutely no personal intercourse whatever, no Chinese minister being able to risk cold shoulder at court for foreign proclivities by visiting a legation on his own account, and no suggestion could make him more uncomfortable than that of receiving at his residence the visit of a foreign plenipotentiary. A member of the Tsungli Yamên a few years ago, as Chinese minister in St. Petersburg, became extremely intimate with Count Cassini—dropping in without ceremony to lunch, driving out with the Count, and so forth. But though the Chinaman afterwards found himself in his own capital at the same time as his former friend—who meanwhile had become minister to China—much to the Count's half-amused disgust, he carefully avoided the Russian legation, except when visiting it with his colleagues as a unit of the Tsungli Yamên; nor did he ever show sign of remembering the old days on the Neva.

The New-year visits were often attended by amusing incidents, which might, had the occasion occurred more frequently, have developed into closer relations. On a day fixed beforehand, the Chinese ministers, presidents of the various boards, and others—forming a formidable column of sedan-chairs and outriders—ran the gantlet of all the legations in one afternoon. No light undertaking this! At each they were regaled with choice vintages and cakes, of which etiquette compelled them in every case to partake. However soberly they might set out for the Belgian legation, the first to be visited, they arrived rumpled and flushed at that of the United States, at the other end of the line. All ceremonial, all stiffness had by that time dissolved, the habitual masks had been discarded, and the real men came forth from underneath. At this stage the Confucians were to be tickled by a straw. Solemn viceroys would evince a disposition to change hats with their foreign hosts, and consequential ex-governors of provinces as large as England would find a source of innocent merriment in the elastic properties of the cords of military epaulettes, which they would pull out and then release, amid peals of laughter. Sweets, comfits, and (one lady maintained) even curios, were stuffed into capacious satin boots — for the children—while occasionally a president of the board of ceremonies would stumble into an alcove and give disastrous vent to his pent-up emotions.

No satisfactory relations, then, being cultivable with the mandarins, and no burning questions demanding settlement, Peking life in the halcyon days was one of much leisure for all parties. Two exceptions there were, however — the Russians and the Japanese. Belonging themselves to the Asiatic world, they alone possessed a working clue to the Chinese mind, and were able and willing to play like against like. If in those days you were to pay a surprise visit to the Japanese legation you would find the minister in a *kimono*, drinking *saké* and eating raw fish—very unlike the correct official who, smothered in gold lace, would, a few hours later, welcome you in his stiff, Europeanized drawing-room. A similar visit to your Russian friend would, nine times out of ten, catch him in a frowsy flannel shirt, playing a masterly game of Russian whist with rather greasy cards, the atmosphere, generally, one of Russian cigarette-smoke, *vodka*, and yellow-backed decadent French novels.

Neither Jap nor Muscovite would thus appear very dangerous. They were treated with contemptuous indifference, and yet their legations have proved intelligence bureaus of the highest order. The ground was being prepared for coming events. Long before the outbreak of the war with China, the Japanese legation at Peking had transmitted to Tokio exact surveys of the whole country, with most minute detail—for instance, the width of every water-course, at every important point and at each season of the year. Later developments have shown, among other things, that the intricate network of Russian intrigue has been for years enfolding recruits from among the Chinese officials who might later on prove useful. And while these two legations were thus, mole-like, working for empire, the rest of the community were, without realizing it, filling the rôle of mere spectators.

Winter was the season for every sort of gaiety—dinners, balls, concerts, theatricals following in continuous succession, which derived additional piquancy from the surroundings, so far removed from the commonplace of Western cities. For instance, the setting out, in sedan-chair or mule-cart, for the ball; the ladies, unrecognizable bundles of Tibetan sheepskins, terminating in ungainly "Mongol socks"—loose top-boots of white felt worn over the dancing-shoes, a necessary protection when the thermometer stands below zero. Then the fantastic lantern-lights, revealing for an instant, as one jolted along in ruts and hollows, small impressionist pictures framed in darkness; a moaning beggar curled under a wall, two snarling pariahs, a deserted alley—to be as instantly swallowed up again in shadow. Finally, the entrance, straight from out this mediæval horror and darkness, into the warmth, light, and music of a ballroom—a hundred tapers reflected from trembling chandeliers in the shining parquet, diamonds flashing, the stream of dancers swaying to the rhythm of the waltz, the ripple of merry laughter, . . . who in this scene of fairyland could spare a thought to the frozen squalor of the sleeping city outside, in whose streets, each winter dawn, men are found dead of starvation and cold?

In the British and French legations—formerly princes' palaces, or *fu*—a very happy compromise has been effected between Western comfort and Eastern magnificence, as preserved in the red-lacquered pillars, curved roofs, and pavilion-like character of the buildings, and in the wonderful carved and lacquered ceilings and panels of the saloons. The original occupiers would, however, scarcely recognize in the warmed and elaborately carpeted passages, and the luxuriously furnished foreign drawing-rooms, their naked and draught-swept halls. Other legations have been specially built, somewhat in Chinese style and of only one story, for European occupancy, and are neither very beautiful nor convenient. One alone is of purely European architecture—naturally that of the adaptive Japanese. Most legations have large shady compounds and immense boundary walls; and all have traditional Chinese vermilion-colored gates—ponderous doors in which a wicket is cut for ordinary exit and entrance. Russian, British, and French have also their chapel and surgery within the grounds. Members of these legations can thus cut themselves off, if they so choose, from all that jars on one in the street outside.

So the winter speeds away in a whirl of entertainments. A French comedy at the British legation (where there is a specially built theatre) is succeeded by a *bal costumé* at the Russian, and that again by a concert at Sir Robert Hart's. Dinners follow one another uninterruptedly—varying from the strictly official function of the diplomatic corps to the jolly carousal of a students' mess, where speeches begin soon after the joint, stories with the cheese, and comic songs at one in the morning still find delighted auditors. Card-parties, too, are many, increasing from the mild "dollar-and-quarter" whist at the club to the "ten-dollar limit" and all-night poker-parties in an *attaché's* rooms. Solemn meetings of the

Oriental Society must also be recorded, where profound Chinese erudition used to be displayed to sadly unappreciative audiences; dancing afternoons and riding-parties, gala nights at the skating-rink and bowling-alley competitions, with many other amusements. A specially charming reminiscence is that of the Sunday *tiffin* party—the preliminary sherry and caviar in the study; the luncheon-table bright with chrysanthemums; the *menu*, written on red paper, whose items are so much less difficult to tackle in the concrete than the Chinese characters which represent them; the dessert, including the little apple-shaped *pai li*, a yellow pear of delicate aroma, for which Peking is famous. Then the adjournment—though midwinter—to the sunny veranda, where the patient dealers week after week undo their blue-cloth bundles and, amid a fire of chaff from "sherris-warm'd" hearts, produce their "old" *cloisonné* and *sang-de-bœuf* vases, dainty porcelain snuff-bottles, wonderful satin embroideries, and handsome skins—long-haired Manchurian tiger, wolf, leopard, or Tibetan lamb. The bargainings which ensue are often carried on from week to week; the dealer gradually coming down, the cautious foreigner slowly rising, until they meet somewhere about the fair market price. Time and patience—and plenty of them—are essential to curio-purchasing in Peking.

Among milder pleasures, mention must not be omitted of the winter afternoon walks—chiefly curio-hunting—into the "Chinese City," for instance, or to the great fair of "Liu Li Chang," taking care not to get shut out of the gates at dark. Paradoxically enough, good Chinese porcelain is becoming very difficult to procure *in China*, owing to steady exportation to Europe and the United States for generations past; while, on the other hand, many fine specimens of Louis-Quatorze clocks and watches are to be found in Peking—the jetsam of early embassies and gifts of European sovereigns to the Chinese court.

In the matter of show-places, Peking is badly off, although, like Barnum's, itself the greatest show on earth. The ordinary Peking street-scenes—for instance, the "hung shih" and "pai shih" (weddings and funerals—literally, "red" and "white affairs")—being particularly interesting. The "Llama Temple," the "Temple of Heaven," and the "Hall of the Classics" nearly exhaust the official list. These are, moreover, disappointing, and it is becoming increasingly difficult for Europeans to gain admittance, parties of foreigners having frequently of late been subjected to great insolence, and even violence, in the attempt. A "sight" of more real interest is the extraordinarily fine so-called "observatory," a collection of large bronze astronomical instruments of exquisite workmanship, heaped on the city wall and left exposed to the weather. Some were made by the early Jesuits, but others date back to the time of Kublai Khan. Another place of interest, and not difficult to obtain a sight of, is the literary examination ground, where thousands of open-air cells in rows, resembling cattle-pens, receive the provincial candidates for the metropolitan examinations. The scholars are confined for three days, each in his cell —with a supply of water and such food as he may have brought with him — while writing the essay which is supposed to determine his future career. The elaborate safeguards against swindling are, however, as usual in China, very much of a farce. Lastly, the French Catholic cathedral is worth a visit, if only to see the Jesuit priests officiating in Chinese dress and queue, and hear a congregation of Chinese converts singing the responses. In this connection it may be remarked that Russia has practically sent no missionaries to China.

CHAPTER IX

PAST AND PRESENT—(*Continued*)

In so polyglot a society there could not fail to be a considerable comic element. When, for instance, a plenipotentiary, speaking in French—which was *not* his native tongue—proposed the health of a departing colleague, whom, he said, he loved as a friend and admired as an *écolier*. As to his excellency's wife, he added, "C'est une sage-femme!" Nor were such mistakes always confined to the English-speaking side. A lady belonging to the linguistic Russian nation, describing a picturesque farm-house she had come across that afternoon, waxed enthusiastic over an old sow that had come running up to her, followed by, "Oh, such *de-ar* little hams!" The lady's husband on the same occasion had been "projected" from his pony. There was, before the war, a Japanese minister at Peking who was the source of much innocent enjoyment. He was a tiny fellow, of cheerful countenance, and, not speaking much English, and still less French, he filled in the gaps with peals of most infectious laughter, though not always very apropos—"You fader have die? Ha! ha! ha! ha!" Foreign dinners bored him fearfully. During one long official function at his own table, he took the *punch à la Romaine* as an indication that dinner was ended, and joyfully led the way into the smoking-room. His error was explained to him by a secretary, more versed in the intricacies of foreign *menus*, and the poor little chap returned to his seat most comically rueful. In the matter, however, of the *Chinese* language, the Japanese had a great advantage over other nationalities. Even if they could not speak, they could explain themselves fluently in writing, the Chinese characters being the same as their own. They could appreciate such a present as one of them was fond of displaying in his study, converted on dinner nights into a smoking-room, viz., an autograph scroll sent him by the Empress Dowager.

Pidgin-English is little available in Peking, and the majority of foreigners—being officials and not merchants—speak some Chinese. Absurd mistakes are, of course, constantly being made, especially slips over that stumbling-block of students, "the four tones!" "Are *fish* going to fall?" inquires the budding sinologue; "Must I put on *learning*, or will *blood* do?" (He is, of course, quite satisfied that he has asked whether it is likely to *rain*, and whether he had better change his *shoes* for *boots; Yü*, fish, being spoken in the shrill "second" tone; whereas *Yü*, rain, is in the bass "third," and so on). Fortunately, the demands of foreigners are usually confined to fairly beaten tracks; whiskey remains "whi-ser-key," and brandy only changes to "b'lantee." Usually the word *chiu* (wine) is added, pronounced *djee-o;* and a lady new to Peking, hearing frequent shouts to the servant of, "Na sherry chiu!" (Bring sherry wine!), or, "Na champagne chiu!" concluded the "boy's" name was "Joe," and called him so ever after.

With the month of April comes the spring race-meeting—a great event. The "griffins" (or maiden ponies) have, as a rule, been purchased during the winter, as they arrived in shaggy, travel-worn droves from Mongolia. The race-course, rented for the community by the Tsungli Yamên (to get the awkward foreigner as far removed as possible from the former course, close to the city wall), is situated six miles out of town, towards the hills. The track is of turf and is a mile long. It is surrounded by trees, and boasts a charming grand-stand and paddock. In the background rise the blue mountains, the neighboring country is attractive, and near by are some reedy lakes and ponds, where snipe and duck abound. Leisured Pekingese take up their quarters for the training season in temples, dotted about near the course, and converted *pro tem.* into racing-stables; Buddhas and gods of war making room for likely winners of the maiden stakes, the Union-Jack cup, or the Peking St. Leger (for there is also an autumn meeting). The fact of the purchasing, training, and riding being entirely amateur, lends a picnic air to the whole thing; and he who has spent such a six weeks in the perfection of spring or autumn weather—riding gallops in the frosty morning air, snipe-shooting till lunch, and waiting for the flighting duck at sunset, with interludes for jovial breakfasts and afternoon rubbers—will never remember Peking ungratefully.

At the commencement of June a general move used to be made to "the hills"—since the advent of the railway, to a great extent superseded by the sea-side resorts of Pei Tai Ho and Chefoo. "Pi Hsu" was the concise and classic description used in explaining this exodus to the Tsungli Yamên, to "avoid the rat"—the equivalent of our dog-days. It was, indeed, a great relief to get out of the dust and noise of the sun-baked city and set one's pony's head towards the cool refuge, thirteen miles away, the Simla of Peking. Although the hills themselves are treeless, and barely clothed with grass and boulders, there are here and there ravines where, as in the sheltered hollows of the English Southdowns, woods have sprung up. One of these ravines, known as the Ssü Ping Tai (The Four Terraces), is the retreat to which, for many years past, the legation staffs have retired from June to September.

The Buddhist abbots evidently possessed as quick an eye for picturesque and agreeable sites as did our own monks of old, and wooded ravines like these, where the path zizzags upward along a torrent overhung with ferns, are dotted at successive levels with charming temples—the "Pearl Grotto," the "Pool of the Dragon Prince," and the "Temple of the Goddess of Mercy," while farther along the hill are the "Temple of the Sleeping Buddha," the "Temple of the Azure Cloud," the "Black Dragon Spring," and many others. Submerged in a sea of foliage, their terraces, as it were, floating on the tree-tops, these temples command magnificent views down the valley and out over the plain below, in summer a patch-work of golds and greens, in autumn a brown sea across which the lights and shadows course in a kaleidoscopic series of enchanting effects. It is to look out on a fairy world from an eagle's eyrie!

Guided, perhaps, by a heliographic flash from a glazed tile in the palace roof, the eye can just trace the mathematical square of the gray Peking walls in the shimmering haze of the distant plain. But after allowing the fancy to roam to the far horizon, one turns with satisfaction to the tranquillity of the temple. No surroundings could be more conducive to the quiet abstraction of Buddhistic tenets. The fragrant pine-shaded court-yard, whose gray stones are set off by a few quaint, twisted shrubs and carefully tended flowers; the *Pai Ling*, or hundred-spirited skylark, hanging in airy cage outside the head priest's door; the temple dog, a handsome, bushy-tailed collie, stretched on the cool stone flags; the pigeons cooing from the roof; the sparrows chirping in the branches; the murmur of the stream, mingling with the sough of the *Sung Fêng*, or pine breeze, and, loud above all, the monotonous whir of the "scissors-grinder" (*cicada*) adding to the sleepy peace of noontide. Nothing could be further removed from the madding crowd and the vain heart-aches of the world.

Such, in brief, was life at Peking up to the conclusion of the Franco-Russian *entente*. From that date commenced a change. The happy family circle was broken up into cliques; mines and countermines were sprung; intrigues of all sorts spread bitterness and jealousy. The old-fashioned, chronic questions of transit and audience gave way to fierce threats and demands for territory and special concessions. The French and Russian ministers alternated their daily visits to the Tsungli Yamên, and bullied, stormed, and threatened, until the Chinese—who looked in vain for help from England—were completely cowed. A rude awakening, indeed, from the old days of Sleepy Hollow diplomacy. Concession hunters, syndicates, and adventurers flocked to Peking as vultures to a carcass.

Nor were this rivalry and strife confined by the allies to official matters in which they represented their governments; these were also allowed to tinge their social relations. Under the old *régime*, for instance, no foreigner would negotiate for a temple or bid for a pony for which another foreigner was in treaty. It was Count Cassini who first violated this excellent rule by sending M. Pavloff secretly to outbid the British *chargé d'affaires* for the temple which had been leased by H. B. M.'s legation each summer for thirty years. Every annoyance, petty or otherwise, that the two allied ministers could contrive to spite the hated Britisher, no scruples of good taste or good manners withheld them from putting into execution. English students were even excluded from the general invitations issued by the Russian legation to all Peking. "Vous me faites une guerre affreuse," complained Count Cassini to Mr. Beauclerk, in insolent mockery.

In the French case this want of good manners was not so surprising. The Russian representatives had so far always been gentlemen, which could scarcely be said of their allies. One French minister was recalled, it was believed, on account of the coarse gallantries which had for a number of years been carried on under his nose, but which at last became too notorious even for the Quai d'Orsay. His successor was in turn disgraced for levying bribes upon a French syndicate, the facts being eventually published by a French journalist under the suggestive title of "Les Pots de Vin du Consul." Then came M. Gérard, the zealous colleague of MM. Cassini and Pavloff in all anglophobist matters. This gentleman in turn made Peking too hot for him, and the manner of his downfall is so ludicrous and so absolutely authenticated that one need not hesitate to describe it at some length.

The Peking Club is a charming little institution —the meeting-place of the male community. The club committee is elected by the members, and is chosen with primary regard to business capacity and special qualifications for "running" such adjuncts as skating-rink, race-course, and tennis-court, or assisting the honorary secretary in the management of bar, billiard-room, card-room, or library. If these useful qualities are forthcoming in a plenipotentiary, his presence on the committee is considered especially desirable as lending a certain *cachet* and weight to the governing body. The club being cosmopolitan, it is naturally desirable that the committee should be so likewise. M. Gérard considered that as French minister he was entitled, *ex officio*, to a seat on the committee. This, however, being contrary to the rules, he had to submit like every one else to the hazard of the ballot-box—his own staff, of course, and that of the Russian legation, voting with the solid unanimity of a *claque*. But M. Gérard was not elected. He thereupon resigned from the club, selfishly compelling his unhappy subordinates and the still more disgusted Russians to do likewise. Their secession did not, however—as M. Gérard had hoped—bring the club to ruin. On the contrary, the harmony of the golden days commenced to revive; although, it must be added, Count Cassini and his staff, who had always been popular as club members, were much missed—not for their subscriptions, but for their personal qualities. What were the incredulity and amazement of the members to hear some weeks afterwards, through the Chinese club-servants, that the French plenipotentiary, who had meanwhile made great show of haughty indifference, was in the habit of visiting the club clandestinely, in the early morning, to read the papers and magazines, and even to take them away! When officially taxed by the committee, M. Gérard's sole concern appeared to be lest the story should get into the newspapers. An amusing sketch did, however, appear in *The Rattle*, a Shanghai illustrated comic journal: "Club Library, Peking: 6 a.m. M. Gérard discovered, in pyjamas, devouring *La Vie Parisienne*"!

M. Gérard was soon after transferred, on promotion; and the universal jubilation was neatly expressed by a minister of the Tsungli Yamên: "I am *so* glad," he said, "M. Gérard is promoted (ambassador), although he can, unfortunately, never *now* return to Peking!" (a legation, not an embassy). Count Cassini's secession also terminated with rather less *éclat* than it had begun. Forgetting that the Race Club formed part and parcel of the Peking Club, the Count—an ardent sportsman and first-class pistol-shot—duly sent in his entries for a forthcoming race-meeting. These, to his astonishment, were officially returned to him, as he was no longer a member of the Race Club. French feelings, however, could not be considered where the chances of his ponies were concerned, and he at once rejoined the club, presenting a handsome cup as a peace-offering.

The Franco-Russian alliance and Japanese war, the successive seizures of Kiao Chau, Port Arthur, and Wei-Hai-Wei, have, indeed, wrought a change in the "Peking" dear to old memories. But, more than all, the advent of the railway to the very gates of the city—so long secluded, and only to be reached by a path of difficulty, if not of adventure—has forever broken down the barrier which the Chinese government had stubbornly maintained between Peking and the outer world. Unless other powers feel sufficiently interested to prevent it, Russia may at any moment now lay hands on the Chinese capital, thus bringing about the prophecy of Chinese Gordon to the Tsungli Yamên in 1880. To render Peking secure he recommended the removal of its suburbs. The ministers said that could not possibly be done. "Very well," said Gordon, "the Russians will be in Peking within a month of crossing the frontier." "Then what are we to do?" they asked. "Move your Queen Bee to Nanking," said Gordon.

We may wonder whether those words are ever remembered now by the Chinese as they watch their Fulfilment advancing on Peking—slow as the tide, but as sure.

CHAPTER X

MANCHURIA

At the present moment Manchuria has arrived at an interesting point in her history, for she provides the stepping-stone whereby the Russians, substituting peaceful for warlike methods,* may emulate her own example of two hundred and fifty years ago. Entering China for the purpose of rescuing Peking from rebels, of restoring order, and generally of preserving the integrity of the empire—that is, of protecting China—the Manchus themselves ended by establishing their own dynasty on the imperial throne. The position of Russia, as achieved during the past few years, is already that of virtual protector of China. Whether events will continue to move in a parallel line with past history until ultimately a similar goal is attained remains to be seen.

"Ah, yes! We know the price of protection!" said a Chinese official, in 1897, to the writer, while

* Among these peaceful means is the influence brought to bear upon the Empress, and upon Li Hung Chang, whom the Russians designate "our man." On the cupidity of these two they are playing, on their fears they are working, on their prepossessions they are trading. To the Empress, China means the Manchu dynasty, and the Manchu dynasty her imperial self.

discussing the terms on which Russia had then recently acquired Manchuria; "early in the thirteenth century the Mongolians, or western Tartars, were called to 'restore order'—and conquered the country. And, again, the Manchu Tartars established themselves in Peking in 1644, and in seven years conquered nearly the whole empire." Nor is this view an isolated one. The writer's journey through China, from Peking to the southern borders, made it quite clear that the majority of Chinese literati and officials are now under no delusion as to the price to be paid for protection—viz., absorption—gentle absorption, it is true; none the less real and permanent, however, because the process is disguised by judicious doses of nepenthe. The confessed aim of the Russian people, who look upon themselves as the coming race, is the "sunny and golden South." "China is our India," is the frank avowal of a Russian statesman whose influence is great; and such is the spirit animating a large section of the Muscovite bureaucracy.

The ulterior motive of Russia in acquiring Manchuria is, therefore, obvious. "What a base for further operations!" remarked a German officer in Siberia, with a deep-drawn sigh. And in this connection it may be noted as a feature of importance that Russia's frontier territories, always a source of strength by reason of their effective military organization, generally form a centre for further extension of territory, while Chinese frontier colonists merely settle down as peasant farmers, constitute no reserve of strength for the imperial government, and are, indeed, more than likely to make terms with the enemy. It is, however, a recognized fact that there are also more immediate reasons for Russian expansion. Hindered in her commercial progress in Asia by the intense cold of the long Siberian winter, lasting for eight months out of the twelve—something unknown in any other large tract where men live in a civilized state—Russia has for no inconsiderable time been covetous of the advantages likely to accrue from enjoyment of the fertile lands and the comparatively temperate climate of Manchuria.

A total change has, in fact, come over the spirit of the scene since the magnificent territories of Manchuria and Liaotung have been added to the great inland region. In the eyes of Siberians, Manchuria is paradise, with a climate more moderate than that of Canada, with winters which they speak of with enthusiasm. The acquisition of this new country, so gratuitous, so sudden and so unexpected—at least for fifty years to come—has absolutely intoxicated the Russians, who are hungering to enter into possession. This temper will do more than any dry economical considerations to stir up the dormant ambition of the whole of Russia, will do more to draw the white population eastward and to hasten the full occupation of Siberia than any ukase of the Emperor or prospectus of gold-miners. This rich country—the future garden of Siberia and of Russia—was dismissed in a sentence in a recent report by a British official. "Nothing," he said, "can be expected, commercially speaking, from Manchuria, a desolate region, through which about a thousand miles of the trans-Siberian will run." The best comment on this opinion is that nothing could well be further from the truth, for, whether the country in question be regarded from the agricultural, the mineral, the strategical, or the merely æsthetic point of view, it is a land of promise, flowing with milk and honey; and its possession exemplifies to the full the meaning of that word of glorious augury to every Russian—Vladivostok, the "Dominion of the East."

Russia was quick to recognize, what has been frequently pointed out, not only the great latent strength of China in this province, with its sturdy population and its facile transport service, but also the many natural advantages of the country. A moderately energetic use of these resources would have enabled China, in Manchuria, to defy the strongest force that might be brought to that theatre of war. On the other hand, the neglect of them was certain to throw all those advantages into the hands of a capable invader, while it is evident that the natural richness of Manchuria must ever have been an overmastering temptation to a power owning such a miserably inhospitable territory as the Russian empire.

Attainment of the longed-for prize has given an added impetus, of irresistible force, to the ambition and enterprise of the Russians. Sweeping the hand across the map southward as far as the Great Wall, "All that is ours!" they exclaim, in astonishment, contemplating their extraordinary windfall; and they are hastening to take full advantage of their good-fortune, as is evidenced by the phenomenal activity recently witnessed at Port Arthur, Talienwan, and in the Hinterland, where many thousands of Cossacks and large bodies of Chinese are employed on fortifications, harbors, and railways, and by the increased zeal and energy with which the construction of the trans-Siberian railway is being carried on. Many Russians, indeed, more advanced in their views, already include Tientsin and Chefoo (that is to say, the whole Gulf of Pechihli) and even Peking; and as the first Muravieff, who took possession of the valley of the Amur, obtained the title of Amurski, so Muravieff number two is already spoken of, only half in jest, as Muravieff Pekingski. The alignment of the railway has been several times shifted farther and farther to the southwest, following the rapid succession of diplomatic achievements of Muravieff Secundus. Manchuria and Liaotung are now the objectives of the trans-Siberian railway. No longer on the Pacific coast, but on the inland sea of China, is to be the terminal point; and what was originally laid down as the last stage of the main line—namely, the Kirin-Vladivostok section—will now be treated as a branch. Even the present route cannot be deemed final, for it is by no means the only one available. There is a still shorter cut, from Kiachta to Peking across the grassy desert of Gobi, the route followed by the writer, which may some day also be utilized.

The acquisition of the vast territory on the Pacific, through the daring initiative of Muravieff Amurski, between 1850 and 1856, and what might be called the masterly diplomacy of Ignatieff in 1858 (if to gallop rough-shod over a helpless negotiator may be termed diplomacy at all), has puzzled the world for forty years. How an empire could change hands without an angry shot, without equivalent or consideration of any kind except "drink-money" to corrupt officials, was a mystery. Yet the second Muravieff has deliberately repeated the proceedings of his predecessor, with the whole world of diplomatists and *quidnuncs* looking on; and the Anglo-American peoples seem to be as much at sea as to what has been done, and how it has been accomplished, as the world was forty years ago, without its telegraphs, special correspondents, and ubiquitous newsmongers. It almost seems that the British and United States governments are still unaware of anything particular having happened in Eastern Asia.

While Russian diplomatists, quietly working with a clearly defined end in view, have effected the peaceful cession to their country of a territory so vast in itself, and presenting such great commercial and political potentialities, the British government has been emulating the ostrich. It has ignored all unpleasant facts, and, endeavoring to find protection under an avalanche of words, opposes "stale, flat, and unprofitable" discussions about an "open door," "spheres of influence," and "preservation of the integrity of China"—which bear about the same rela-lation to *realities* as the paper "sycee" so plentifully burned at Chinese funerals does to solid silver—to a policy which aims at and obtains absolute possession, and to a force which, *de facto*, and all discussion notwithstanding, is hurrying on the dismemberment of the Chinese empire. And what is here said of the British government is applicable also to that of the United States, in whom, however, ignorance and neglect of such a question, in view of the fact that they are but just embarking on a foreign policy, are more pardonable.

The diplomatic agents, of course, naturally follow the lead of their governments in their determination to remain in ignorance, and the real dynamic forces pass over their heads, like messages over the telegraph wire, leaving no trace. Wherever one goes in making the overland journey to China the tone is the same. At St. Petersburg the trump card is to get on with Muravieff, and at Peking the instructions are evidently the same—"get on" with your Russian and French colleague. But there is no peculiar merit in getting on with Muravieff. The merest tyro in diplomacy can do it. All that is necessary is to let Muravieff have his own way in everything, for then he will be found the mildest-mannered man that ever built up one empire by undermining another.

It is unnecessary here to recall in detail how the famous Cassini convention was flouted by Lord Salisbury and derided by Sir Claude MacDonald up to the very day when Port Arthur was occupied.

Indeed, it is supposed that they still please themselves with the fancy that there was an element of fiction about that classic document. The habit of vehemently denying, instead of taking thought and acting on, the truths which are brought to their notice, is still rampant among British representatives, which is partly accounted for by the fact that they possess no intelligence department. It seems hardly credible, but it is nevertheless true, that during the last few months of 1898 stirring and tragic events happening in the imperial palace at Peking and occupying the intelligence agents of some of the legations there, scarcely even penetrated the thick wall of the British legation. The air was filled with schemes of reform, and the arch-reformer, Kang-Yu-Wei, spent months in Peking and was known to many there. Will it be believed, then, that his very name was unknown at the British legation until the explosion of the *coup d'état* and the order for his arrest? It was from no desire to hide his light under a bushel that Kang-Yu-Wei was a stranger to British officials, for his chief English confidant, a man entitled on his own account to every courtesy, was refused admittance to the minister, to whom he wished to impart information as to what was going on in Chinese official circles.

All this is part and parcel of our system of letting Asia shift for itself, a system which is such an enigma to all on-lookers, whether friendly or otherwise. For instance, the Russian consul-general at Urga, and others in Siberia, absolutely refused to credit the writer when he had to acknowledge that in the British government administration there was no Asiatic Department. They evidently drew the inference that what did not appear on the surface was worked more efficiently under ground. It is true that some Anglo-Indian officers are now being sent to Peking to study the Chinese language; but the fact remains that in the north of China, at the present time, the British have not one man, military or civilian, who is able to speak Russian.

And while such a condition obtains in the British service, a scheme is now under consideration by the Russian government to establish an Oriental Institute at Vladivostok, for which candidates who have passed through a secondary school will be eligible, the institute having for its aim the special education of those who are preparing for official posts in the civil service and for commercial pursuits in Asiatic Russia and the neighboring countries. It is intended that the course of education shall be of an entirely practical character, for the benefit of those to whom a working knowledge of the Chinese, Japanese, Korean, Mongolian, and Manchurian languages will be not only an advantage, but a necessity. The course of study is to be of four years' duration, and all students will be compelled to learn Chinese, to which no fewer than twenty-eight hours weekly are to be devoted, while the most promising in all classes are to spend their holidays in China, Korea, or Japan. Besides the regular students, there will be admitted to some of the lectures strangers holding a certain social position or of certain occupations. A boarding establishment will be carried on in connection with the institute, where thirty students will reside as state-pensioners. In addition, four officers will be annually selected by the governor-general of the Pri-Amur province to attend lectures which he shall select, and these officers will be required to submit themselves to examination with the rest of the students. Among the special subjects to which attention will be devoted will be general instruction as to each country dealt with. Thus, in the Chinese-Japanese division the Japanese language will occupy a prominent place; and so on in the other divisions.*

From what has been said it must be evident that the most important events may be incubating in China without the least intimation of their purport reaching the ears of any British agent. Under ex-

* From the beginning of the second year of study, the subjects of instruction will be divided into four groups: Chinese-Japanese, Chinese-Korean, Chinese-Mongolian, and Chinese-Manchurian. The subjects common for all divisions are theology, Chinese, English, and French (the latter not obligatory), a general study of the geography and ethnography of China, Korea, and Japan; a general review of the political and religious organization and customs; the political organization of contemporary China, and a review of its trade and commerce; the history (during the nineteenth century) of China, Korea, and Japan in connection with their relations with Russia; and the commercial geography of Eastern Asia, and history of the commerce of the Far East. Political economy, international law, the organization of the Russian state and of one other European country; elementary civil and commercial law, book-keeping, and mercantile knowledge generally, are also included in the curriculum.

isting conditions, who can wonder at the surprises with which British ministers are continually being confronted! What has happened before will happen again, unless there be drastic reform in our system.

In order to rightly understand the present position of affairs, some little insight into the past history of Manchuria is necessary.

It is, perhaps, known to a few that China is now for a third time ruled by a Manchu dynasty, although very little interest has been felt hitherto in the country which has given her so many rulers. The first invasion by Manchu Tartars was merely one of the overflows which seem to have taken place more or less frequently, China being overrun first by the Mongols, who, beaten back by the Manchus, in turn got the upper hand again. The second invasion led to the founding of the Kin dynasty, which held its own for more than a century, until expelled by the Mongols under Genghiz Khan. Under the Kin dynasty the present method of shaving the head and wearing a queue was introduced and enforced with the utmost rigor, and the "pig-tail," which to the average Westerner is exclusively Chinese, is in reality worn under protest, and is still regarded as a sign of subjection to the Manchu conquerors. Indeed, it is customary, in some of the revolutionary secret societies with which China is honeycombed, to cut off the queue of a candidate for admission, and, as the non-wearing of it would at once proclaim the rebel, to braid on a false one, which is worn in the outside world! The tight sleeve, instead of a full, open one, was also introduced and made compulsory by the Manchus.

But who were these redoubtable Manchus, who were able to impose their will on a people so much more numerous than themselves? Originally, no doubt, they were connected with the great Mongol family, and partook of the warlike qualities and nomadic habits which characterized the people of Genghiz Khan. They were also, however, of Tungusic origin, and from an early period seem to have been actually the rivals of the pure Mongols, with whom they contested, as we have already noted, the north of China for many centuries. The name "Manchu" was not known to, or adopted by, them at the time of the second invasion, but was taken later by the successful chief of one of the tribes, who, having overcome most of his neighbors, extended his own tribal name to all his tributaries.

When the third invasion took place, the victorious Manchus adopted this as their reign name, in contradistinction to that of the previous dynasty—*i.e.*, *Ming*, signifying brightness, as of light; while *Manchu* means clearness, as of water. The word "Manchuria"—a merely geographical term, it may be mentioned—is unknown to the Manchus themselves, and also to the Chinese, whose name for the country is Kuantung ("east of the barrier") or San Tung Sheng ("the three eastern provinces").

With the exception of a few wandering tribes, there are now no nomad Manchus. The whole race, indeed, although retaining in its native country certain of the old characteristics, such as courtesy and generosity, is becoming more and more commingled with and absorbed by the Chinese. Even now, in some of the frontier districts it is difficult to distinguish between the two races, and the love of speedy justice, hatred of corruption, and respect for women which used to characterize the Manchus have long since vanished. Although the conquerors of China, their influence on the nation has not been of a lasting character. On the contrary, the Chinese have themselves forced their way into the lands of the Manchus, who have gradually been driven farther north, and, as a nation, are rapidly becoming extinct. Indeed, owing to this Chinese immigration, and to the exodus of natives for the purpose of serving in the Chinese army, the proportion of pure Manchus in Manchuria itself has been for some time steadily decreasing and now probably constitutes only about five per cent. of the entire population. There are several tribes, varying slightly in characteristics and customs; of these, the Solons, or Salons, a brave and good-natured people, are the best representatives of the primitive Manchus, having preserved many national customs and observances of their ancestors; as, for instance, the burning of their dead and the subsequent suspension of the ashes in sacks on the branches of trees. The members of this tribe, rejecting Buddhism, still believe in the Shaman wizards and their rites. They are, nevertheless, capable of adapting themselves to fresh surroundings and of assimilating new ideas.

GROUP OF TUNGUZ AND TENT

Buddhism is the chief religion of the Manchus, but they have grafted on it many of the doctrines of Confucius, and not a few of their own ancient superstitions. The Chinese, with whom the Manchus are being so rapidly merged, have three religions, which they frequently profess at one and the same time, selecting from the tenets of each whatever appeals to them most forcibly. This triple creed is made up of Confucianism, which is purely Chinese, and appeals to the moral nature; Taoism, also indigenous, and entirely materialistic, ascribing miraculous powers to all sorts of plants, to the elements, and to combinations of time and space; and Buddhism, which was transported from India, and is intensely metaphysical.

There are also Mohammedans, who have their temples and priests, but, as a sign of submission to the reigning power and official religion, each Mohammedan mosque contains a tablet in honor of the Emperor. This is sacrilege, of course; but although the Manchu Mohammedans, as in southwestern China, practise circumcision, and are acquainted with some of the outward forms of their religion, yet they are deplorably ignorant of the doctrines of Islam. They are, nevertheless, as a rule, a kindly and courteous community, and at Yunnan Fu, near the end of his journey, the writer was very well received and entertained by Mussulman leaders.

Christianity does not seem to make much progress with the Manchus, for as early as the first years of the present dynasty in China certain Jesuit missionaries had not only introduced the faith, but had acquired much influence over the monarch and court by their knowledge of medicine and science. They afterwards fell into disfavor, probably because they had not the wisdom to refrain from meddling in politics, and, although their missions are found even to the present day, they have undergone much persecution, and were at one time ordered to leave the country. There was a still earlier mission of Nestorian Christians to China which has an extremely interesting history, although its records are far from complete. The most ancient Christian monument found in Asia, and one of the most valuable relics

GOLD WOMAN, "FISH SKIN" TRIBE

in all China, is the Nestorian tablet, which contains the only record of this mission. This places the date about the sixth century, and shows that Christianity was at first well received and largely adopt-

BURIAT WOMAN IN FÊTE DRESS

ed, although subsequently it disappeared, like the monument which tells of it, buried during the great persecution, and not coming to light until centuries later. Although this has not, strictly speaking, anything directly to do with the history of Manchuria, it has a bearing on it, since the frequent irruptions of the Manchus into China doubtless brought them under such influences as have been described.

The total population of Manchuria has been estimated at widely varying figures. Twenty millions, however, would appear to be a moderate and probable estimate, and would tally fairly with the sum total of the three provinces taken separately. The Sungari basin is thickly peopled, and another populous district is Southern Manchuria, especially the valley of the Liao-he River. The three races to be found are the Tungusian (including the Solons, the Golds and Manchus generally, and also the Koreans); the Mongolian (including the Buriats); and the Chinese (by far the most numerous). The Manchurian language is only preserved from entire disuse by the fact that it is the native tongue of the ruler, and, as such, must be spoken at court and in diplomatic circles. The written characters were originally borrowed from the Mongols, and are founded on the Syriac forms which, it is supposed, were introduced by the Nestorian missionaries to the Uighur Turks, and adapted by the Mongols to their own language. These were largely modified and improved. The language differs in many respects from the Chinese, belonging to the Turanian group and being polysyllabic. There is very little Manchu literature, only about two hundred and fifty works in all, many of which are literal translations of the Chinese classics.

In Europe, and perhaps still more in the United

States, it is little understood how recent has been the rise to power of the Manchus. Even as late as 1624 Manchuria (at that time a rising state known as the "Land of the Northern Barbarians") recognized China as the suzerain power, and paid tribute to her. When required, the Manchus in return re-

GROUP OF BURIAT WOMEN AT THEIR NATIONAL FÊTE

ceived the assistance of troops to help them against the invading nomad tribes from the valley of the Oxus. But at this time the Ming dynasty was tottering. Like all Chinese dynasties, it had begun amid war, securing the throne by the violent means of rebellion. Later, peace and prosperity reigned, battles and warlike expeditions were few in number, and directed only against troublesome border tribes. It had now reached the last stage, when, believing the imperial power to be well and firmly established, the Emperor is apt to lapse into effeminacy and luxury, while his court becomes corrupt and the state is neglected. It was not long before the empire was thrown into hopeless confusion, one of the frequently recurring rebellions culminating in the suicide of the "Son of Heaven." The commander of the frontier forces invited the Manchus to come and help in the restoration of order, and Dorgun, regent of Manchuria and uncle of the boy-king, Shun-Chi, complied with the request. He marched an army to Peking, and succeeded in quieting the country; but, when asked to return to his own land with a gratuity, he declined, and proclaimed his nephew Emperor of China. Thus, in 1644, was founded the dynasty which to-day is ruling in Peking.

But a totally unforeseen result accrued. The moving of so large a body of Manchus into China, while denuding Manchuria of the flower of her population, also opened that country to numbers of Chinese immigrants; and the process has been since aggravated by the necessity of maintaining garrisons throughout the Chinese Empire, while the Chinese have poured into Manchuria in ever-increasing numbers. These immigrants were at first of a far from desirable kind, usually escaped convicts, outlaws, and, indeed, bad characters of various sorts who had found the mother-country inhospitable. Political offenders also found in this Alsatia an asylum. At the same time the natural advantages of Manchuria, with its fine climate and its virgin soil, attracted the Chinese, and especially the trader, who, notwithstanding the many difficulties he had to contend with, especially the lawless state of the country, and despite the fact that colonization was only permitted by law since 1820, has by degrees established himself firmly in Manchuria. To-day not merely all the merchants, but the artisans, gardeners, and working-classes generally, are purely Chinese.

The effect produced on the Chinese as a nation by the Manchu conquest has been to considerably alter their former customs and practices. Before that time they had been liberal and enterprising in dealing with foreigners, and records are extant which prove that the advantages of foreign intercourse and trade were fully appreciated by them. With the advent of the Manchus, however, things were altered.* Foreigners were as far as possible excluded, trade being limited to Canton. Anti-foreign feeling, in fact, began when the conquering race found the foreign trader no longer powerless and suppliant, but strong and self-assertive; and to this day it has been the policy of the Manchus to represent Europeans as a race seeking only commercial gain, and that at whatever cost to others.

* See *China in Transformation*, pp. 34, 35.

Many other exclusive measures were introduced, all designed with the object of maintaining the Manchu power and of upholding the dynasty. No mandarin, for instance, was allowed to hold office in his own province, nor to remain in one place for any considerable time. Thus it has come about that the Chinese as a race have unjustly acquired a character for national exclusiveness and immobility, and many customs introduced by the conquerors have been ascribed to a survival of Chinese antiquity. This Manchu policy of exclusiveness can at the present day be most clearly seen in the case of Tibet, which is still closed to the world. It is not to be assumed, as is usually the case, that the inhabitants of the Flowery Land submitted tamely to the Manchus, any more than they accepted the wearing of the queue, or pig-tail, without a murmur. They bowed to fate, as the Chinese always do when once mastered, but they opposed the Tartars for many years throughout China, and for eighteen years a large portion of the southern provinces was in rebellion, before complete submission was enforced.

The Manchus have been so far successful in their policy that, even with their small numbers, they have been able to maintain peaceful and absolute domination over an empire which, whether considered from the point of view of numbers or extent of territory, is the vastest in the world. But, with the Western powers coming into closer and closer contact, such a state of affairs clearly could not last. As wrote the Abbé Huc, in a fine passage: " These foreigners, these barbarians, whom the government of Peking pretends to despise because it fears them, will eventually become impatient before the obstinately closed doors; one fine day they will cause them to fly in splinters, and will find, behind, a people innumerable, it is true, but disunited, without power of cohesion, and at the mercy of any one who chooses to seize a whole or a part."

Even before the establishment of the Manchu dynasty in 1644, the Russians had cast covetous eyes on the rich country separated from them by the river Amur. Hitherto they had never ventured up the Sungari, but in that year, having heard of the fertility and productiveness of the country it drained, they organized expeditions, under the command of Stepanov, to examine the *terra incognita*, and began to buy provisions, collect tribute, and so forth. The Peking government, mustering a force at the mouth of the Sungari, put an end to these invasions. Stepanov was murdered in 1658, and for two centuries no Russian again appeared on this river. During the following years, however, several trading settlements were founded on the Amur delta.

It is a noteworthy fact that China—at that time superior in wealth and in civilization, and possessing a strong and intelligent government—in her early dealings with Russia always gained the advantage in settling questions of frontier. The White Tsar's ambassadors to Peking were treated in the same way as were other "tribute-bearers." As their northern neighbors became stronger, however, the

Chinese court was gradually growing weaker and more effeminate; the people were oppressed, and brigandage flourished. On the conclusion of the Crimean War, Russia, able to devote more attention to her Eastern affairs, proceeded to secure her position. The great Proconsul, Muravieff Amursky, who was the chief promoter, if not actually the originator, of the Trans-Siberian Railway scheme, obtained for Russian subjects (by the treaty of Aigun, in 1858) the right to navigate the Amur and its tributaries, the Sungari and Usuri. The treaty was signed merely by local officials, and was not ratified by the imperial government until two years later (1860), when, Peking being in the hands of the Anglo-French forces, and China *in extremis*, Count Ignatieff saw his way to obtain still further concessions. Making full use of her opportunity, Russia demanded and obtained the cession of the Manchurian sea-coast, extending for six hundred miles, and of the country stretching between the Usuri and Amur rivers and the Sea of Japan, for the first time acquiring, on the Pacific littoral, harbors which were not ice-blocked for six or eight months in the year. Thus, merely by diplomatic pressure skilfully applied, without even a consideration of any kind in return, a magnificent territory, the northern approach to China, was made over to Russia; and China voluntarily closed to herself forever all access to the Japan Sea, an act, referred to elsewhere, which was a turning-point in the world's history. In spite of the treaty concluded, the Chinese government stubbornly resisted every effort of the Russians to navigate their vessels on the Sungari, or otherwise to introduce their trade. Various attempts were made by private individuals and firms to ascend the river, and to trade with the natives of that fertile region; but, owing to the hostile attitude of the government at Peking, these expeditions were all failures and cost more than one trader his life.

By reason of the rapid economical growth of the Amur province, and the recently arising necessity to obtain provisions for the laborers engaged in the construction of the Northern Usuri section of the Siberian Railway, it became imperative for Russia to develop commercial relations with the inhabitants of the Sungari region. In 1895, therefore, the Tsar's representative in Peking took steps towards obtaining from the Tsungli Yamên an order to the governor of the Kirin province to render every assistance to Russian traders, and with a successful result. Utilizing this opportunity, the first trading expedition was undertaken by two merchants, Boganoff and Tifontai, accompanied by Captain Grüler (of the general staff), which penetrated to the extreme west of Manchuria and was well received by the Chinese authorities. A still more important mission was despatched later, when Matunin, Zimoreff, and Dobrividoff (members of the Imperial Geographical Society) collected valuable information about the country in general and the Sungari and its tributary, the Nonni, in particular, paying special attention to the commercial aspect of the question. The privilege already acquired by Russia of trading on the Sungari, of which she at last was able to avail herself, gave her access to the very heart of Manchuria. This advantageous position was further assured, in 1897, by acquisition of the right to build railways and to station troops throughout the country—everything in connection with the railways being Russian, except the figure-head in the form of a Chinese president—and by the establishment of Russia, under the guise of a "lease," at Port Arthur and Talienwan.

At the present time the country is still divided, for purposes of government, into three provinces: Fungtien (*i.e.*, "Ordained of Heaven"—a name given by way of compliment, after the Manchus became rulers of China) or Shengking, with Mukden as capital, in the south; Kirin in the centre, the chief town bearing the same name; and Helungkiang in the north, with Tsitsikar as capital. Fungtien is governed on the same system as is customary in China, the two other provinces being under military government and both having a commander-in-chief. Since 1878, however, the Chinese agricultural population has been practically under civil law alone. The official posts are all given to Manchus, the army is exclusively composed of them, and, notwithstanding the fact that they are being gradually merged in the Chinese race, the country has hitherto preserved a sort of political and racial independence, being directly subject only to the Emperor—an independence which has, naturally, been fostered by the reigning dynasty for its own advantage.

It must have become painfully apparent, however, to the Chinese people that, with the whole of Manchuria, including Mukden—always held sacred by the

MANCHU WOMAN

Manchus as the burial-place of their early khans—in the hands of Russia, the power of the "Son of Heaven" is rapidly declining in favor of that of the "White Tsar." Assuredly, Russia herself is not slow to recognize and take the fullest advantage of her opportunities. She is gradually pushing her battalions, both infantry and cavalry, farther and farther south and southeast, and forming a chain of military posts commanding the whole Chinese frontier from Blagoveschensk to Port Arthur, and another series from Blagoveschensk, along the Sungari River and its tributaries, to the Great Wall itself. The old and for many years neglected high-roads to the frontier are being repaired, new ones constructed — among others, one from Aigun to Mergen — and other routes are receiving attention, the great road from Kirin to Peking being, indeed, entirely under Russian domination.

To add to all these powers of menace against China, Russia has still another advantage in the truly magnificent waterways provided by the three great Manchurian rivers; while, to crown all, her railway, when completed, will give her complete command over her newly acquired territory, and will admit of her introducing troops, ammunition, and provisions without limit—a portentous outlook for China, and not only for China, but for the whole world.

CHAPTER XI

MANCHURIA—(Continued)

Because China is so vast, and Manchuria is (to borrow the Chinese phrase) merely a "cut-off region," remote from the world's chief highways, people in Europe and the United States have been in the habit of thinking of the latter as a paltry territory of no great value. If one considers merely its geographical position and climate, an appreciation of its size alone, without special regard to its natural resources, should suffice to dispel this view. Amid so many conflicting estimates, and in the absence of a proper survey, it is difficult to ascertain the exact size of the country, but it is probably well over 363,000 English square miles. It is more than twice the area of Japan, and nearly as large as Austria-Hungary, one-fourth the size of China proper, and over six times the size of England and Wales. Turning for comparison to America, it is considerably more than twice the size of the North Atlantic division of the United States, including Maine, Massachusetts, New York, New Hampshire, Rhode Island, New Jersey, Vermont, Connecticut, and Pennsylvania.

It is bounded north and east by the Amur River

and its tributary the Usuri; southeast by the highlands and solitudes separating it from Korea, and by the Yalu River; south by the Yellow Sea; while westward, towards Mongolia, there are no natural frontiers. The border-line here was once delimitated by a line of palisades, the first of which was erected four centuries ago by the Ming dynasty to keep out the Mongols from Liaotung. A second was designed to keep out Manchu and Tartar robbers. They had, however, no strategic importance, serving simply as a "sort of magic circle traced round the land, which was thus placed under the protection of the terminal deities." These palisades can no longer be traced, only an occasional mound or row of trees marking where they once stood, and this region remains a veritable "No Man's Land."

The northwestern portion of Manchuria, comprising the highland of the Great Khingan Mountains, has not been fully explored. A much-used route runs across this tract from Kailar to Tsitsikar—the line of the Trans-Manchurian Railway—but outside this particular region we have scanty information as to the nature of the country. The soil here, however, is remarkable for its porous qualities and power of retaining water, so that swamps and bogs—not the ordinary mossy peat-bogs—are exceedingly common, and even occur on steep hills, but (the sub-soil being stony) are not deep. West of the Great Khingan range stretches the Mongolian Desert, which is gradually encroaching to the east and south. The

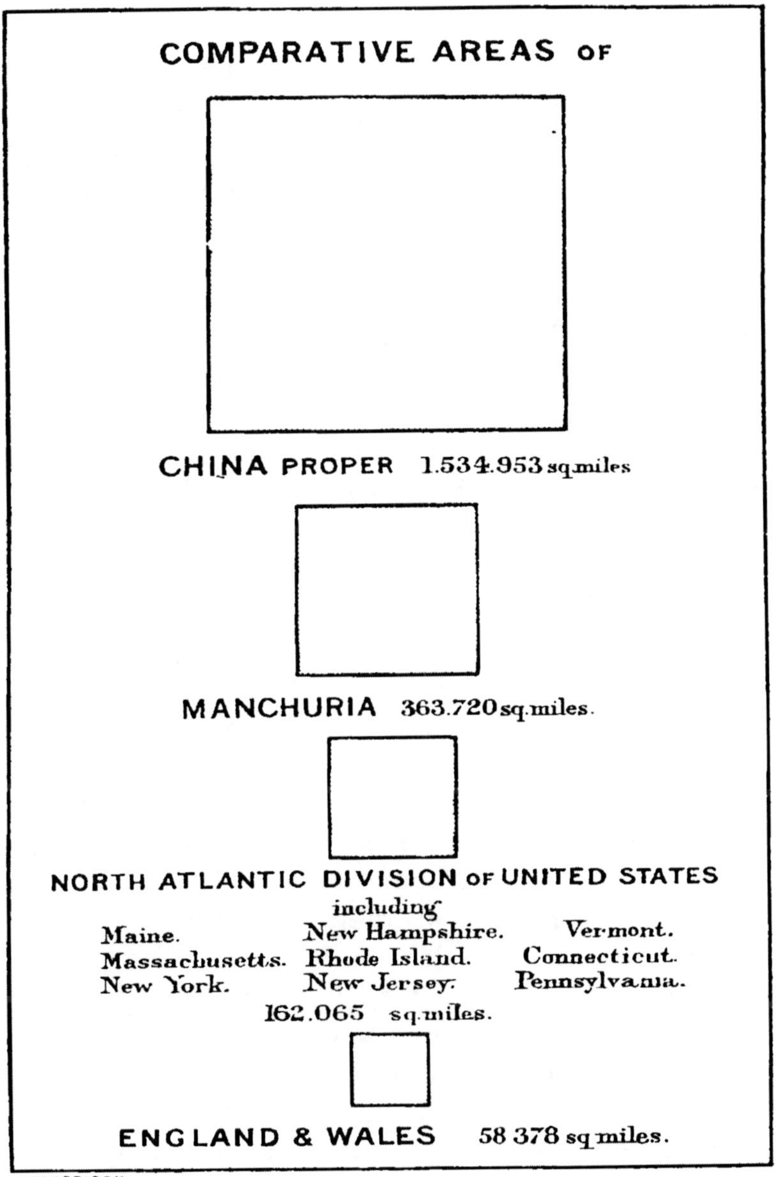

COMPARATIVE AREA OF MANCHURIA AND OTHER LANDS

other chief mountain ranges are: 1. The Lesser Khingan, in Northern Manchuria, which forms a sort of boundary to the sandy steppe enclosed in the fork of the rivers Sungari and Nonni. 2. The Kenteh-alin in the east, parts of which are covered with fir forests. 3. The Chan-guan-tsai-lin, in Central Manchuria, the top of which, so far as known, is a great uneven table-land, covered with thick forests and full of swamps, but with fertile valleys. 4. The Chang-pai-shan or Shan-alin, otherwise the "Long White Mountains," which lie to the north of Korea. These, the sacred mountains of the country, are the favorite subject of the Manchu poets, who love to sing of them as the revered home of their forefathers—"the fairest land in the world, with its woodlands, sunny glades, and sparkling streams all bathed in the bright atmosphere of heaven." The formation of the range is partly volcanic, and in the centre is a lake enclosed in the crater of an extinct volcano. They are the highest mountains in the country, some peaks being considerably above the snow-line, and, standing out impressively in their white garment of snow, they probably derive their name not merely from this fact, but also by reason of their limestone formation, which renders them dazzlingly white. The summit of the highest peak is of pumice-stone, pieces of which are carried down several hundred miles, floating on the surface of the waters of the Yalu, and greatly astonishing the simple natives.

Another interesting range is the Kwanguing, which skirts the west side of the Liaotung Gulf.

These mountains are also sacred, one of the peaks (Mount Wulin) having been from a remote period considered one of the "nine guardians of the empire." Here is still shown the hermitage where Yenwhang, one of the most renowned of Chinese princes, passed his days, "far from the madding crowd," surrounded by books and manuscripts. Every notable mountain in Manchuria has one or more monasteries, either Buddhist or Taoist, some of extreme antiquity, and tracing back their existence for at least a thousand years, the former being the more splendid and the latter the more numerous. European and American missions have as yet scarcely made their influence felt in Manchuria, and with the advent of the Russians will probably disappear, as is the case elsewhere whenever Russian authority is established. The Greek Church, even with all the weight of Russia behind, is not likely to err on the side of overzeal or indiscreet interference with the ancient institutions of the Chinese, as has too frequently been the case with both Roman Catholic and Protestant missions.

The most important waterways are the Sungari, with its tributaries, and the Yalu; the basin of the former being, in parts, the most fertile and densely populated district in the country. To decide the question as to how far the Sungari is navigable has been the object of various expeditions since it was nominally opened to foreign trade by the treaty of Aigun. It seems certain that in the summer season, between the middle of April and the end of October, it is navigable as high as its tributary, the Nonni, thus providing a waterway right across Central Manchuria. It is possible, indeed, to go by water as far south as Kirin, where boat-building is a large industry, but only this at certain periods. The Nonni itself, too, is navigable as far as Tsitsikar, while another large tributary, which runs southward from Sansing, is also available for small craft. In some places the Sungari, over a mile wide, increases greatly in volume during the summer, when the snow is melting on the White Mountains. During the floods it resembles an inland sea dotted with islands and covered with flocks of geese, swans, and other wild fowl. The basin of the Usuri, a tributary of the Sungari, forming the eastern boundary of Manchuria, suffers much from these floods, which entirely spoil this region as a country for colonization, despite its numerous natural advantages. The water rises suddenly to a great height above the ordinary level, and sometimes even submerges the houses, notwithstanding the fact that they are built as high as possible.

The Yalu River (or Liao-he),* which drains southward to the Liaotung Gulf, is chiefly important as affording the only practicable water outlet possessed by Manchuria to the China Sea. It is not, however, at present navigable, except in its lower course, and then only by small boats. The soil of the valley is in parts extremely fertile, and as one of the granaries of Manchuria this region has always been

* Where two names are given for towns, mountains, and rivers, the first is the Manchu name, generally used by Europeans, and the second that in common use among the Chinese.

jealously guarded by the Chinese government, as it will be, but in more effective fashion, by its new owners.

Remains of ancient forests are said to be in existence on the right shore of the river, but at present the lower portion of the valley is very sparsely wooded, chiefly with poplars, willows, and elms, which the people have planted round their houses and graves. The upper parts of the basin are covered with fir-trees, which are felled and floated down the river, the carrying-on of this industry being at present the chief use to which the Yalu is put.

The climate of Manchuria has been likened to that of Canada by those who have had experience of both, and the two countries are, indeed, similar in other respects. "How important has Canada been esteemed," said a Russian officer of high standing to the writer, repeating the very words employed many years ago by Williamson, a most acute observer, "and how poor is our appreciation of Manchuria, yet the latter is perhaps the richer country of the two." To briefly sum up the matter, the Manchurian climate may be described as a Canadian winter and summer, with this difference only, that there is a blue sky throughout the year. On the whole, and especially in South Manchuria, it is extremely healthy, and well suited to Europeans. Extremes of heat and cold are felt, in summer the temperature varying between 70° and 90°, and in winter between 50° above and 10° below zero. The rivers are frozen over soon after mid-November, and are not again navigable till towards the end of March. A great difference distinguishes the regions north and south of the Sungari, the former belonging to the Siberian world, while the latter, both in climate and vegetation, is similar to that of the Flowery Land.

Judging from the scanty information afforded by travellers, chiefly English and Russian, and from the existence of indisputably valuable mines, one may conclude that Manchuria is exceedingly rich in minerals; gold, silver, lead, iron, coal, and salt being all found in varying quantities. Indeed, now that Russia is practically in ownership and is opening the country, the great natural riches seem to make it possible for Manchuria one day to rival South Africa or Australia. So far, however, little has been done to develop her resources, and such mines as already exist are worked in a very elementary and unscientific way.

Gold has perhaps the largest range, being found along the river Amur and its tributaries in the north, on the Sungari and its tributaries in the centre, and in the Chang-pai-shan Mountains and Liaotung peninsula in the south. There are, besides, many isolated gold-fields, some of which are hardly worked at all. It has always been the policy of the Chinese government to suppress gold prospecting and mining in Manchuria, partly, no doubt, from superstitious reasons, which make it unlucky to disturb the configuration of the earth, and thus to "open the dragon's veins," but chiefly because they feared that the gold-digging communities, never easy to control wherever met, would some day prove unmanageable. At all events, the illicit gold-digger and the robber were until recent times on the same footing in Manchuria, and when captured were generally put to death. All the gold-fields are a government monopoly, which results in their being worked in an unprofitable manner. The monopoly has been but indifferently respected, for, apart from the bands of Chinese illicit gold-seekers, the Cossacks have on occasion engaged in this commerce.

The best-managed gold-fields are worked by an organized community, presided over by an elder elected by the most respected members and styled the *da-e*. He has one or two assistants, and is the supreme authority in the community, being empowered to punish evil-doers with whipping or even death. In the latter case, however, in order to preserve a somewhat superfine distinction, no blood must be shed—and the victim is therefore buried alive or drowned! The *da-e* receives all the gold which is found and distributes it again, and also has charge of all widows and orphans. The members are free to leave the community and join another, but, having left, they cannot be readmitted. An organized community like this, with its strict discipline, is the more remarkable in a robber-infested country like Manchuria, ruled over by a decadent dynasty and a corrupt officialdom. The existence of such a self-constituted and law-abiding little kingdom illustrates the manner in which men of all races and ranks, drawn to one place by a common pursuit, will band together for mutual control and defence, and out of the most heterogeneous parts evolve a coherent whole—a characteristic of mining communities which may be noticed in all parts of the world.

The Chinese government once, and once only, tried the experiment of opening one of the Manchurian fields to all comers, and with disastrous effect, owing no doubt largely to the incapacity and weakness of the local officials. In 1889 the gold-fields on one of the Sungari tributaries were thrown open to all, on condition that ten per cent. of the washed gold should be paid to the Treasury. Swarms of gold-plunderers were at once attracted, chiefly Chinese, from Vladivostok and the South Usuri districts, and serious disturbances arose. As soon as the news reached Peking the order was cancelled, and soldiers were despatched post-haste to evict the diggers. Little resistance was offered, but about a thousand men died meanwhile of typhus and dysentery, brought on by overcrowding and bad hygienic conditions, and the evicted miners spread over the neighboring districts, adding to the number of tramps and robbers. This gold-field is still being worked, but in a most primitive manner and without machinery, the output being inconsiderable. When visited some years ago the community was small and not very prosperous, but it is difficult to get any reliable information, on account of the suspicious attitude of the miners, who are naturally inclined to conceal any success they may have. At Guan-i-san (on the Amur) is a gold-mine worked by private capitalists, by special permission of the government, where, according to the Russians, a more satisfactory output is obtained. In Southern Manchuria the richest gold-fields seem to be in the Chang-pai-shan Mountains, where is also situated a silver-mine, probably of considerable value, but handicapped by want of fuel, as well as by the usual lack of proper machinery and mechanics.

To summarize the scattered information gleaned from various sources, gold is found (1) in Northern Manchuria: on the Russian frontier, along the rivers Urga, Sheltuga, and Fabira, all tributaries of the Amur; also along the Amur itself; (2) in Central Manchuria: in the Ninguta district, along the Sungari basin, and on the river Tun, or Davokha, which drains the Lesser Khingan; (3) in Southern Manchuria: at Tsai-pi-how, in the Kulah Mountains, Kirin province; in the Chang-pai-shan Mountains; in the eastern part of the Liaotung peninsula.

In the extreme south of Manchuria, in the Liaotung peninsula, lead and copper mines exist, but they do not seem to be extensively worked. Iron is found in the same region, and also at Kirin, where it is used for the government arsenal, and still farther north again at Sansing, where it is reported that there was once a flourishing cast-iron foundry.

Numerous coal-beds are found throughout Manchuria, but from the somewhat meagre reports it does not seem, on the whole, that coal, especially in the north, is of a first-rate quality,* though some seams are both extensive and good. In many cases, however, the beds are only worked on the surface, and in the same district as some of the largest seams there are silver-mines actually unworked because of "lack of fuel." The principal coal seams now being worked are found in the Liaotung peninsula and on the adjacent islands; in the southern province of Shengking; in at least ten places in the province of Kirin; in the eastern part of Northern Manchuria, where there are open beds; and on the left bank of one of the Sungari tributaries, opposite Sansing. A reference to the map will show how general is the distribution. In the Liaotung Gulf salt is also found in large quantities. The method of obtaining it is very simple, the sea-water being merely run into square pits, which are closed when full. The heat of the sun causes rapid evaporation, and a certain amount of salt is left, which the owner gathers into heaps and covers with mats. There is said to be mineral salt at Ninguta, but there is no positive evidence of this. Sulphur would seem to exist in the southern districts of Manchuria, and also in the north, not far from Mergen. It was near the latter place that earthquakes happened in 1720, in the neighborhood of the Sakuanshan, or "Sulphur Mountains." There is every indication that

* The mines in the hills southeast of Mukden supply the town and metal-works, and also the steamers plying in the Yellow Sea. This coal is said to be superior to that of Japan and equal to the best Cardiff.

in the remote past earthquakes were severe and volcanoes active, and in the neighborhood of Ninguta there are numerous lava-beds, which emit a hollow sound when walked upon. The foundations of the stronghold of Kuantien, in South Manchuria, are built of black lava, found close at hand; in the same region also occur great blocks of "pock-mark stone," as the Chinese call it. A coarse white marble is fairly common, and is burned for lime in the south; and some sixty miles east of Newchwang is found a variety which is largely quarried and made into ornaments, pipe mouth-pieces, and *articles de luxe*, which find their way all over China. This marble is creamy white, irregularly patched or streaked with light green, and bears a resemblance to jade. Agate is common on the Amur, and in Eastern Manchuria a conglomerate of peculiar hardness is found, which takes a polish equal to granite. Gneiss is not uncommon, but basalt and granite, both red and white, are more general.

Although possessed of natural resources in profusion, there is not as yet any large manufacturing industry in Manchuria. The most important is the distilling of bean-oil, which also constitutes the most important export. It is made wherever there is a sufficient crop of beans or pease, from which the oil so universally used in Chinese cookery is expressed. The residuum is pressed into cakes, which are used for cattle or transported as manure for the sugar-canes. The beans are also ground into pulp, and concocted into a dish known as "bean-curd," which is considered a delicacy. The chief oil factories are found in the Sungari basin, where there are sometimes as many as forty or fifty in one town. Oil is also made from many other plants besides beans and pease. For food and lighting it is extracted from hemp and from the ricine plant; the sesamum or *sutai* yields the so-called grass-oil, much used in Chinese kitchens, and even the kernels of peaches and apricots are utilized for this purpose. Distilling is carried on in the same districts, the smaller distilleries being situated in private houses, while the larger are in special buildings surrounded by walls and groves of trees, and guarded by armed men, so that from a distance they present the appearance of small forts. A spirit distilled from *sorgho* is much drunk by the people, "to the forgetfulness of good and evil," as their saying is. Pottery for home use is made in most parts, the largest works being in South Manchuria. A special kind of large glazed pot is worthy of mention, being used in every Chinese household for keeping salt provisions, pickles, vinegar, etc. Fur-dressing has attained to great perfection in Manchuria, and is very general, tanneries being found in most towns. The leather is good, sheepskins being particularly well dressed. The procuring and dressing of sable-skins is a fairly large industry, part of the yearly tribute to the government being paid in these. They are, however, getting somewhat scarce, and are dark in color, the fur being by no means equal to the Russian variety. A special kind of foot-gear, called *u-la* or *wu-la*, not met with elsewhere, made from one piece of leather and roughly rounded at the heel and toe, is found throughout Manchuria. These shoes are fairly waterproof and are in great demand in swampy and mountainous districts, being invariably worn by hunters. Wool-felting and carpet factories are found in some of the large towns, the greatest number being at Petuna, in Central Manchuria. The carpets are made from sheep wool, mixed with camel and cow hair, and are cheap and poor in quality. A coarse kind of paper is made at Petuna from hemp-combings, a better sort being manufactured farther south. Snuff-boxes and pipes, which play such an important part in the social life of the Manchus and Chinese, are made of various substances, the most sought after being of stone, though sometimes they are of chalcedony and carnelian, which are found on the banks of the Amur, and are elaborately worked and very valuable. Every Manchu, as well as every Chinese, thinks it his duty to possess a stone mouth-piece to his pipe.

Mention must also be made of the factories for making maccaroni and starch, the latter manufactured from maize. The curious pasteboard figures of men horses, bulls, etc., covered with fringed paper to look like wool, which are made in most parts of China, and burned by the Chinese in memory of their dead, are produced in large quantities in Manchuria. There is also a manufacture of a rough sort of cotton texture much used by the people, made from native cotton, as well as from Indian yarn, the import of which increases yearly.

From time immemorial, according to Chinese history, Manchuria has been celebrated for its pearls, said to vary in size from half an inch in diameter to the size of a millet seed, which are chiefly found in the Sungari and its tributaries, and in some of the smaller lakes. The fisheries are a government monopoly, and are strictly forbidden to private persons, with the inevitable result that at present the pearl trade is almost *nil.* All the rivers in Manchuria abound in fish of various sorts, and fishing forms the occupation of a considerable part of the inhabitants. One of the tribes, the Golds, who live along the banks of the Sungari and Usuri, make their livelihood entirely by hunting and fishing, catching salmon, sturgeon, and various small fish. The salmon of the Sungari are so large and plentiful that the Golds use their skins for clothing in the summer, the women embroidering them elaborately; hence their Chinese sobriquet, "The fish-skin people."*

The thick and extensive forests with which Manchuria was originally covered, on all her mountain slopes, are gradually disappearing with the increase of population. Indeed, so largely have they been destroyed by the system of "brand-tillage" in vogue,

* The salmon, called by the Russians *veta*, and locally *tamakhg*, is darker than *salmo salar*, and has not its silvery shimmer. During the season all the Golds are occupied, the men in catching the fish and the women in preparing what is called *khola*—*i. e.*, dried fish.

that in some parts the character of the country is quite changed and even the climate affected. The work of demolition has been carried on without any particular method, and consequently is of no advantage to the country. Under this plan, where the timber is got rid of and the ashes serve as dressing—a system still to be seen in many parts of Indo-China and India—the land is cultivated for a couple of years and then abandoned for a new plot. There is no regularly organized forest trade, and when there has been an unusual demand for timber it has actually been found easier and cheaper to import lumber from the United States than to transport the home growth for a dozen miles or so in a roadless country. There are, however, still vast unexploited forests on the slopes of the Great Khingan and Chang-pai-shan; and when proper forest regulations are enforced, as, doubtless, they shortly will be under Russian rule, these should prove a vast reserve of available wealth.* The forests in most parts of Manchuria are full of birds, generally of species analogous to those of Western Europe. Ravens are found in large flocks and are held sacred, as the Manchus believe them to be the spirits of their ancestors. There is also a peculiar bird, only found in

* The trees found in Manchuria include the larch, willow, oak, ash, birch, poplar, elm, cedar, common fir, and hazel; there are varieties of well-known brushwood, while the ordinary wild flowers of an English wood, the blue-bell, larkspur, dog-rose, and hawthorn grow in abundance, as do the Scotch-thistle, ferns, mistletoe, etc. The largest trees are the larch, oak, and black birch.

Manchuria, resembling a lark in appearance, but having the faculties peculiar to a mocking-bird.

Wild beasts still infest the forests of this country. Panthers, the man-eating tiger (or "lord," as the natives call him), wild boars, bears, foxes, wild-cats, and pole-cats are numerous, and in the northern forests the squirrel and sable are so abundant that the hunting and trapping of them is a staple industry for a large section of the population. The abundance of mountains and forests in Manchuria offers great attractions to the professional hunter, notwithstanding the bad roads and the scarcity of population; but the mere sportsman has been deterred by the rough life involved, and by the difficulties in the way of procuring safe-conduct.

The roebuck, which is found in many parts, is valued for his young horns, called "panty," as well as for his sinews. The young horn is composed of a very tender vascular substance covered with a thin skin, while bearing which the animal avoids touching the trees and bushes with the horns, and prefers, though at grave risk, to remain in the open spaces. After several months the skin begins to scale, causing irritation to the animal, who then rubs the horns on the tree branches, the moss-covered bark, or other soft things. This helps the scale to fall off, and then begins the second phase in the development of the horns, which now become harder. Some time after reaching full development they fall off, to be replaced by new ones. The change takes place every year, beginning from the fourth year of age of the animal. The horns obtained in the first period of their growth, particularly in June, are held by Chinese doctors to be a very efficacious remedy in strengthening weakened constitutions, especially in a damp climate, and experiments recently made have confirmed the Chinese opinion. The remedy is used in the form of a glue, which is extracted by boiling the "panty." According to some authorities, a pair of young, tender, and vascular horns, about a foot long, is worth £50 to £60 sterling, whereas a pair of fully developed horns is worth only about seven shillings. The Russians, however, put the price of the best "panty" in the South Usuri province at 300 rubles, or about £30. In the Kirin district experiments have been made to tame roebucks, but the "panty" got in this way was not so valuable. Besides roebucks, the kabarga, found in the northeastern part of the Kirin province, is hunted. The males have under their belly a little pouch, about one and a half inches in diameter, which contains musk, the best quality being got from fully developed animals. The very young have nothing in their pouch, and the old ones musk of an inferior quality. Tigers are valuable, not merely on account of their skin and claws, but also for some of the bones. The skin of the Manchurian tiger, with its long, silky hair, is even more highly prized than the Indian.

Before the conquest of China by the Manchus, the profession of arms was the only one held in any respect in Manchuria, and agriculture, like other industries, was little practised, the raising of crops being left mainly to women, as the men were all engaged, directly or indirectly, in the army. Under such circumstances irrigation was neglected, no attempt was made to clear the land of timber, and only the pressing needs of the individual family were provided for.

From the agricultural point of view, the country may be divided into two chief sections—the northern and the southern.

In Northern Manchuria some parts of the country offer great possibilities in the way of agriculture, while others are practically useless. In the centre, between the rivers Nonni and Sungari, is a barren steppe, to the east of which again lies the basin of the Sungari, the most fertile portion in the whole of Manchuria. The worst cultivated district of this neighborhood is near Kirin, where the country is mountainous and boggy, while a little lower down the river the people devote themselves more to fishing than to agriculture. To the west is the basin of the Nonni, also fertile, though not cultivated to the same extent as the Sungari district. Tsitsikar and Mergen, in the eastern and northern districts, are the best cultivated portions of Manchuria. North of the steppe already mentioned lies the thickly wooded Lesser Khingan range, and, still farther north, the basin of the Amur, where the severity of the climate makes agriculture difficult. In Southern Manchuria there are two distinct regions—a plain, and an elevated country with high mountains. The somewhat monotonous plain is well cultivated, and, on the whole, fertile. The mountainous portion, abounding in vegetation and affording grazing-land for cattle and goats, is picturesque, its scenery a varied panorama of waterfalls, hills, and valleys. The soil generally is unlike that of the neighboring countries, although the formation of loess in the southern parts, which is in active progress, connects it intimately with China; indeed, the Great Plain of China extends for many hundreds of miles into Southern Manchuria. The most fertile soil resembles a mixture of clay and sand, and is so rich that in a virgin state it will act as manure. Eastern Manchuria is mountainous, the rocky surface of the land being but thinly covered with soil, and is liable to droughts, which occur every few years.

The plants most commonly cultivated in all parts of agricultural Manchuria are: millet, bean-plants, various cereals, wheat, oats, buckwheat, and maize; tobacco, indigo, the ricine plant (of which a fine variety, equal to a famed Japanese rice, grows in the north), potatoes, and all kinds of vegetables, which form a large proportion of the food of the natives, and are very cheap. Millet is a popular food among the poorer classes, and a drink called *kanshin* is distilled from it, while some varieties are only used for cattle. Beans, black, white, and red, are largely used for oil-making, as are the larger kinds of pease. Tobacco grows almost everywhere, especially on the middle course of the Sungari. Manchurian tobacco is highly prized throughout China, while the local consumption is enormous, the inhabitants, both men and women, beginning to smoke from the age of eight or nine and continuing the practice almost without intermission during the whole course of their lives. Cotton is cultivated to a certain extent in the southern districts, on the shores of the Liaotung Bay.

After the conquest of China, the Manchus adopted in their own country the method found in use in the Celestial Empire of reserve stores or granaries for corn, of which there are two kinds—the government, and the village or communal. The former, situated in large towns and managed by officials, are intended to supply the whole district in case of need. Owing, however, to official corruption and mismanagement, which have been, if possible, more rampant in Manchuria than even in China, these stores are of very little service, and in case of famine are generally found to be empty. The village stores are really useful, each being managed by a representative elected in the village. No one who has not contributed is entitled to receive help in time of need, and the community itself decides the percentage to be stored each year, which in ordinary times does not exceed one per cent. of all the crops.

The cultivation of the poppy for opium, which dates from quite recent years, about the "sixties," has already attained large proportions and has begun to compete seriously with the import from India. The poppy, in fact, flaunts its red flag in almost every part of Manchuria, more especially in the

Sungari region, and is the most profitable crop an agriculturist can raise. It is, therefore, inevitable that, with the Chinese arriving yearly in increasing numbers, the opium trade will rapidly reach even greater proportions. There are no less than five inducements for the development of poppy culture: the increasing habit of smoking opium; the expensiveness of the foreign article; its easy transportation in a practically roadless country; the increasing export of the native opium, especially to the Chihli province; and the early ripening of the poppy, which makes it possible to rear a second crop on the same ground. The use of opium as money is in some parts very common; the laborer coming from the north preferring to be paid in opium, which is easily carried in his wallet and increases in value as he makes his way southward.

Formerly Manchuria produced a great number of medical plants, roots, grasses, and bark,* chief among which the highly prized *ginseng*, now the more sought after because it is becoming very rare. In its native state it has a very narrow range and is a government monopoly, although a large amount of secret illicit selling takes place. So scarce and costly has it become that attempts are being made, not without success, to raise it artificially. The extraordinary virtues ascribed to this plant by the Chinese are manifold. It is believed that it will prolong a man's life, and, notwithstanding the opinion

* Agassiz specifies sixty sorts, while Colonel Putiata, a Russian authority, names as many as two hundred.

held by Western doctors that it is of a very ordinary character, the people cling tenaciously to their belief in its miraculous healing power.

Sericulture is practised in the south and south-east, being especially common in the large towns on the Liaotung peninsula. It is entirely a primitive home industry, without any attempt at division of labor or investment of capital. In quality the silk is good, but inclined to be dark in color, for, owing to the amount of soda used in its preparation, it will not take light dyes. The export has hitherto been to China only, but this will probably soon be altered, and a large increase in the amount woven will, doubtless, be the result of a determined effort on the part of foreigners to develop this industry. Many of the dyes used are rendered fresher and brighter by the application of a sort of extract of mushrooms. These are called *mu-err*, and, being much used in cooking, afford a means of livelihood to a considerable number of people, who hunt for them in the woods. Before being cooked they are soaked, thus producing the extract used by the manufacturers of silk. This trade is chiefly developed in the eastern mountains, where the oak forests have been greatly injured by the practice of cutting down the large trees in order to grow good crops of mushrooms on their stumps.

As Manchuria may now be regarded as practically Russian, only a few words are necessary regarding the taxation which has hitherto been enforced. In former times no such thing as a land tax existed in the country, but one was introduced in the early days of Chinese immigration, and now the only exemption is in favor of land belonging to temples. Every one is free to occupy as much land as he can pay for, the local authorities having merely to grant permission and register the occupation. Useful laws hinder the accumulation of large land properties by individuals; for instance, if arrears for six years are not paid, or if the ground is allowed to remain uncultivated for three years after occupation or registration, the land lapses to the government.

Gardening is as yet little developed in Manchuria, and there is no trade in garden produce. The fruit-trees most cultivated are pear, apricot, and cherry; apple-trees are also met with, and, in a few orchards, the raspberry is grown. Manchurian pears are celebrated, and attain an enormous size in the Sheng-king province, where grapes, chiefly wild, are also found in the mountains. They are, however, cultivated in some parts of the province, and wine of very fair quality is produced by the missionaries. Latterly there have been some not unsuccessful attempts to develop the wine-making industry on a larger scale.

Cattle-breeding in Manchuria is practised only on the steppes and in the extreme west, in the "no man's land" bordering Mongolia, where is a vast upland altogether unfitted for agriculture. This region is specially favorable for cattle-breeding, because of its great extent, nutritious grass, and comparative abundance of water. On this plateau cattle-breeding is practised, not merely on the steppes, but also in the valleys, where, however, the grass is too watery and not sufficiently salt, and therefore not so good for cattle. The highland cattle are of the same species as those of Northern Mongolia, where they feed on dry saline grasses. The horned cattle are of the big species, but the horses are of small growth, distinguished, however, for their powers of endurance, like those of the Mongolian breed. In other parts of Manchuria, also, cattle-breeding is carried on, but to a very limited extent, the only demand being for agricultural work in spring and summer, and for carrying purposes in the winter.

CHAPTER XII

MANCHURIA—(Continued)

As in the case of agriculture, commerce was held in contempt by the Manchus, but with the advent of the first Chinese settlers began a new era. At the outset, however, the lawless and unsettled state of the country offered a most serious obstacle to trade, one that has indeed continued down to the present day, owing to the lax rule of the Manchus, who were entirely preoccupied with enforcing their supremacy in China. Many of the Chinese immigrants were outlaws and escaped convicts, and these, joining with the worst class of the natives, formed themselves into organized robber bands, such as that of the *Hunhutze*, or Red-beards, called by the Russians "Kunkhusi," who even now are a constant menace to peaceful settlers of the districts where they have established their strongholds. They defy the Chinese authorities, and, having smuggled improved weapons across the Russian frontier, invade villages and farms, and their red flag, with the inscription "Vengeance," still strikes terror into the poor up-country trader. In the old days, and till quite recent times, these robbers were so audacious in their calling that they found themselves in danger of altogether losing their means of livelihood—no one would dare the risks involved in trading with inland towns, and, therefore, there was nothing to steal. They accordingly established a sort of insurance office at Newchwang, where the merchant who paid toll to them—and every one took care to do so—was supplied with a little flag, which fluttered on the front of his cart, a magical passport which gained him an unmolested path through the robber-infested country. It is still customary to insure goods before sending them inland, and although the underwriters would doubtless repudiate with scorn the idea of having any connection with the present-day Red-beards, yet the same little flag still flies on the front of the carts, indicating with which office they are insured. Whatever the secrets of local insurance may be, the first condition of successful trading, safe and swift transport, has been sadly lacking in Manchuria, a fact hardly to be wondered at, since a not dissimilar state of affairs has till recently obtained in Northern China,* and may be said to continue to this very day. An instance of the insecurity of traffic in China, even on the high-roads, was the case of Mr. Burlinghame, then the lately appointed United States minister, who, in 1863, was stopped and nearly captured by a band of robbers quite close to Peking. The prices of provisions in Manchuria have been known to rise one hundred to two hundred per cent. because the

* See *China in Transformation*, pp. 300–302.

Hunhutzc were interfering with the shipping of corn on the Sungari. At the time of the Tai-ping rebellion no man went about without arms. Field laborers carried spears and matchlocks while working, and robber gangs held to ransom high officials and even towns.

Even now the brigands, sometimes known as *Hongus*, who infest the country between the Usuri and the Amur, are a source of great trouble to the Russians, by reason of their unprovoked attacks on Russian subjects, of which the recent massacre of a band of Cossacks is by no means an isolated example. The Russian government, in connection with the construction of the railway through Manchuria, made the protection of the laborers against the attacks of these bandits their reason for quartering troops all over the country, and each massacre of Cossacks will certainly furnish a reasonable pretext for the introduction of a still greater number of Russian soldiers. Chinese troops invariably take to flight on the approach of the robbers, whose horses are so fleet as to carry them rapidly beyond pursuit of even the trained Cossacks.

Travel in Manchuria is a slow and tedious business. The ordinary two-wheeled Chinese carts, drawn by mules and ponies, are the usual means employed in transport traffic. The cost of conveying goods is small, but, on the other hand, the charges for passenger traffic are very high, and the rate of progress extremely slow.* The best times for

* A cart capable of carrying three tons of produce, drawn by six

trade are the autumn and winter, when the roads are good and the agricultural population is not employed on the land. There is then a constant stream of caravans along the great roads, especially those connecting the fertile lands of the Sungari with the Lao-khe River and Liaotung Gulf, while the inns, empty in summer, are crowded with people and animals. In winter sledges are much used for passengers, and are quicker and more comfortable. The roads, as a rule, are extremely bad, though they have been improved since the development in colonization; on the whole, the best road—or, rather, the least bad—is that between Peking and Mukden. At one time, when Chinese troops were gathered on the northern frontier of Manchuria to repel the Russians, it was proposed to construct a waterway across Manchuria from south to north. The project, of course, like so many Chinese projects of recent times, came to nothing, but is still quite feasible. No attention is given to keeping the roads in good condition; irregular and uneven, they usually consist merely of ruts, gradually becoming impassable but for the rains, which convert them into a common puddle. When the rain ceases the carts form fresh tracks, which harden in the sun. Inns, of a primitive character, it is true, but welcome

mules or ponies, and accompanied by a driver or conductor, can be hired for about 5*s*. per day. Such a cart could travel twenty-five miles a day on a long journey, and more on a short one. A passenger-cart of the common kind, drawn by three ponies, can only accommodate one passenger; its hire is 3*s*. per day.

enough to the traveller on Manchurian roads, are found plentifully in this country, as in China. Here shelter, fire, and hot water are provided, the traveller bringing his own provisions, and, if he likes, his cook. These hostelries have the merit of being exceedingly cheap.

The advantages to be looked for in the construction of railways in Manchuria were first pointed out by the Scotch missionary Williamson, who suggested a line from Talienwan Bay, with its rich coal-field, through Kin-chow, Fu-chow, Kai-chow, Hai-ching, Liau-yang, and Mukden—the whole course rich in minerals, terminating in the pulse and indigo producing districts in the north, and thus commanding the entire commerce of the country. He expressed the opinion that in the construction of such a line there would be few difficulties to overcome, the excellent harbor at Talienwan being open nearly all the year round, and the country on the line of route consisting of a series of valleys running north and south, with here and there a few insignificant ridges, and requiring no tunnellings or cuttings. This is practically the very line now adopted by the Russians, who in this, as in so many other instances, have profited by information acquired by Englishmen.

Railway projects here, however, no less than in China, have often met with opposition. Even when, in 1885, the Emperor of China had at last been induced to consent to a line between Tientsin and Peking, local opposition brought about the abandonment of the scheme; and in Manchuria, after the country had been surveyed and the route marked out for a trunk-line from Peking to Mukden, an obstacle was encountered in the objection raised by the military governor of Mukden that the line would pass too near the Imperial Tombs in that district. The contemplated route was to pass these tombs at a distance of twenty miles, but the geomantic* influences were not to be disturbed, a compromise had to be made, and was eventually provisionally accepted, by which it was arranged that the railway should pass the tombs at a distance of *twenty-three* miles! The telegraph, which has been carried across Manchuria for a distance of over two thousand miles, and connects Port Arthur, Kirin, and the chief towns with Newchwang, which again is connected with Tientsin and Peking, was mainly used by the Chinese officials, and could not be relied on.

* Geomancy, the *Fung shui* of the Chinese, is a superstition which has an enormous hold upon all classes throughout the empire. It is based on the rudiments of natural science, to which have been grafted various doctrines from Confucianism and Buddhism, while it retains some of the Taoist superstitions. The worship of ancestors is a part of it, and it ascribes all kinds of occult influences, powers, and properties to the elements. No enterprise can be undertaken without consulting the geomancers, who make an excellent living out of the gullibility of their clients. An amusing instance is given, arising from an event which occurred when it was proposed to construct a telegraph line between Canton and Hong-Kong: Canton is the City of Rams or Sheep, the mouth of the river is known as the Tiger's Mouth, the district opposite Hong-Kong is the Nine Dragons (Kaulun). What more unpropitious combination could arise—a telegraph line to lead the sheep into the Tiger's Mouth and among the Nine Dragons!

As generally throughout China, so in Manchuria, but in a greater degree, taxation forms a substantial hinderance to commerce. Besides the regular government taxes, the local officials levy dues quite arbitrarily upon goods going to or coming from the interior.

If, under such unfavorable circumstances, commerce is carried on at all, it is owing to the personal qualities of the merchants, who are nearly all Chinese from the province of Shansi. The natives of this province are distinguished as being among the best traders and quite the best bankers in the empire, and are noted for their sagacity, temperance, economy, and *esprit de corps*. Their assistants are invariably also Shansi men. In the absence of any effective government, the local merchants have formed themselves into guilds for mutual protection and guidance, somewhat like the great trade-guilds of the Middle Ages in Western Europe. Their method of self-government, by which certain members are chosen yearly from the large firms, to settle all questions which may arise, and to represent the merchant class before the authorities, is based closely on the practice obtaining in China. These firms have the right to issue credit notes.

In some parts of Northern Manchuria, in those districts where the nomadic and hunting population is found, markets are held from time to time, giving the people an opportunity of exchanging their various goods. Such are held at Sansing in June and July; at Tsitsikar usually in the same months, when the yearly "tribute" of deer and sable skins, exacted by the Chinese government from some of the Manchu tribes in lieu of military service, is brought to the treasury, and gifts are bestowed in return. Another big market is held at Ganchur in August and September, at the time of the pilgrimage to the local convent, and people come very long distances to dispose of their goods here, chiefly by barter, silver being very little circulated, while tablets of tea are largely used.

The trade of Manchuria mainly consists of—

1. Exports of the produce of the country.

2. Imports of foreign goods from Europe and the United States.

3. Imports of Chinese goods and produce.

The most important export is that of bean-oil; tobacco and a particular kind of silk being also largely exported to China.

Cotton goods of various kinds are the most considerable import. British yarn, we are told, is being supplanted by the Indian. Manufactured cotton goods come chiefly from Britain and America, but also from Holland, India, and, since 1894, from Japan. Notwithstanding the extreme cold of a Manchurian winter, woollen goods are not in much demand—the lower classes, as in Northern China, keeping themselves warm in sheep-skins, cotton-cloth, or wadding—and there is practically no woollen manufacture in the country. Both demand and supply, however, might be further developed. A cheap, rough woollen cloth, as Agassiz remarks, would probably command a good sale, and with the opening up of the country the purchasing power of the inhabitants will of course rapidly increase. As regards such articles as kerosene, matches, sugar, etc., Europe and America have a great advantage over Russia, on whose imports a heavy duty is levied.* The local Russians consider this duty a mistake, being of the opinion that a remission of such prohibitive excise, which would tend to considerably increase both import and export trade, would be greatly to the advantage of Russia generally.† With the occupation of Manchuria by the Northern Colossus a magnificent opportunity for developing the trade of Great Britain and the United States has passed away.

While the actual currency is much the same all over the country, and resembles the Chinese, the value of the "cash" (the English term for the *tsien*, the most used coin) varies in different parts, there being, it is said, three distinct methods of reckoning.‡ Paper money is circulated by one private

* The American kerosene, however, is said to be very superior to Russian, and to hold its place by virtue of its superiority.

† Matunin gives a list of Russian manufactured goods which might find a market in Manchuria. This includes several kinds of cotton material, drills, calicoes, reps, etc., black and colored cloths, plush, and flannel. He emphasizes the point that they must be cheap, for, ready money being scarce, the people do not look for quality.

‡ The three methods of reckoning seem to be:

1. In Western and Central Manchuria (from Aigun in the north to I-tun-chau in the south), 1 coin=2 cash; 49 coins=100 cash; 490 coins=1 dao. This varies a little; for instance, in Sansing, 500 coins

firm, and the notes issued by the loan banks are in great request, the banks, as in China, working under a system of mutual guarantee. There is also a silver currency of a primitive nature, the silver being made in bars, which are cut into pieces when necessary. The Russian paper rubles have for some years past circulated in the north, and are generally in use, being much preferred to the silver ruble. Mexican dollars and *dao* are also used as small change. Much of the Manchurian trade, however, as explained elsewhere, is still done by barter, and tea-tablets are frequently used as money, while in the poppy-cultivating districts laborers are usually paid in opium.

The incompleteness and insufficiency of the information at present available concerning Manchuria is startlingly evident to any one who examines closely into the subject. Taking into consideration the vast extent of the country, the ethnic variety of its inhabitants, its natural resources, and the rapid development which has taken place during the last few years, under conditions which at first presented grave difficulties, it is matter for surprise that the Western world should be content with so meagre

=1 dao; in Bayansusu, 1 cash=2 coins, 1800 coins=1 dao. This reverses the relative value of cash and coins.

II. In Southern Manchuria, 1 coin=6 cash; 16 coins=100 cash; 160 coins=1 dao. (N.B.—The reckoning has to be done approximately in *sixes*.)

III. (Used only for very small payments.) 1 coin (tao-tsien, or dan)=1 cash.

Spoiled and defective coins are not taken at all.

The *dao*, or *tao-tsien*, nominally contains 1000 cash.

a knowledge of Manchuria as they at present possess. No doubt the indefinite nature of our information as to the country is in great measure owing to geographical and political conditions, but it is also in part due to the lack of interest shown by the Western peoples as regards Far Asia, and to the casual character of the expeditions which have from time to time been undertaken in Manchuria, for the most part accomplished by individual Englishmen and official Russians. The importance of studying the country is now, however, more fully recognized by the world at large, and the lack of knowledge at present prevailing as to this vast region—this Eastern Canada, with its magnificent geographical position and immense resources—will soon be a thing of the past.

When the trans-continental railway through Siberia and Manchuria is completed, Russia's relations with the rest of the world will be materially altered, for she will then occupy a commanding situation in the Gulf of Pechihli and a powerful position on the Pacific. It is probable, however, as already suggested, that her advance into China will be gradual and by peaceful means. It may be assumed that her present occupation of Manchuria, although preeminently a military one, is not altogether due to a passion for conquest, but is in part the outcome of geographical circumstances, and of that moving force which compels a vigorous and dominant people, hemmed in by the ice-locked northern seas, to push a way for themselves towards the open sea.

Russia, in the Far East, as in Central Asia, is aiming at the south—always the south. Whatever changes may take place in the system of government, this movement, as the writer has always maintained, will not, in the nature of things, cease, unless checked by a resisting force—that is to say, by some power as strong and as determined as Russia herself.

In Manchuria, as elsewhere, her progress will be marked by the incorporation of the subject races. Whatever her military and commercial aims, she does not neglect social and religious matters. Her Church, indeed, takes a leading part in the moulding of the conquered peoples, confession once in two years being the only obligation imposed on a convert, and many adherents being gained. Nearly all Koreans immigrating into Manchuria become converted, the Chinese alone remaining obdurate in this respect. It would be unjust not to note the fact that the general influence of Russia in the territories she has acquired in the Far East has been for good. Not only has she introduced a higher degree of civilization, but she has opened up vast regions to commercial, scientific, and general development, not shrinking from the initial expenditure involved in the construction of roads and other means of communication through difficult and often dangerous territories. And these benefits are already apparent in Manchuria, where, from the very commencement of the Russian occupation, a silent transformation has been taking place and is now proceeding at lightning speed.

CHAPTER XIII

EASTERN MONGOLIA

On leaving Siberia for China, the season of the year is a matter of great importance, and has naturally much to do with the rate of travelling. There are certain months when the Russians say there are "no roads," and they do not think of making a journey during that period, except on a matter of life and death. What is called "the commercial road" from Irkutsk to Kiachta, the one used by the writer, though shorter than the old postal route, is so broken and hilly that the rain and snow of the autumn render it extremely arduous. The writer encountered some serious difficulties on this portion of his journey, the *yamtschik* (driver) refusing to proceed on more than one occasion when the weather got bad. There are also many more hinderances to travellers than on the regular government postal roads, where are generally provided ample relays of post-horses, as well as accommodation of a primitive kind; and the inconvenience in question is not always to be commuted for money. "*Schimpfen oder bezahlen*" (abuse or pay), said a Russian officer to the writer. But, judging from experience, "*und*" might well be substituted for "*oder*." The knowledge of even a very limited vocabulary of Russian is extremely useful on the road—indeed, necessary—when travelling without the aid of an interpreter. Mongolia should be avoided even as early as October. Snow, ice, and atrocious weather must then be expected, as the writer can testify from experience, and it is bitterly cold, even with the wind behind. The traveller must equip himself, Russian fashion, with felt, furs, or sheep-skins, and, if possible, should carry a small charcoal brazier of Siberian or, even better, Japanese manufacture.

On reaching Kiachta, the writer was compelled to interview a Chinese police official through the medium of a small boy from the local "hotel" (a confectioner's house). He spoke in Russian to the officer, and, receiving the replies of that personage in extremely broken Pidgin-Russian, translated them again for the benefit of the writer's limited intelligence—a conversation not likely to lead to any clear understanding. The Chinese here, as at Peking, look upon the Mongols as an exceptionally stupid people, an altogether inferior race. But it is not merely the Mongol, it is hardly necessary to say, who is thus regarded by the Chinese. All the benighted beings who have the misfortune to hail from the "cut-off regions"—that is, from anywhere outside the Chinese Empire—are held in like poor esteem. At this place it was necessary, as already mentioned, to invite the assistance of the Commissioner of the Frontier towards procuring the necessary transport for the journey from Kiachta to Kalgan. He, however, found himself unable to move in the matter, such facilities being only accorded to officials on service, or to those provided with special letters from the St. Petersburg authorities. The writer's object was to enlist the sympathetic co-operation of the Commissioner's wife, a lady who spoke both French and German, but with no successful result, and it was impossible to procure either horses and tarantass (the quickest means of conveyance), or even camels. The only thing to do, therefore, was to telegraph to the British ambassador at St. Petersburg, but even he was unsuccessful in his kindly efforts at assistance. Eventually it was found possible to get away by means of a judicious use of the ruble, a cart drawn by camels being secured to proceed as far as Urga, where fresh arrangements had to be made for the continuance of the journey to Kalgan. While endeavoring to engage the required conveyance — tarantass and horses — at Kiachta, the writer underwent the experience of driving a bargain with a patriarchal old man who made a livelihood out of such transactions, and whose venerable appearance and air of transparent honesty were somewhat discounted by a pair of beady, cunning eyes. He asked three times the price which he ultimately agreed to accept. Next day it was found possible to make other arrangements, and he was offered part of his price to cancel the contract, but he would not be satisfied with this; he demanded the whole amount, declaring that he had been put to great expense, and using many similar arguments. His demand being refused, he went off, calling upon all the saints in the calendar to witness the ignoble conduct of this Englishman. An Austrian, the sausage-maker of the place, and an important personage in his way, intervened, and advised a settlement of the difficulty, saying: "Don't let it get to the police office; he is a friend of the old man's, and, in any case, you would have to give so many tips that it would cost you many rubles to get clear of the business." Advice which, there is reason to believe, was thoroughly sound.

On entering Kiachta, a traveller from Siberia is at once reminded of his near approach to a foreign and Oriental land by the continual procession of camels through the streets, the mingling on all sides of Chinese and Mongols, and the unintelligible language which prevails. The streets are, on the whole, well kept, at least so they appear in dry weather, the sidewalks being generally of wood. Situated on the Russo-Chinese frontier, this town is of considerable importance as the headquarters of the rich merchants engaged in the overland tea trade, and also as the residence of the Russian government commissioner and other officials. The inhabitants of the Chinese town Mai-mai-cheng, separated from Kiachta by a neutral zone, are all officials or Chinese traders, and are forbidden by law to bring their families with them.

The journey between Kiachta and Peking is tedious to a degree, and yet there is a certain charm about it, mainly, no doubt, the charm of novelty. The most interesting point on the route is on arrival at the great Mongol headquarters, or "camp," at Urga* (known among the Chinese as Kuren, or "the great enclosure"), where, as stated by the Russian consul-general, there are more than ten thousand llamas congregated in the two huge llamaseries, which are separated by the deep ravine through which the post-road passes. The population of the town, about thirty thousand, is dependent upon these monasteries and on the regular transport of tea between China and Russia. Urga consists merely of a straggling collection of huts, or, as they may be called, tents, situated on the river Tola (a tributary of the Orkhon), at a distance of about six hundred miles from the northern frontier of China at Kalgan, and about two hundred and fifty miles from the southern frontier of Russia at Kiachta. It is divided into two parts—the Mongolian quarter (Bogdo-Kuren) and the Chinese quarter of Mai-mai-cheng (place of trade). Among the many temples in the Mongolian quarter is that dedicated to *Maidari*,† and in this quarter also is situated the palace of the Kutukhtu, or "living representative of the Di-

* From the Russian *Urgo*, a palace, otherwise known as Bogdo-Kuren or Ta-Kuren (sacred encampment); known also among the Mongols as "Hurae"—*i.e.*, enclosure or encampment—the full Mongol name being "Bogdt Lama en Hurae," the "enclosure or encampment of the supreme Llama."

† *Maidari*, according to Yule, is the Mongol form of the Indian *Maitreya*, the name of the Buddha next to come, and who will be the fifth of the present World-period.

vinity." The whole town of Urga is surrounded by mountains, some of them thickly wooded; the climate is good, but cold winds are prevalent.

The commanding site in the town is occupied by the Russian consulate, or "Green House," which stands on an elevation to the south, overlooking the river Tola, and midway between Mai-mai-cheng and Bogdo-Kuren. Here the writer received the greatest kindness and hospitality from the consul-general, a cultured and travelled gentleman, the sojourn there leaving very pleasant memories. The Russians have had a consulate here for forty years, and it is one of the significant features in connection with the territorial aspirations of that nation that during all that period the Chinese territory as far south as Urga has been included in the maps published by the government at St. Petersburg or elsewhere. The Chinese themselves have practically no maps of their outlying positions. During all this time a process of silent, imperceptible assimilation has been going on between the Muscovite officials and merchants and the Mongolian herdsmen, who supply all the transport animals for goods and travellers, and in sundry other ways find it to their advantage to serve the Russians. The natural result of their intercourse has been a steady strengthening of the ascendency of Russia, and a corresponding diminution of the power and prestige of China, so that, in the event of any political upheaval in that part of the world, it may be expected that the Mongol tribes will go over in a body to the Russian standard; and even should no such upheaval occur, they will be gradually leavened by the Russian yeast.

Till very recently the principal medium of exchange at Urga was brick-tea, first moulded and pressed solid, sawed into small lumps, which buyers either carried in their arms to the market or brought lashed to their saddles, bartering it for other goods. For a sheep, for instance, they would pay from twelve to fifteen bricks, and for a camel from one hundred and twenty to one hundred and fifty. Latterly, however, Chinese brass cash has been introduced as a circulating medium in the retail trade. Perhaps the feature in Urga which makes the most impression upon a traveller is the presence there of a certain class of mendicants who, taking up their quarters in the cold, bleak market-place, accept what charity comes their way, and remain exposed in all weathers. They are regarded with indifference, and when they die their bodies are removed to some ravine at a little distance from the town and left to the dogs, while their rags and any other possessions are appropriated by some of the surviving beggars.

The greater part of Mongolia consists of a vast arid steppe known usually as the Gobi,* the Chinese name, however, being Shamo—literally, the "sandy desert." This desert traverses Central Asia obliquely, and is for the most part bounded by mountainous

* The word "Gobi" in Mongol literally means a waterless, barren plain, almost devoid of grass; the word for steppe is "Tala."

regions. In size, that part of it which belongs to the Mongols, if we include Northern Mongolia, almost equals the whole of China Proper. In the general configuration of the land it is unlike that country, from which, moreover, nature has separated it widely by climatic conditions.

The traveller crossing the Gobi leaves the last stream, the Tola, behind him at Urga, and here, too, he may say good-bye for a time to all trees and shrubs, for no rivers cross the wide expanse of the desert, and it is possible to ride six hundred miles without seeing even a stream. Here and there are dried-up watercourses in the bed-rock, and these are filled with sudden torrents by the summer rains, but the fierce winter gales, hot, dry winds, and rapid evaporation make it impossible for a permanent stream to develop. The Gobi must, therefore, forever remain a dreary waste, where, for the most part, even grass can scarcely grow, where trees are so rare as to be beheld with awe by the wandering Mongol, and where only birds of prey can exist in large quantities, feeding on such camels and men as fall victims to the thirsty desert, and on the few wild animals which are found there.

The grass called by the Mongols *dirisun*, common also in Russian Turkistan, which is found in some of the more favored spots, is the most flourishing vegetation, being from four to five feet high; but, as a rule, only a few weeds or small flowers or a kind of wild leek are found growing in the sand. These, with an occasional patch of scrub, are the only things

CROSSING THE GOBI DESERT

that break the terrible monotony of the interminable waves of sand which stretch away as far as the eye can see. The distance is not infrequently rendered deceptive by the mirage, which dances forever on the horizon and seems to take a malicious pleasure in deluding the traveller and puzzling him by the quaint shape of the objects it reflects. All traces of habitation gradually disappear, until at length even the road ceases, and a region is reached whose desolation is emphasized by the black rocks projecting from the ground on all sides. The soil is a reddish gravel or sand, mixed with various stones, the celebrated "Gobi stones"—quartz, pebbles, agates, carnelians, and chalcedony—and these, with their greens and blues strewn together, make a welcome change from the monotony of color presented by the sea of sand.

The climate varies from Indian to Siberian, and that sometimes in a few hours. In summer the desert is swept by a hot, dry wind—the southeast monsoon—and in winter by a fierce northeasterly gale from Siberia, which uproots all vegetation and drives the sand into deep drifts. The intense cold of the Gobi winter at one time led travellers to estimate its elevation at far too high a figure. As a matter of fact, it varies from four thousand to five thousand feet above sea-level in the east, to considerably less in the west, while in the region of the Kiachta-Kalgan caravan road it actually drops to about two thousand feet, continuing at this level for some sixty-five miles. On the whole, the Eastern Gobi, which borders Manchuria, is not so barren and desolate as the other parts.

If vegetation is scanty, animal life is still more so. Herds of *dzeren*, belonging to the antelope species, about the size of a goat, are sometimes met with, and are found principally in the eastern portion of the Gobi. They are generally seen in herds of from fifteen to forty, but in those rare spots where there is good pasturage the herds number hundreds or, occasionally, even thousands. They avoid man, are very swift, and have great intelligence. One of their greatest enemies is the wolf. During the winter they often travel hundreds of miles to get away from the snow, and they will also cover great distances in search of food. choosing always the best pasturage, but keeping entirely to the plains. Their avoidance of thickets, high grass, or any kind of cover, renders it a matter of extreme difficulty to get near enough to shoot them, and when merely wounded they generally escape. The method adopted by the Mongols is to dig pits at intervals in those parts where the *dzeren* are plentiful, and these are left for some weeks, so that the animals get accustomed to the sight of them. After this some of the hunters armed with matchlocks conceal themselves in the pits, while others make a circuit round the herd and gradually drive them towards the ambush, no shot being fired until the animals are within fifty paces of the guns. Another method is for a Mongol to ride over the desert on a camel till he sights a herd of *dzeren*. He then dismounts, and, concealing himself as much as possible behind the camel, approaches the herd, sometimes getting within as close as a hundred paces.

In addition to the *dzeren*, a small animal of the marmot species is found, which burrows its way in most parts of the steppe, but as a rule no sign of life is seen in the desert save the wheeling flocks of ravens and crows, on the lookout for a meal. These birds are held sacred by the nomads, who call them "the Sepulchre of the Mongol," and will not kill them. Consequently they are very bold and rapacious, and will almost enter tents, while they peck open the packages of food and often attack the camels by tearing at their humps. Sand-grouse, which lay their eggs, three in number, on the bare sand, are fairly plentiful, and are seen flying at great speed in search of water, after their morning meal of various grass seeds.

Wild animals are numerous in Mongolia, and include the tiger, the panther, a wolf of great size and ferocity, and the brown and black bear, the ounce, elk, stag, wild goat, wild ass, hare, and squirrel. The yak also, the "long-haired" or "grunting" ox, is found near the Tola River, although it was at one time supposed that this animal was peculiar to Tibet. The wild duck and the merganser, which make their appearance in such large flocks in the neighborhood of Peking and Kalgan during the month of March, forming quite a distinct characteristic of the scenery, set out in flocks for the Mongolian desert and Siberia as soon as the temperature in these places gets warm.

The lack of agricultural enterprise among the Mongols has prevented the resources of the country from being exploited, but in the lower valleys of the mountainous regions oats, potatoes, and barley are grown, and in the southern parts the ordinary products of Northern China. Indigo, the poppy, and the mulberry-tree are reared in the east, on the borders of Manchuria. The plains are for the most part covered only with prairie grass; but, in the south and southeast especially, as one descends from the plateau into the valleys towards China Proper, the country is fertile, and in summer there is an abundance of wild flowers. The grass and flowers, however, bear no comparison in coloring or luxuriance to those of the meadow-lands of Europe, and a couple of days' journey northward from China brings one again to a desert country covered only with scrub. The southern valleys themselves are populous and thriving, and far from presenting an uncheerful aspect. Monotony and melancholy are, however, the chief features of the Gobi Desert.

The desert stretches south almost to the verge of China Proper, from which it is separated by the Great Wall. This structure has long since ceased to form a real boundary to China, owing to the immigration of agricultural Chinese, who, establishing themselves in the valleys which slope down from the Gobi, have reclaimed a portion of that desert, which they call Tsaoti or "Grassy Lands." As the writer, late at night, reached the Great Wall, some twenty miles from the Chinese frontier town of Kalgan, a

MONGOLIAN DESERT—TOMB OF LAMA, ENCAMPMENT, AND CARAVAN

Chinaman put his head into the cart, and, to the great astonishment of the writer, addressed him in Russian: "Vi-li Gospodin kotori dolshen pribit Kalgan?" (Is master going to Kalgan?) The man had been sent by one of the Russian tea firms at Kalgan to meet the "foreigner." On passing from the Gobi into China, and as the Great Wall is left behind, the climate gradually becomes warmer, the streams more plentiful, the whole scene more animated, until at last we are in the Flowery Land, with its numerous villages, busy roads, and industrious population. And, *pace* M. Huc, the first sign of China is the pig, the hideous black pig beloved of the Chinese, "gavorting" in the distance; and *not* the "all-pervading musk," as the Abbé says.

And here it may not be out of place to remark on the striking similarity of type, noticeable as one passes southward, between the Buriat, the Mongol, the Chinese, the Shans, and the Burmese. Their singing, especially, has a strong resemblance. A Mongol cameleer crooning to himself was the first thing to make the writer thoroughly realize that Russia was left behind, and that one was moving in the direction of China. Music, indeed, plays an important part in the social life of the country we are now entering. The travelling minstrel, with guitar or flute, can pick up an easy living among the *yourtas* of the Mongols, who gather round to hear him chant in monotonous tones, but with a note of wild pathos, the songs of the country. Some are love ditties, but most have reference (like the Norwegian Saga and the folk-songs of so many countries) to the daring exploits of warrior ancestors in the past—perhaps of Genghis Khan and his victorious armies. The modern Mongol, sunk in indolence and apathy, must still have a spark of the divine fire left, since he loves to remember the days of bygone glory. Such a lay is the "Song of the Black Colt," the most popular in all Mongolia.

The Chakhar country, as the south of Mongolia is called, is a belt about one hundred and thirty miles wide by three hundred in length, forming a sort of neutral zone between China and the Gobi, and is inhabited very largely by Chinese, or by a mixed race, the offspring of Chinese fathers and Mongol mothers. This region, besides being agricultural, affords good pasturage. Its inhabitants are largely employed by the Chinese government as a sort of frontier militia, whose *raison d'être* would seem to be to supply a considerable number of officials with more or less lucrative positions.

Mongolia is peopled partly with nomadic and partly with agricultural tribes, all claiming descent from the ancient Scythians and Huns, whose sphere of action, far from being confined to Asia, spread to the very sea-coast of Western Europe. These ancient conquerors gradually made their way to the borders of the Chinese Empire, and in the third century before Christ became so formidable that the Chinese built the Great Wall to check their inroads. No other people ever so greatly disturbed the neighboring nations, and, while acting up to the spirit of their proud motto, "Erein mor nigen bui" (A man's path is only one)—namely, through sufferings, boldness, and valor, to attain eternal glory—they were in-

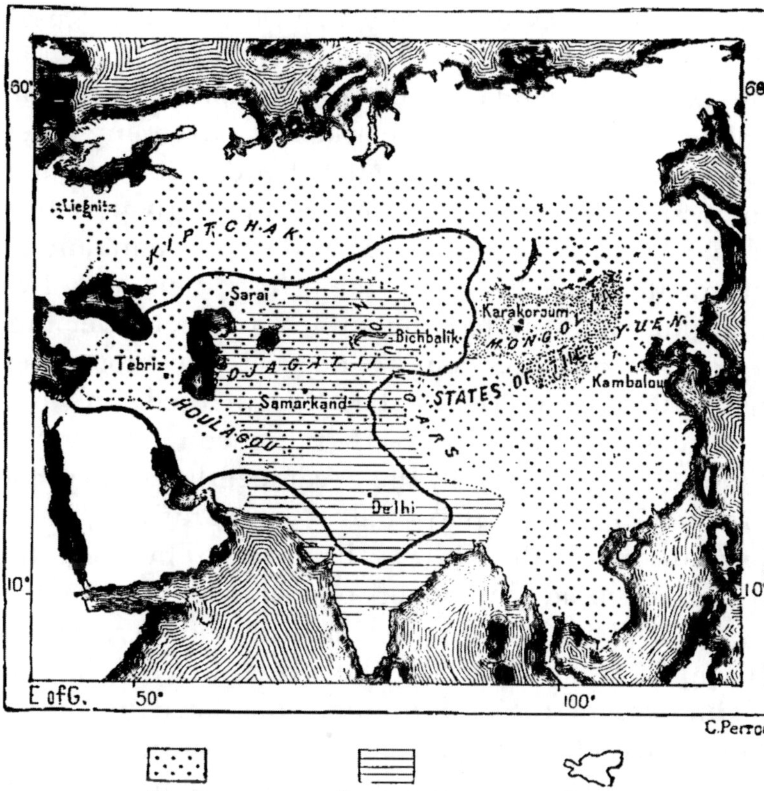

INVASIONS OF THE MONGOLS AND CONQUESTS OF THEIR SUCCESSORS

superable. Their dominions at one period extended from Poland to Hungary in the west, to China in the east, and the Mongolian court of Kublai Khan at Peking was considered the most magnificent in the world; for a considerable period the Mongols in Russia, under the name of "The Golden Horde," exacted homage from all the States, including Muscovy, which was eventually to rule not only Russia in Europe, but a vast empire in Asia, including the very descendants of these same Mongolian tribes. But, though the success attending their arms was extraordinary, their tribal divisions made it impossible for them ever to become a great nation. Some great warrior, some leader of commanding personality, could band them together and lead them to conquest, but the campaign once over they broke up again; then by degrees they lost their national characteristics, became merged on their frontiers with the peoples they had conquered, were themselves subdued in the seventeenth century, and are now merely a part, and a comparatively unimportant one, of the Chinese Empire. There is a frequently quoted saying of one of the ministers of Genghis Khan (the great Emperor and hero of the Mongols, from whom all the present-day "princes" claim descent): "The kingdom has been gained on horseback, but it cannot be governed on horseback," a motto which betokens a surprising amount of enlightenment for the time at which it was uttered. It has frequently been said, and seemingly with truth, that the ancient Mongols showed greater consideration, especially in the matter of religion, to the nations they subdued than did the conquering hosts of many Christian and Mohammedan countries. Such moderation points to a degree of civilization which is lacking in the Mongol of the nineteenth century, who, were he capable of conquest, would certainly be incapable of using his power rightly.

The prevalent impression that the influence of the Mongol conquerors on Russia was slight and superficial is inaccurate. Russia was, in fact, in the position merely of a vassal state, having no Mongol or Tartar population scattered throughout her territory, but being compelled to send her princes to attend the Mongol Khans, even at Karakoroum, in Mongolia, when called on. From these princes homage of the most humiliating character was exacted; for instance, they were forced "to lick up any drops which fell from the Mongol's cup as he drank." And this state of affairs continued till the year 1478, when, for the first time, the Tsar refused homage to the Khan of the Great Horde. In addition to this exaction of homage, the Mongol power extended to the collection of a poll-tax, and also to the requisitioning of military contingents. The Grand Dukes had to obtain a *yarlik*, or firman, from the Khan before they could ascend the throne, and they could not wage war without the sanction of the Suzerain. Thus the Muscovite nobility became partly Orientalized, and one of the Tsars actually was of Mongol origin, while Russian dress became gradually more and more Eastern in character, as witness the long, flowing *kaftan*, or over-robe. The Mongol influence was naturally most powerful in the case of the Russian rulers and aristocracy, who were in close contact with their Mongol suzerain. The style and ceremony of the court were modelled after Asiatic forms, and the Russian nobles even shaved their heads and dressed as directed by their conquerors, wearing skull-caps similar to those now in use in Central Asia, while the very crown, called the "cap of Vladimir Monomakh," is nothing but a Kirghiz cap ornamented with precious stones.

Not merely in externals — dress, manners, and habits of life—did the Russian princes and boyars, the officials and richer merchants, imitate the Tartars. The very spirit of the people was affected. During the whole of the "Moscow period," up to the time of Peter the Great, the control and the statecraft generally were Tartar. The Tartar immigrants, drawn into Russian service, in the second generation usually became orthodox Russians. But to placate those who might object to such a process, a special Khanate was founded—the Kingdom of Kasimof—where for two hundred years Mohammedanism was the state religion. Two things generally cited as consequences of Mongol domination would appear to be attributable to other causes. The severe punishments formerly in use in Russia came from Constantinople with the ecclesiastical law, which became included in the civil law; and the Mongols did not seclude their women, for they appeared in public on all state occasions. The knout, however, was probably introduced by the Mongols, as was also the custom of the *praviozh*, or public flagellation of defaulting debtors.

The southern Mongols, especially those who live on the borders of China Proper, have so much intermarried with the Chinese that the national type has been considerably modified. Unfortunately, the worst traits of both people seem to perpetuate themselves, with the result that the Mongol has lost his energy and martial spirit, while he has acquired much of the cunning and *finesse* of the lowest type of Chinese. The combination is not attractive, and to these characteristics must be added the childish credulity of ignorance, and the slavish superstition of a priest-ridden nation. This degeneracy, however, must not be attributed entirely to the mixture of Chinese blood, for even in the Mongols proper (if any be really entitled to that name), such as the Kalkas, who occupy the northern and northeastern regions, there is a noticeable falling off in character. These are mostly tribes of the more strictly nomad description—whose flocks and herds provide for their daily needs, the cattle being exchanged with town-dwellers, and the wool being spun and woven by the women —who are simpler and less suspicious than their southern brethren. The crafty Chinese make great profit out of their stupidity and inability to understand business. In his *Souvenir d'un Voyage*, the Abbé Huc gives an admirable description of the way in which the Chinese beguile the Mongol who has come to a Chinese city, probably to sell his tea or dispose of cattle. "Tea is prepared for him at once, his cattle are attended to, a thousand little attentions are shown him; he is caressed, flattered, almost mesmerized. A good meal is served him free of charge in the room behind the shop, and this finally convinces him of the devotion of the Chinese confraternity. No sooner have they become friendly with the poor Mongol than they never leave him. They give him spirits in abundance, making him drink till he is almost intoxicated. They keep him thus three or four days in their houses, never letting him out of their sight, making him eat, drink, and smoke, while the shop assistants sell his cattle at their pleasure, and buy him such things as he may need." Not altogether unlike the poor up-country prospector and miner or ranchman in Australia and California, who is subjected to much the same sort of treatment as long as anything remains in his pocket! As for the Russian opinion of the Mongol, it is graphically illustrated by their proverbs, "The Tartar, like a dog, has no soul — only vapor," say they, while their favorite epithet for the Mongol is "Swine's ear"—peculiarly offensive, as the pig is considered unclean.

The Mongols have the childish inquisitiveness of the savage, and pester a traveller with the most trifling questions, the answers to which they often do not understand, for the extremely conservative order of their minds and the monotonous existence they lead, out of touch with any world but their own, makes it difficult for them to grasp anything outside their ordinary experiences. Still, the common people, or "black folk," as they are called, when uncontaminated by Chinese or priestly teaching, are kind and simple-minded; but their extreme laziness, lack of enterprise, and abnormal gluttony make them but degenerate descendants of a race of great warriors, who in their time mastered so considerable a section of the world.

Love of money characterizes nomads and agriculturalists alike, and bribery is not only common but invariable. Few things in Mongolia can be accomplished without it, and nothing is more characteristic than the extreme circumlocution with which a bargain is accomplished. Tea-drinking and general conversation invariably precede any business on which a would-be purchaser and seller meet, and very gradually, and with great precaution, the subject is led up to, when, of course, the buyer offers less and the seller demands more than he is prepared to agree to. As the proverb says: "When the seller cheats up to heaven in the price he asks, you come down to earth in the price you offer." The whole affair takes several hours, being concluded without word of mouth. The bargain is struck by merely a pressure of the fingers, concealed by the long, hanging sleeve, so that the utmost secrecy may cover the whole transaction. The matter is not even then ended, for the silver offered and the scales in which it is weighed come in for the most searching scrutiny! The Mongol is evidently persuaded that honor must not be expected, even among thieves.

Gluttony is another common failing, and this in an extraordinary degree, mutton (of a most delicious quality, it must be owned) being the favorite dish.

Mutton, in fact, is a passion with the Mongol, and the highest praise he can bestow on anything in the world is to say it is "as good as mutton." Even the lovelorn Mongol swain can find no more enthusiastic description of his Dulcinea than to put her in the same category as his favorite food. The Mongols also eat the flesh of goats and horses, and, more rarely, of cows and camels, while they dislike fowl or fish, which they consider unclean. The lamas, or priests, who refuse ordinary meat, have no objection to carrion, especially if at all fat. Cookery in Mongolia is a very simple business indeed. The usual method of preparing the mutton is to boil it, the breast being sometimes roasted as a delicacy. When frozen, as is the case on a winter's journey, and therefore requiring a long while to cook, they slice off pieces from the surface, which are eaten half raw, returning the meat to the pot—a disgusting performance. The extent of their appetites is stupendous. A Mongol will eat more than ten pounds of meat at a sitting, and some have been known to devour an average-sized sheep in the course of twenty-four hours! On a journey, when provisions are economized, a whole leg of mutton is the ordinary daily ration for one man. Another favorite food is "meal tea," a compound made with "brick tea," fat, and meal (and of about the consistency of porridge), which is eaten in the morning and at mid-day. Snow and ice are melted for cooking purposes in the winter-time, ice-blocks being carried on one of the camels; and it is characteristic of the Mongol that, with a wooden shovel always carried for the purpose, he gathers up the snow round his tent, without any qualms as to its cleanliness.

If the Mongol is a glutton, he is even more of a drunkard, and in engaging a servant it is useless to stipulate that he should be sober. As with Siberian servants, one can only hope that he may drink rather less than usual. The most innocent beverage is milk, which is got from cows, goats, sheep, camels, and mares. The mares' milk is kept till it is sour, each day's pailful being emptied into the last, and the whole being frequently stirred up. In Southern Mongolia it is kept in earthenware jars about four feet high, and in Central and North Mongolia in skin bags of the same dimensions. This soured mares' milk, a kind of *arrak*,* if drunk in great quantities, produces intoxication; it is also used to distil a species of whiskey, largely produced and much drunk, supplemented whenever possible by the Chinese spirit, which is a good deal stronger. This spirit is much prized by the Mongols, who rarely visit China without bringing some back; and the itinerant Chinese trader, who travels from tent to tent bartering his goods, usually balances accounts with some of his whiskey, which costs *him* very little, but is a costly luxury to the poor Mongol.

* The *arrak*, according to Gilmour, is put into a huge pot, covered with what looks like a barrel with both ends knocked out; a vessel is suspended in the middle of the barrel, and a pot kept filled with cold water is set at the top; after a few minutes' boiling the vessel inside the barrel is found filled with pure and good spirit.

The most repulsive feature of the Mongol's character is his dirtiness, which is simply unspeakable. The least uncleanly Mongol (it would be a mockery to talk of the cleanest) does not wash any portion of his person more than once a day, and that in the most elementary manner, while many never attempt to wash at all. A little water is poured into the ever-present wooden cup, from which it is either emptied little by little into the hand, or taken into the mouth and squirted out as needed. It is usually considered quite sufficient to wash only the face and hands, while, for drying, the Mongol uses anything that comes first, and, as may be imagined, little time is wasted in the cleaning of pots and cups, which are simply licked out after each meal. The natural consequence of such habits is skin-disease, which is very prevalent. In defence of the Mongols it is said that these peculiarities are partly due to a superstitious belief common among them that if they use too much water they will become fishes. Be this as it may, they certainly avoid, in their more permanent *yourtas*, or tents, the proximity of water, preferring even to have to carry from a distance what they need for cooking purposes. When on the march they are obliged, for the sake of pasturage for their animals, to encamp not too far from a stream or well, and on such occasions they display a remarkable instinctive knowledge of locality, varying the length of their journey with much skill in order to halt at a good grazing-place.

It is pleasant to turn to at least one good feature,

and a highly attractive one, in the Mongol character—their extreme hospitality—which is especially noticeable among the poorer people. No matter who he may be, the stranger alighting at any tent will always be warmly welcomed and given food, and his horse or camel attended to; and all without any thought of remuneration, except, perhaps, the gift of a little tea, should he happen to have any with him. Any Mongol who refuses to offer hospitality, or even gives a cold welcome to a traveller, is stigmatized as "not a man, but a dog"; and it is a great grievance with many Mongols that, having entertained Chinese and foreigners to the best of their ability in their own homes, they have been given "the cold shoulder" on presenting themselves at the Peking houses of their former guests. The highest honor which can be paid to a guest is to set before him the rump of a sheep with the tail attached, because, each animal having only one tail, it follows that the sheep must have been killed to make the dish, and also that it must have been a good one, for otherwise it would not have a tail fit to be seen.

The snuff-bottle plays a very important part in general social intercourse. These bottles vary in value according to the rank and wealth of the owner, the cheapest being of glass and the better ones sometimes of stone, beautifully made. The etiquette attaching to the use of snuff prescribes that the visitor should first offer his bottle to the host (in the case of a foreigner who does not carry snuff, the Mongol entertainer will present his), which must be received in the palm of the hand, carefully carried towards the nose, the stopper lifted, and a sniff taken; then, the stopper being readjusted, the bottle is with the greatest care and gravity handed back to the owner. The possession of a large and well-filled snuff-bottle is a *sine qua non* and a male prerogative, but the Mongol woman apes her lord by carrying a small, flat bottle, mostly unfilled, which she will also present to a visitor. Politeness forbids that the emptiness should be noticed, and the same ceremony is gone through with due deliberation. While it is proceeding, questions are asked as to the health of the cattle, which every one by courtesy is supposed to possess, and not until these questions are answered does the personal welfare of host and guest become a matter of mutual interest.

Besides his cattle, but *longo intervallo*, the two most interesting subjects of conversation to a Mongol are medicine and religion. As regards the former, he is always interested to hear of new cures, and the foreigner is to him a wonderful person, chiefly on account of his knowledge of disease and its remedies. The Mongol is very credulous in such matters, and easily imposed upon by the Chinese doctors, while the dash of fatalism in his character makes him accept calmly, if it comes, the news that his case is hopeless. As to religion, it is here only necessary to mention that it plays so important a part in the lives of these people — among whom every third man is priest or lama, and where every family when travelling (and they are on the move a great portion of the year) carries its own priest with it—that, necessarily, the miracles and ceremonies of their faith enter largely into their lives and form one of the chief topics of their conversation.

CHAPTER XIV

EASTERN MONGOLIA—(Continued)

THE pre-eminence given to cattle in the interchange of social amenities is only natural, considering the important position which the breeding and tending of cattle occupies in the life of Mongolia. Agriculture, except in the south, is little practised, and as a rule the Mongol spends the whole summer, when his animals are out grazing, in riding from tent to tent, drinking tea, and gossiping, and only exerts himself in the autumn and winter, when the camels must be collected for the tea transport. The exposure he can endure is extraordinary; he will sit for hours on his camel in a cold wind with absolute unconcern. Every Mongol, at least among the nomads, is a born horseman, and understands every point of his animals. Girls are seen everywhere mounted on horses and camels. Horse-racing is a favorite amusement, and it is said that some years ago, at the festival held in honor of the birth of a Mongol Buddha, there were actually over three thousand competitors in the races. In traversing even the shortest distances a Mongol will ride in preference to walking, and invariably herds his cattle on horseback. Even when intoxicated he can keep his seat and perform gyrations which would dismount any ordinary horseman. In the south, flocks of goats are kept on the hill-sides, and the herdsmen use a curious crook with a bend in the end, by means of which they can sling stones to frighten refractory goats and prevent their getting into dangerous places.

The most usual and on the whole most convenient method of travelling in Mongolia is by camel caravan, and, though oxen can be used in some parts of the country, there are districts and times of the year in which only the camel is possible, while for rapid transport it is at all times indispensable. The camel cart is a square wooden vehicle with two wheels, long enough to enable the traveller to lie at full length should he feel so inclined, though the roughness of the roads, the lack of springs, and the cramped nature of the vehicle do not exactly woo one to repose.* The ox-carts are cheaper and are much used for freight, but are, especially to the Western mind, terribly slow. The speed of a camel, if such a term can be applied to its progress, is a little over two miles an hour, allowing for stoppages to adjust loads and for the animals breaking loose, and other interruptions incidental to travel in the remoter regions of the Far East. The journey from Kiachta to Peking, a distance of about one thou-

* The appliances usually carried consist of a wicker jar of oil for the wheels, an iron lantern and stock of candles, and an arrangement for blocking the wheels, when, the camel taken from the shafts, the cart remains resting on a support in front.

sand miles, can, however, be accomplished in twenty-five days (which means travelling sixteen hours to cover forty miles a day), or even less, and for such a speed the traveller is charged a higher rate, the journey usually taking about thirty days.

As may be supposed, a journey through Mongolia, though possessing some interest at first, soon becomes to the ordinary traveller almost unendurably monotonous, the slow and tedious progress through interminable undulating plains being wearisome in the extreme. Of the various methods of travel, horseback in summer-time is least open to this objection. Hill and vale, temples, Mongol tents, oxen, are passed with greater rapidity, and the journey may perhaps be varied by a chase after some unexpectedly encountered herd of startled deer, with afterwards a rest and a meal at the tent of some hospitable though filthy Mongol. No one with fastidious tastes would appreciate travelling in Mongolia.

The camels found in Mongolia are of the two-humped Bactrian species, the one-humped camel common in Turkistan being quite unknown here. Their endurance is remarkable, and is only equalled by their power of assimilation. Some will eat anything that comes in their way—leather, old tents, and even saddles, while most of them can find sustenance in the sparse and wiry vegetation of the desert, and regard the onion and the *budarhana* as positive delicacies. Salt is, however, a necessity of life, and a dry atmosphere is the only one in which they can flourish. Patient, helpless, timid animals these, without much intelligence, and incapable of defending themselves from the attacks of wolves or birds of prey.

Before the departure of the caravan in autumn, the camels, which have been at grass all summer, and have put on too much flesh, are prepared for work by being fastened with their halters to a long rope stretched along the ground and secured at the ends to two poles driven firmly into the ground. In this way they are kept standing without any food for ten days, or even more, only receiving a little water every third or fourth day, a practice which hardens them and takes down their spare flesh. A Kalgan merchant is reported to have actually kept his camels in this way without food, watering them only every other day, for seventeen days! In March they begin shedding their coats, and by the end of June the hair has entirely disappeared, leaving the skin quite bare. Grotesque-looking animals they are at this period, when they are susceptible to cold, rain, and every change of weather; and so weak are they that even a small load soon galls their back. But a fine, short, mouse-like hair soon begins to cover their whole bodies, and by the end of September the new coat is fully grown. On a winter journey they are hardly ever unsaddled, but on arrival at the halting-place are at once let loose to graze. In summer and hot weather the saddles must be removed every day, and even then, with all due care and precaution, sore backs cannot always be avoided.

The Mongol is almost a part of his camel, and

on its back can sleep, read, and even write. The writer's chief camel-driver was wont to rest his head on the front hump (as if it were a pillow) and systematically go to sleep, and the Chinese who accompanied the expedition as Mongol interpreter—although, as a matter of fact, he knew nearly as little Russian and quite as little Mongol as the writer himself, and was, moreover, in a continual state of warfare with the drivers—remarked: "Mongol man can walkee top-side camel all day, all night." Indeed, what the Mongol would do without his camel it is impossible to say. The invaluable animal supplies him with milk, and with wool for his clothing, besides being his faithful companion and frequently his means of livelihood. It "pays the rint" far more literally than the proverbial Irishman's pig, and, being a long-lived animal if well treated (frequently attaining the age of thirty or even forty years), it will last its master the greater part of a lifetime. In damp weather it often suffers from coughs, and occasionally from glanders, but the commonest form of ailment is the mange, known as *homun* by the Mongols.

Postal communication through Mongolia was established by the treaties of Tientsin (1858) and Peking (1860). These treaties gave to Russia powers to organize regular transmission of mails between Kiachta, Peking, and Tientsin. Russian post-offices have been established at Urga, Kalgan, Peking, and Tientsin, the post being carried from Kiachta as far as Kalgan by Mongols, and afterwards by Chinese.

Light, horse-carried mails leave Kiachta and Peking three times a month, the journey occupying about twelve days. For the benefit of the Russian political and clerical Missions at Peking, the Chinese government carries monthly, by means of camels, a heavy post (not over twenty-five hundredweights), which takes from twenty to twenty-four days. The Russian government spends on this service annually about £2400, while the total receipts are only about £430. On special occasions, such as the transport of important official documents between China and Russia, Cossacks act as couriers, travelling with relays of horses in a two-wheeled Chinese government cart. The journey, about one thousand miles, occupies nine or ten days, the only payment made being a gratuity of three silver rubles (about eight shillings) left by the courier at each station.

The tea-carrying trade between China and Russia is carried on to a large extent by the Mongols, the tea being brought from Kalgan to Urga(the great centre of the trade), where it is examined by Russian agents, who then engage fresh carriers to transport it to Kiachta. The necessity of having officials to preside over this trade led to the establishment of a Russian settlement at Urga, where, however, the number of Russians is still small, being only augmented when, for political exigencies — or, as the Russians might put it, owing to the unsettled state of the country — the subjects of the White Tsar may require additional protection. It may here be noted that the chief exports of Urga are hides and timber, the principal imports being tea and clothing material.

The Mongolian language has no relationship to the Chinese, but in its written form resembles that of the Manchus, who founded their writing on the Mongol characters, originally borrowed from the Uighur Turks of Kashgaria. This was the form of writing used by Genghis Khan and his successors, and was probably brought into Turkistan by Nestorian missionary monks, who adapted it from the old Syriac. The characters were somewhat modified in the thirteenth century, and an attempt was made to supersede them by Tibetan forms in the time of Kublai Khan, but eventually the Uighuresque characters were more or less perfected, adopted at the beginning of the fourteenth century, and remain in use to this day. The colloquial language is very different from the written, abounding in dialects and in modifications. A line of Mongolian writing is said to be like a knotted cord, while the people themselves say it resembles water poured from a jug. As an illustration of the difference between the spoken and the written languages of Mongolia and Manchuria, it is curious to note that, although their writing is closely allied, their colloquial language is quite different. There is practically no Mongolian literature, except the sacred books and liturgies, for the Mongol is so absorbed in his religion that it would seem to him waste of time to write or copy anything on other subjects. The lamas and princes are the only people sufficiently educated to take any interest in books, the poor people being as a rule quite illiterate.

The dwelling of the nomadic Mongol is a *yourta** made of felt. This tent is round and cone-shaped, having a skeleton of wooden laths made lattice-wise, to expand or shut up. A sort of chimney is constructed at the apex with poles, which are attached to the laths and stuck into a hoop at the top. Usually one or, in winter, two sheets of felt are drawn all round; a space about three feet square is left in the laths for the doorway, which is closed in with felt, and the chimney affords light and air. The fire burns constantly in the centre of the tent, and round it felt is laid down, while in the wealthier *yourtas* there are carpets for sitting and sleeping on, and the tent is lined with silk or cotton. The domestic utensils and the household gods (*burkhans*) complete the furniture, which has the merit of being exceedingly portable. When a Mongol wants to move he has no difficulty in packing up his home, while on the whole this primitive form of dwelling is warmer in winter and cooler and dryer in summer than might be expected. The traveller must be careful not to approach a *yourta* except from the front, making a wide *détour*, if necessary, in order to do so. He must also shout vigorously to the inhabitants to protect him from their dogs; otherwise he may find it a matter of some difficulty

* *Yourta* is the name used by foreigners. The Mongols call it *gi-rai*, as distinguished from a travelling-tent, which they call *mai-chung*.

to ward off the attacks of these animals; but the "fierce Mongol dog" of travellers' tales is not to be met with. The agricultural Mongol does not live in tents, but builds himself houses and villages much like the Chinese. The houses are sometimes round, but mostly on the Chinese model, and are built of mud, or bricks made of mud, and furnished with tables and chairs in the Chinese fashion. These people are more civilized than their nomad brethren in that they bury their dead, whereas the nomads leave the bodies to be devoured by wild beasts and birds of prey. The agricultural implements used are like those of the Chinese, only rougher, the carts being particularly uncouth, with great solid wooden wheels, seldom circular, and wooden axles, not quite straight, the whole primitive and unfinished.

The Mongolian women, unlike many of their Kirghiz sisters, have none of the attractions, at all events to a Western eye, which are usually expected in their sex; nor is their position an enviable one. They are household drudges, and take little care of themselves, with the result that very little is bestowed upon them by their lords and masters. The marriage laws give as much freedom to the idiosyncrasies of the contracting parties as the most ardent Western reformer could wish, only they betray a partiality for the sterner sex which is not surprising in a country where woman is still the mere accessory of man and by no means his equal. The Mongols have proverbs similar to the Russian ones: "Love your wife as your own soul, and beat her like your fur"; "It is my wife, my thing." Thus a Mongol can have but one lawful wife, but if the marriage turns out badly he can divorce her, without returning any part of the

KIRGHIZ WOMAN

dowry—usually the *yourta*, with all its fittings—which he has received with her from her parents. He can also divorce her merely for whim or caprice, but in that case must return some part of the dower. On the other hand, a woman may leave her husband if he is not "affectionate"—that is, presumably, if he works her too hard and beats her too often; but in that case she must repay part of the antenuptial settlement. As this, however—whether cattle, clothing, or cash—has been handed to her relatives, who naturally may not have the slightest desire to return it, there is every probability that the average wife will have to put up with her husband, whether "affectionate" or not. Somewhat reversing the order of a Western wedding, the only people of importance at a Mongolian bridal are the husband's relatives. As a preliminary to the ceremony, the stars are consulted, and, should they prove unfavorable, the wedding will not take place.

The Mongolian type of countenance is not intellectual, being distinguished by a low, narrow forehead, and, except when modified by Chinese intermarriage, by a somewhat childish expression. The high cheek-bones and small, dark, elongated eyes resemble the Chinese, but the nose is not quite so short and flat nor the face so rounded. The Mongols have coarse, black hair,* very scanty in the beard and whiskers; large, protuberant ears, a dark, sun-burned complexion, and, lastly, a stout, thick-set figure, rather above the average height of Asiatics. Their distinctive characteristics are their general gravity of expression and cautious, inquisitive mode

* There is a Russian proverb which says: "The red-haired Zyranin is created by God; the red-haired Tartar, by the devil."

of address. Those who live in the immediate vicinity of the Great Wall, and who have intermarried with the Chinese, have also adopted to a large extent their dress and manners; but the true Mongol is very conservative, and his costume and habits have varied little indeed since they first became

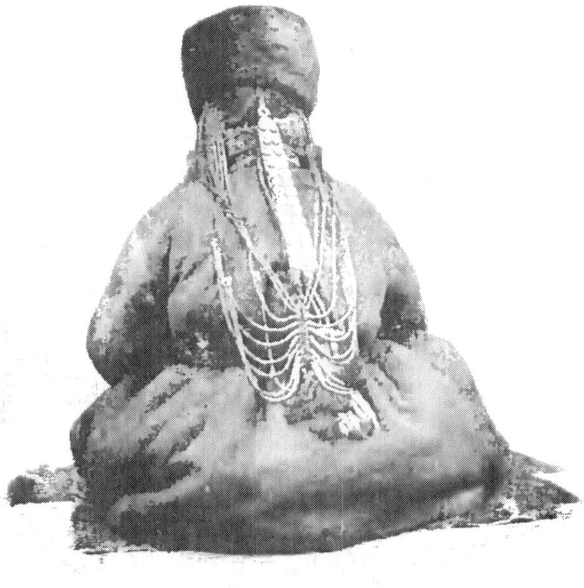

COIFFURE OF A KIRGHIZ BRIDE

known to history. There is little difference in dress between the sexes. In winter the clothing is of blue *daba* (Chinese cotton stuff), with outer garments of skins, while in summer silk is worn. The details of dress, especially among the women, vary in different districts, but the outer garment of both sexes is invariably a wide, roomy coat, with ample sleeves, which reaches to the ground, the women allowing it to hang loose from the shoulders, while the men wear a belt. This coat is used as a blanket at night. Gilmour gives an amusing description of the surprise of a traveller watching a woman who, mounted on a camel, was leading another harnessed to his cart. "Her hands disappeared, and inexplicable leanings and movements were seen about the shoulders till at last the gown slid off and revealed another more suitable for the heat of the day. The girl had actually managed to change her dress while riding one camel and leading another." The lamas invariably wear and carry, as originally prescribed by their great teacher,

> " . . . three plain cloths,
> Yellow, of stitched stuff, worn with shoulder bare,
> A girdle, alms-bowl, strainer,"

and at prayer-time they don special yellow mantles and tall caps, according to their rank. Like the Chinese, the Mongols shave the head, only leaving sufficient hair for a long pig-tail behind. The women plait their hair in two braids, and decorate it with ribbons and glass beads or strings of coral, their love for such ornaments showing that they are not altogether devoid of the weaknesses of their sex. Silver brooches (fastened in the hair above the forehead), ear-rings, and bracelets are also customary.

Though the freedom of intercourse between people and officials is a matter that has often been remarked on—they smoke and chat together without restraint—it must not be imagined that class distinctions have no place in the life of the Mongols. They are divided into four classes: princes, nobles, clergy, and common people. The first two form an exclusive aristocracy, by which the common people are held in a sort of serfdom. These "princes" are so numerous that the Russians usually address all Mongols ironically as "prince," and have a quaint proverb which exhorts the "prince" to perform the most menial duties: "Prince, O prince, take a pitchfork and help to rake the dung-heap!"

A cattle tax is the only one levied, except on special occasions, such as the visit of a prince to Peking, or the marriage of one of his children, when a special collection is made. The inhabitants of Inner Mongolia consist of forty nine families or clans, called "banners," each one having its own chief and distinguishing flag. These chieftains all claim descent from Genghis Khan, and pay no tax to China, being merely bound to military service. On the contrary, the Chinese State subsidizes them, allowing each one so much a year, in return for which he is bound in allegiance to acknowledge the Emperor as his over-lord, and not to enter into any relations with a foreign power without reference to Peking. There is a yearly assembly of princes, presided over by one of themselves, when local questions are decided, but this assembly is under the control of the governor of the nearest Chinese province. Each prince must appear at court two or three times in the year, and take with him gifts, such as camels and horses, in return for which he receives presents of far greater value.

The lamas are exempt from military service, and form a class apart; it is no doubt partly owing to the large numbers of this celibate priesthood and to the diseases which, unchecked, ravage Mongolia, that we must attribute the sparseness of the population in comparison with the size of the country. It has been variously estimated at between two and three millions, but, whatever the exact figure may be, there can be no doubt that the purely Mongolian race is being rapidly assimilated by the Chinese.

The religion of Mongolia is Lamaism, which has been called the "Romanism of the Buddhist Church." In its complete development of the priestly prerogative and assumption of temporal as well as spiritual power, it has generally much in common with the Church of Rome. The similarity, indeed, goes much further, and becomes in many particulars so remarkable, and in some cases even so grotesque, as to have been the cause of much dismay and perplexity among the missionaries of the Roman Church from the days of the early Jesuits down to our own time.

It is to be regretted that this religion, which has taken such a hold upon the people that in one of the large cities it is said that every third man is a lama, and that every Mongol family has its own priest, does not exercise a better influence on the manners and morals of the people. In Tibet, the lamaseries are served by nuns, who perform all housework. These women dress as do other Tibetan women, with the exception that their dresses are of the same material as that worn by the priests. These nuns, who frequently live with their own families, are treated with great respect by the people. They are supposed, as are the priests, to devote themselves entirely to the service of Buddha—a theory which, according to common report, is not too strictly carried out in practice. The lamaseries are not famous for a high standard of morality: "The monastery faces the nunnery; there's nothing in that—yet there may be!" says the cynical Chinese proverb. Theoretically, Buddhism has many excellent doctrines, but its practical effect is to delude its votaries as to moral guilt, and to encourage the sophisms with which men are only too ready to gloss over their evil deeds. The ultimate goal of Buddhism is Nirvana, Eternal Rest and Peace, the shortest path to which—according to the degenerate Buddhism of the present day—is a life of complete non-doing, a stagnant existence, passed merely in fruitless contemplation. This chimes in exactly with, and largely accentuates, the natural indolence of the Mongol. What a falling off from the original teaching of Buddhism, which contains so much that is right and noble! Truly the "Light of Asia," which began with such worthy aims, is setting in obscure darkness.

There are four ranks of clergy, the word "lama," properly speaking, being only applied to one of the higher grades. An examination in the Buddhist books must be passed before the candidate can attain the first two ranks. The head of the whole Buddhist hierarchy is the Dalai Lama, residing at Lhassa, who is practically sovereign of Tibet, but owes fealty to China. An able and enterprising Dalai Lama could easily excite his people to revolt, but, though the Lama nominally appoints his own successor, China is careful to see to it that the choice shall fall on some one of insignificant personality whom they can easily dominate, and, if necessary, crush. The Kutukhtu, or third person in the Tibetan patriarchate, lives at Urga, which is the sacred city of Mongolia, and only second in the opinion of the Mongols to Lhassa. The Dalai Lama and the Urga Kutukhtu, in Lama doctrine, are the living representatives of the Godhead, and when they die their souls are reincarnated in newly born boys. These Kutukhtus, or Gigens (who never make use of the expression "at my death," but always "at my renewed birth"), are found in all the temples throughout Mongolia and in Peking, all being lower in rank than the one residing at Urga. The lamas educate them, and, in order to preserve their own ascendency (as any one of these boys may become the High Priest of the order), do not encourage intellect or character among them.

Since the introduction of Buddhism, Tibetan has been the Mongolian sacred language, in which all the services are held and sacred books written. There are three services a day in the temples, the call to prayers being the blowing of trumpets made from large sea-shells. When the worshippers are assembled the lamas seat themselves on the floor or benches, and in a monotonous drone chant passages from the sacred books. Their chanting is occasionally broken by an exclamation from the presiding lama, or by the clash of cymbals or brass plates, which are beaten at intervals. On festivals a more imposing ceremonial is observed.

The divinities worshipped are not in all cases borrowed from Tibet, and, consequently, from the Hindus, as is the case with the purer form of Buddhism. The *Yaman-dag*, or Goat-face, for instance, is of national origin, a reminiscence of the old devil worship, and is represented as of a dark-blue color, with a horned head adorned by a coronet of human skulls. He is supposed to vomit flames, and has twenty hands, all grasping human limbs or some instrument of torture. In common with other uncouth divinities, he is regarded with veneration by the Mongol, who is profuse in propitiatory gifts at his shrines.

Superstition is rife in Mongolia, being an integral part of the religion of the priest-ridden people, whose solitary, desert life is no doubt in part responsible for their strong belief in the supernatural. The Mongol has firm faith in soothsaying and augury, and wastes large sums in propitiating the *shamans*. No exposure of their fraud will convince him that it is idle to rely on magicians and sorcerers, and his every-day life is regulated by a series of the most absurd superstitions. A journey must never be discussed beforehand; milk must not be sold in cloudy weather, lest the cattle should die; and many other such rules must be followed if ill-luck is to be avoided. The worship of the streams and lakes, of the spirits of the wind, rain, clouds, water, and hills, is still continued; nor is this strange, when such worship is officially recognized even throughout China. This is particularly noticeable in the north of Mongolia, the original home of the people, where all the rivers and mountains are especially worshipped as gods. Many are the legends connected with the mountains. Both in Mongolia and in China there are many traces of fetichism, as evidenced by the number of sacred heaps of stones, known as *obo*, or single stones and trees, to which offerings are made. In both countries these possess "mystic potency"—the *ling* of the Chinese. The Mongol holds them in great reverence, and never passes without adding to them a stone, rag, or tuft of camel's hair. In summer they are the scene of religious festivals and the meeting-place for the people on holidays.

It is probable, as already pointed out, that out of every family one member at least, if not more, will enter the priesthood. The Chinese government encourages this system, fearing that if the country became too populous it would be unmanageable. Quite the contrary policy seems to be followed by Russia, since among the Buriats, as the Mongols farther north are called, lamas are comparatively rare. Whether this is accomplished by official pressure or by moral suasion, the fact remains. Unlike China, Russia does not fear her ability to cope with a rap-

U

BURIAT LAMAS, WITH CHINESE INTERPRETER

idly increasing population; on the contrary, she looks to them to aid her, when the time comes, in overthrowing their present masters, the Chinese. The Greek Church, supported of course by the Russian government, has taken an interest in the country, and has sent several missions to work in that field; so far, however, Christianity has made but little headway.

At Kalgan, the town which guards the entrance to the Great Wall, are three famous theological schools for Mohammedans. It is said that the "faithful" in this town are far from being strict in their religious observances, and will at times smoke opium, and even eat pork, "if only sold to them as mutton."

All travellers in this country seem to agree that the barbarous condition of the Mongols, and many of their worst characteristics, are due to the malign influence of a debased religion. The sacred city of Urga is famed for the number of its temples, one of which, in the extreme west of the town, and on a higher level than the other parts, is, with its immediately surrounding houses, regarded as so peculiarly holy that, according to report, no layman and no woman is allowed to live there. Throughout the town are placed praying-wheels, a turn given to one of these being looked upon as equivalent to repeating the prayers with which it is covered; and "falling worship"—*i. e.*, lying down flat on the face and marking with the forehead or with a piece of wood the next place of prostration—is much resorted to.

With scrupulous exactitude, too, does the Mongol carry out in the letter the teachings of Buddhism as to the sacredness of life. Even when one of the small eagles, which hover over the outskirts of the market, swoops down and makes a snatch at the meat carried by a returning purchaser, he will, if it has not been carried away, merely stoop down and pick it up, and will then resume the interrupted telling of his beads as he proceeds on his way. And yet Urga is described as the wickedest and most worldly city in the country, while the lamas, themselves brought up to a life of laziness—"only those become bonzes who can't get a living," says the proverb—with little learning, but immense influence over the people, act as a sort of evil leaven, corrupting the whole mass of Mongolian society. They can hardly be said to live up to the description which has been given of them:

> "The noble order of the Yellow Robe,
> Which to this day standeth to help the world."

On the contrary, it is their policy, in order to preserve their ascendency, to manage that the common people should remain so ignorant as not to be able to recognize their true character; and so the whole race is retarded in its progress, and rendered more and more incapable of mental or moral development.

CHAPTER XV

THE YANGTSZE VALLEY

THE northern section of the writer's journey, from the Baltic to the Gulf of Tongking, having as its object the examination of the main line of Russian approach to China, has now been dealt with. Siberia, Mongolia, Manchuria, and Peking have been glanced at, and the reader, it is probable, will have found many of his views regarding this northern section of Asia modified or even completely altered, and will, it is hoped, be in a position to better appreciate the transformation of Asia which is now taking place.

From the north, starting from Peking, it had been the intention of the author to make his way overland to Szechuan, but the disordered state of that province made it necessary to change the route and to proceed southwards by sea to the Yangtsze. That great artery, traversing the so-called British sphere, a region immediately concerning not merely the British but all English-speaking peoples, was ascended once more by the writer, who made his way to Chungking in Szechuan, close to the navigation limit. On arrival there the province was found to be extremely disturbed, and all idea of travel in Central Szechuan had to be abandoned. There remained the last portion of the writer's journey, namely, that across Southwestern China, with a view principally of once more examining on the ground the question of communications from the south—on the one hand from British India and Burmah, and on the other from French Tongking—a question which for many years had engaged the writer's attention.

It is unnecessary here to give any description of the Yangtsze River, of the marvellous resources of that wonderful waterway, or the beauties of its upper reaches. Those who are anxious to know something of this region can find information of a varied nature in published works.* Sufficient here to note that the majority of travellers only ascend as far as Hankau, and see but an uninteresting portion of the river, while the few who enter the lower gorges above Ichang, fine though these are, still remain unacquainted with the most striking cañon scenery of the river. Away from the banks, which alone are seen from the steamer deck, the country is to them still a *terra incognita*. In this chapter an impression of the political situation obtaining in the Yangtsze region is given, while in the succeeding pages will be found information of a varied character regarding Southwest China and Tongking.

When all the concessions and counter-concessions extorted by foreign powers from China since the Japanese War have been balanced up, there remains to the credit of Great Britain the territorial exten-

* *China in Transformation*, by the author; *Yangtsze Gorges*, by Archibald Little; and Mrs. Bishop's last work.

UPPER YANGTSZE GORGES—CHINESE PATROL BOAT

sion of the island colony of Hong-Kong to the limits necessary for its effective fortification; the lease of Wei-Hai-Wei, which is in any case a burden —and, if it is to be made tenable as a place of arms, a rather serious burden—on the British exchequer; and, finally, the Yangtsze Valley as a "sphere of influence" or of "interest," or an open market for British (and American) merchants.

During the session of Parliament of 1898–99 the nature of Britain's claim to that open market was concealed by her Foreign Office, the government pledging its word to Parliament and the country that it was a valid and valuable acquisition. The country was scarcely satisfied with bare assurances, and eventually the demand for the document itself, conveying our rights, could no longer be resisted. In response to this demand the title-deed, so to speak, of British interests in the great Yangtsze Valley was produced, and never, probably, was a more remarkable State paper issued to the public in a more remarkable manner. It was no Convention signed and sealed by the ministers of the two governments, scarcely even an official declaration, but an off-hand reply to a query of the British minister in Peking as to whether the Chinese government would consent to alienate the great central zone of the empire. "Of course not," was the laconic and only possible reply of the Tsungli Yamên. It was an absurd question to ask, and, as was observed at the time, it was not unlike England being asked if she had any intention of alienating the valley of the Thames. Such was the charter of British rights and liberties in the Yangtsze Valley! How it was edited for publication, with the famous "strictly speaking this is not grammar" annotation, is too well remembered to need further reference than to remark that the binding was worthy of the book.

To put the case without circumlocution, the alleged interest of Britain in this part of China rested on no concrete basis whatever. It was not a title—*quâ* title—on which a usurer would have advanced money at fifty per cent. interest. And yet, for all that, the title was good and inexpugnable—on conditions. It did not rest on anything which an imbecile government might grant, but on what a vigorous government might take. The concession, so called, might be treated as a blank cheque, which a strong power might fill in as it found convenient. Most or all of the concessions obtained by Great Britain on behalf of her subjects, in the form of treaty rights from the Chinese government, concessions which include a number of legal or legitimate bases for claims in China—such as the managing of railways, the opening and working of mines, the navigating of rivers, the trading at certain ports without let or hinderance, and the carrying-on of sundry other activities—may prove to be of no practical value unless, and in so far as, they are made good by actual enforcement. They are legal titles against all the world, but, in order to be effective, must be made good by action—perhaps by force. It scarcely appears that the British government has even

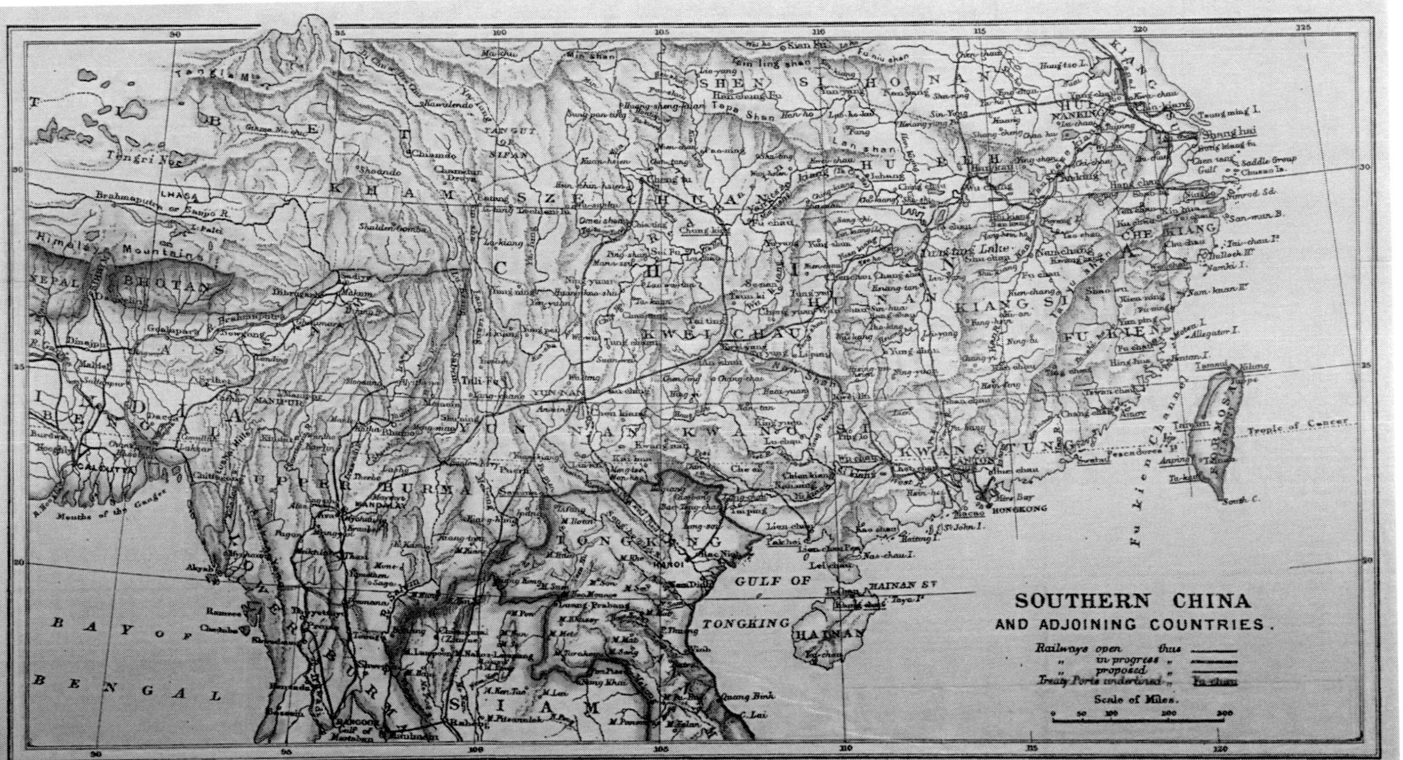
SOUTHERN CHINA
AND ADJOINING COUNTRIES.
Railways open thus
" in progress "
" proposed "
Treaty Ports underlined " Fu-chau
Scale of Miles.
BAY OF BENGAL
GULF OF TONGKING
HAINAN ST
HAINAN
HONGKONG
Tropic of Cancer
Fu Kien Channel
FORMOSA
SHEN SI
HONAN
HUPEH
AN HUI
KIANG SU
CHE KIANG
KIANG SI
FU KIEN
HUNAN
KWEI CHAU
SZE CHUAN
YUN NAN
KWANG SI
KWANG TUNG
TONGKING
SIAM
UPPER BURMA
LOWER BURMA
TIBET
KHAM
INDIA
BENGAL
ASSAM
NEPAL
BHOTAN
Himalaya Mountains
LHASA
CALCUTTA
Mouths of the Ganges
MANDALAY
RANGOON
Gulf of Martaban
HANOI
NANKING
Shanghai
Tungting Lake
Tung-ting Lake
Tali-Fu
London & New York: Harper & Brothers, 45 Albemarle Street, W.

yet realized the inchoate and imperfect character of these rights and concessions, or the fact that before they can be developed into valuable realities a period of intense energy, of political crisis, and possibly of conflict, may have to be traversed. One understands the economies of truth which are imposed upon responsible ministers. Weak and evasive as had been their defence of the drifting policy in the Far East, one could make some allowance for a government so completely insensible to the more remote interests of their country as was the British administration a couple of years ago. Under the circumstances, no one could cavil overmuch at the subterfuges by which ministers sought to appease the country, *if* only it was certain that, in spite of their illusory speeches, they were at last really awake, and were doing their best to remedy past neglect. With regard to the Yangtsze Valley, no practical man ever attached the smallest importance to our paper title. Whether grammatical or not was perfectly immaterial; the real title lay in the will and resolution of the British government and in the enterprise of British merchants. The value of the field lay not even in exclusive *legal* possession, but in effective occupation.

The interesting and only practical question now is: What steps have been, or are being, taken to establish British influence or interests in the valley of the Yangtsze?—What is the British government doing? What are the manufacturers, financiers, engineers, and miners doing to occupy a field whose paramount importance has been fully recognized by all who have given any attention to it? A question as to what they are not doing, what they are neglecting to do, would admit of a more categorical answer.

The provincial authorities in the Yangtsze provinces, though subordinate to the central government, nevertheless wield enormous power; in fact, under normal conditions the power of initiative is left wholly in their hands. In the present condition of the country, and during the paralysis of the central government, this local initiative must of necessity be more and more asserted. Behind the viceroys and governors are the mass of the people, industrious, orderly, and peace-loving. Whoever intends to do anything useful in the Yangtsze Valley must reckon with these two forces, and if the British government had entertained any serious idea of following up its own repeated declarations it would have taken steps to cultivate relations at least with the government authorities, an obvious measure which has been so far entirely in abeyance.

The Court of Peking, the Tsungli Yamên, and Li Hung Chang monopolize our whole attention, while the men who actually rule two-thirds of the empire are ignorant and neglected. Some of these high functionaries are patriotic according to their lights, and though they would gladly rid the country of all foreigners whatsoever, they discriminate accurately, and perfectly realize that, of all the foreign powers who are knocking at their gates, the Anglo-Saxons represent the minimum of danger to China. Undoubtedly these men need guidance and enlightenment, and it would be highly politic for the British and United States governments both to cultivate their sympathies and to assist them to clearer views of their duty. Nothing at all, however, has been done in this direction. Indeed, the British government has, by the attenuation of its consular staff, taken steps to put it out of its own power to gain influence in these important central and southwestern provinces. At those very points where it is most important that Great Britain should be strongly represented, she is not represented at all. Consuls Hausser and Jameson, the British representatives at Tengyueh and Ssumao, were drafted off to the Burma Boundary Commission, and, what is even worse, the only British official in Szechuan—Mr. Litton, vice-consul at Chungking, the most important point in Western China—was sent on a wild-goose chase to Kweiyang, the capital of another province, by orders from Peking. A wild-goose chase it may be called, because such inquiries into the murder of a missionary, where the British are concerned, are quite well understood by all the parties concerned to be mere pretexts for evading action. When the other powers have missionary outrages to deal with, they proceed in a wholly different fashion and make an entirely different kind of impression on the Chinese. France and Germany are known to mean business, and receive prompt satisfaction accordingly, while the despatch of a young man to prosecute inquiries in a nest of Chinese conspiracy and intrigue is a clear indication that the British mean no more than to "save face." The proceeding is, in fact, reduced to the level of an official speech in Parliament. Mr. Litton was compelled to leave the consulate at Chungking absolutely tenantless, for there was no office assistant there. In fact, in the whole vast province of Szechuan, which is at present of such crucial importance to Great Britain, there was, when the writer passed through it early in the year 1899, neither consul nor vice-consul to represent British interests. No clearer proof could be given that neither the minister at Peking nor the government at home had at all realized what the Yangtsze Valley means.

There is strong evidence that this lukewarm, negative policy has tended to alienate the provincial magnates of the Yangtsze provinces. They were at one time pro-British, seeing in Great Britain their only hope of being saved from the domination of aggressive and tyrannical powers, and it would have been easy for a few capable men, without any great subtlety of diplomacy, to enter into an arrangement with the viceroys of the Yangtsze which would have given Britain a footing there befitting the importance of her interests. Such politic procedure, however, as has been said, has up to the present time been neglected. What is certain is that Chang Chih Tung, who may be considered the leader of the provincials, being a man of strong character, official purity, real patriotism, and, above all, having the courage of his convictions, has become very sceptical as to the probability of Great Britain asserting her right to a legitimate position in the Yangtsze; and unless he and his *confrères* regain confidence in the strength and resolution of Great Britain, they will feel themselves compelled to follow the example of the invertebrates in Peking and purchase safety by throwing their weight into the scale of the strongest power.

China has now passed into such a condition that indifference is no longer possible for her, neither will it be long possible for us. It is pre-eminently true in China that whoever is not for Britain is against her, and the alternative must soon be faced by the most reluctant of governments: shall they vindicate the interests of the British—and of the Anglo-Saxon race generally—vigorously, manfully, and straightforwardly, or submit to their being completely crushed by the powers who are pressing forward their own claims to the entire exclusion of those of Britain? It is not, moreover, merely a *negative* policy in the Yangtsze Valley that has to be deplored. Instead of active steps having been taken to win the favor of the officials and people, every opportunity has apparently been sought to incur their aversion—as, for example, in the collection of likin dues. The Chinese provinces, as is well known, had little sympathy with the central government in the prosecution of the war with Japan. They were, indeed, among its most unsparing critics. But the British have undertaken to levy from these provinces a special heavy contribution towards the indemnities extorted by Japan. The interest of the Anglo-German loan was secured by a collection of likin dues in the Yangtsze Valley, of which the customs had undertaken to make a collection. The likin collection throughout China is, after the missionary question, the most thorny subject in any intercourse with the provincial authorities. It is their special source of revenue, and they naturally object very strongly to its being taken from them in order to provide tribute money for foreigners. But the British made a great point of these collections in the Yangtsze Valley being hypothecated for the service of the loan. That would have been sufficiently odious to the officials and people so mulcted, but it was furthermore insisted that the collection should be actually made by the hands of the Maritime Customs, which to every Chinese mind is a distinctively foreign institution. Moreover, at the same time the British government also went out of their way to attempt to make the customs service not only foreign, but British, having claimed of the Chinese government that the head of the service should be of British nationality.

Thus we have the spectacle of a tax, obnoxious in itself, on the double ground of its proceeds being unfairly withdrawn from the provincial budgets and of its appropriation to an odious purpose, being collected by Englishmen, and, as the people say, paid into a British bank. That the Yangtsze provinces should make a grievance of this is only what was certain to happen. Was it not, then, a short-sighted policy to impose this special taxation not only on British trade, but on the particular provinces in which it was Britain's paramount interest to appear rather as the protector than the oppressor? The tax-gatherer, never a popular character, is most hateful when, as Mr. Gladstone said of Ireland, he appears "in foreign garb," and to insist that the foreign garb should be no other than British was clearly hardly the way to conciliate the not unnatural feelings of the Yangtsze populations. But this leads up to the question of the general relations between the British government and the Chinese customs service, which cannot be here discussed in detail.

Various reasons might be given for Britain maintaining towards China her habitual attitude, one in particular being that a succession of ministers had grown accustomed to rely entirely upon what they deemed a special source of information, a special vehicle for exercising influence at Peking, and a special protection for British interests. They had come to believe, in short, that the inspector-general of Chinese customs was an unpaid British agent on whom they could rely far more than upon their accredited representative. It never seemed to enter their minds that a faithful servant cannot serve two masters, and that it was impossible for a man of the high character of Sir Robert Hart to use his position as a trusted employé of the Chinese government in order to further exclusively British interests. Such fallacies, however, not only exist, but are very tenacious of life. Even the recent revolutions were insufficient to undeceive the British government, who considered it a great score against the massive aggressions of Germany and Russia that an Englishman was confirmed in his post as collector of Chinese revenue. This line of argument has been repeated every time diplomatic successes have been recapitulated by members of the government, though in what manner Britain was to benefit by the arrangement no one, either in the government or outside of it, has been able to explain. In what way has the inspectorate of customs been of advantage to her in supplying information, advice, or assistance of any kind, since it has been put to the test? In the only way in which it could have been of service to her without perfidy to its paymasters. No one can now be so blind as not to perceive this, for even the Anglo-Chinese papers are beginning to reflect on the evil influence which the fetich has exercised over the British government, and to preach on the text "No man can serve two masters."

Intimately connected with the development of the Yangtsze Valley is the right of foreigners to navigate all the inner waters of China. This has been treated by the British government as a special concession to Great Britain, and was hailed by the mercantile community in that country and in China as the one item of value among the so-called concessions in which the British people were interested. The satisfaction felt with regard to this promise of new openings for trade was, however, always expressed with the qualification that its value depended on how it was to be carried out. The government itself, it must be confessed, made no such reservation, but declared with repeated emphasis the plenary character of the Chinese concession. Those who had experience of Chinese practices and of the way in which previous advantages had been allowed to lapse, with the connivance of the British representatives, were still sceptical until the reality of the new concession could be tested by experience.

Their misgivings seemed to be more than justified by what took place with regard to the West River, connecting Yunnan with Canton. After many years of vain efforts, the opening of that waterway had been announced as a triumph of British diplomacy, for which the government accepted full credit. But it soon appeared that exultation was somewhat in advance of fact, for, the French having intimated an objection to the opening of the one important mart on the river—namely, Nanning—the British government apparently acquiesced, temporarily at least, in the restriction to the lower reaches of the river of their right of trade and navigation. Such a staring object-lesson would not be lost on the Chinese, who would naturally suppose that a power which would thus yield to the objections of the French might certainly be relied upon to give way to the more legitimate objections of the Chinese themselves in the case of the other water-routes which are nominally thrown open to foreign enterprise.

So it comes about that the right of inland navigation has not yet received effect. Nor will it become a reality unless the British government honestly wills that it be made so. In the present state of feeling among the provincial officials, and in view of the incipient anarchy in Central China, all enterprise on the part of British pioneers will be nipped in the bud unless assurance is given to them that the capital they may invest shall not be exposed to pillage and spoliation. If inland navigation is to be carried out anywhere at all in China, it is in the region drained by the great father of waters, the Yangtsze, for into that main artery flow navigable streams innumerable, traversing vast tracts of well-peopled country, offering tempting facilities for traffic. But in order to utilize these promising channels, some assurance of protection must be given to the adventurers. This can easily be done by arrangement with the high provincial authorities, backed up by an effective patrol of light-draught gunboats carrying the white ensign. If some measures of this kind be not taken, then not only is the one important concession obtained by British diplomacy rendered a dead letter, but before long the absence of this preservative force, and the consequent dissolution of the bonds which keep the Chinese administration together, will open the door to quite another kind of enterprise — that of filibusters and pirates.

The revolution in China is proceeding with great rapidity, and though it is impossible for any one to foretell the issue of the various disturbances in the provinces, any more than to foresee the outcome of the palace feud in Peking, yet it is folly to shut one's eyes to the fact that the elements of great changes are in active conflict, and that unless controlled and guided by some strong but kindly influence they cannot but lead to widespread calamity. The prestige of the dynasty has been shattered, first by the shock of the Japanese War, and next by the bullying of Russia, France, and Germany.

The viceroys and governors are necessarily paralyzed by the recent events in Peking. Not knowing which side would eventually issue triumphant from the struggle, they have mostly assumed the attitude of sitting on the fence. As regards the relations to foreigners, they are particularly circumspect, and wait to see whether hostility or friendship with them is likely to be the winning card. The people are no less unsettled, for, though entirely devoid of political passion, they are keenly alive to their own material wants and to the sanctity of their hearths and homes. What they see before their eyes and what they hear rumored from distant parts, greatly exaggerated, of course, fills them with forebodings. Outbreaks which the authorities are unable or unwilling to suppress give encouragement to risings all round, and one rising begets another. If the working people should be driven to arm themselves for defence against brigands, the temptation is great to use such new-found courage and force for aggressive purposes. There are no large bodies of men in the world so docile and so easy to govern as the Chinese, but once the social and family bonds which hold them together are loosened the artisan may as easily become a brigand as the laborious fisherman becomes a pirate.

The process of dissolution is going on. The anarchy which has been the nightmare of all who have studied Chinese affairs for the last twenty years is looming in sight. Great events are in course of incubation. The process cannot be arrested without the application of a vigorous hand, and it will not wait the convenience of any lukewarm onlooker. The truth of the matter is that Britain's inheritance in the Yangtsze Valley will be in a state of chaos, that the slumbering embers will be all ablaze, before she thoroughly rouses herself to apprehend its value.

The question naturally arises: "What must be done to save the situation?" Faults of omission have already been partially indicated, and before entering on the positive side of the question it will be interesting to see what the other powers are doing. Russia, not content with the absolute possession of Manchuria and the military occupation of Newchwang—a treaty port in which the British are largely interested—and the assumption of control of all the territories north of the Great Wall, is exceedingly active also in the centre of the Yangtsze Valley. Cossacks were already to be seen at Hankau when I passed through early in 1899, and have distinguished themselves by their interference with

English trading firms in that place; while the redoubtable Pavloff, who recently established such a distinguished record in Peking, at the end of 1898 paid a visit to that city ostensibly to "settle the land question," which needed no settlement. If he intended to meddle with the land question at all, it may be taken for granted that he would be more likely to "unsettle" than to "settle" it.* For many years the Russians have been laboring to establish themselves in Hankau, and M. Pavloff's visit was certainly not unconnected with Russian aspirations in that quarter. No doubt the immediate object was to confer with the French agents and to concert common action with them. The French were then and are still absolutely dependent on the support of Russia, and, though Russia approves generally of French aggressions, she claims the right of checking the pace; and as she will not be ready for several years to come—that is to say, until the completion of the Siberian Railroad and its branches—to afford France material assistance, she does not wish her partner to force her hand by bringing matters to a rupture prematurely. No doubt the assertion of British prestige at Fashoda temporarily inspired caution in both allies, and recent "amicable" communications between London and St. Petersburg had also probably something to do with the peaceable character of M. Pavloff's visit.

But France can do an immense deal without

* The question has been decided in favor of Russia (Jan., 1900).

bringing matters to a crisis. By means of the Roman Catholic propaganda she is driving a wedge through the very heart of Chinese government and administration. The sole interest that France has ever had in China has been the protectorate of Christians. It was seen how, more than twelve years ago, the tentative attempts of the Vatican to appoint an Apostolic Delegate at Peking were frustrated by the interference of France, who delivered her ultimatum to the Pope, declaring that if he did not abandon that intention the republican government would confiscate the revenues of the Church in France. It was almost with tears in his eyes that the Holy Father eventually declared his inability to carry out the proposed measure, saying: "Much as I love the Church in China, I cannot sacrifice my children nearer home."

The account of this transaction given in the *Revue des Deux Mondes** puts the matter plainly enough: "M. Lefebvre de Béhaine opposa nettement le veto gouvernement de la République au dessein que les anglais et les allemands avaient su inspirer à Pekin et faire accueillir au Vatican. Le pape céda; il fit imprimer et envoyer aux évêques français une brochure où il expliquait pourquoi, malgré son vif déplaisir et malgré l'avantage qu'il avait espèré pour la foi catholique de la création d'une nouvelle nonciature, il daignait condescendre au vœu de la fille âinée de l'église.'" It is

* September 1, 1898.

reported that the Apostolic Delegate is actually to be, or has been, sent, but entirely shorn of his independence. He is, in fact, to be the head of the French propaganda.

The blood of the martyrs is in China the seed of French aggrandizement. France uses the missionaries and the native Christians as *agents-provocateurs;* and outrages and martyrdoms are her political harvest. What the preponderance of her commerce does for England the Catholic protectorate does for France, so that the influence of their respective positions *vis-à-vis* the Chinese is nearly balanced; but France makes ten times more capital out of her religious material than Great Britain has ever done out of her commercial. Under the fostering care of the French government the Catholics have become a veritable *imperium in imperio*, disregarding local laws and customs, domineering over their pagan neighbors, and overriding the law of the land. Whenever a Christian has a dispute with a heathen, no matter what the subject in question may be, the quarrel is promptly taken up by the priest, who, if he cannot himself intimidate the local officials and compel them to give right to the Christian, represents the case as one of persecution, when the French consul is appealed to. Then is redress rigorously extorted, without the least reference to the justice of the demand. The assurance that this kind of interference on the part of a foreign power is certain to follow, leads, of course, to the grossest abuses being perpetrated by the Christians. And while the French missionary may go far, the native Christian goes infinitely further in browbeating the authorities and tyrannizing over the people.

A recent example of this, one of many, was related to the writer when travelling on the Yangtsze recently. A Roman Catholic priest (Chinese) was riding into a town, when some of the country people cursed him. He at once got out of his sedan-chair, called for the leading men of the town, and told them that unless they paid him $100 he would denounce them to the magistrate. Ignorant of what the consequences of their getting into the hands of the mandarins might be, the people collected the ransom demanded and paid it to the priest. It is said that he invested the money in a house in the neighborhood, and settled down in it to propagate the doctrine. It is not surprising that arbitrary proceedings like this should cause the Christians to be feared and hated, and we need not wonder at the occasional murder of a priest when such feelings are spread generally throughout the country. Every such incident, too, is utilized by France to extort more and more privileges and concessions in the Yangtsze Valley. She has at the present moment in her current account the following debit entries against the Chinese government: One hundred murders, two of them being foreign fathers; twenty thousand Christians driven from their homes and reduced to beggary; and 5,000,000 taels' worth of property destroyed. This heavy bill is being added to daily, and in the liquidation of it France has a magnificent game to play. She can either wring whole provinces from the central government, or lie in wait for local reprisals, or combine the two—as Germany did in the case of Kiaochau—which procedure may take the form of heavy drafts on Yangtsze territory or of such exclusive claims as may effectually bar the development of that region by any of the really commercial powers, for in her Far Eastern policy France cannot be called commercial.

Thus, through Britain's abstention on one side, and the energy of her rivals on the other, she may come to find that her position in the Yangtsze Valley is this: that Britain is the only power who will eventually be excluded from it. If we realize the fact that France claims jurisdiction over more than one hundred thousand converts in the province of Szechuan alone, besides large numbers in Hunan, Honan, Hupeh, and in other of the Yangtsze provinces—every individual convert being as the grain of an explosive which is able under skilful handling to burst China in pieces—if we realize this, we shall see that the peaceful development of this great central zone of China will never be accomplished by a merely lukewarm policy on the part of Great Britain. France is working at high pressure for the disintegration of the existing polity, and it is a significant circumstance that the same agent whose machinations in Upper Burma had so nearly cut off the British hinterland—which the Indian government was forced, against its will, to annex—

had been, when the writer passed through Chungking early in 1899, and has since been, working like a zealot to foment disturbance in Szechuan, out of which France may find occasion to prosecute her great scheme of aggression. It is another interesting circumstance that, while this very active French consul has been making such strenuous exertions at Chungking, the British consulate in that important city was for a time left without a consul or British representative.

What the French scheme is has been sufficiently obvious in various parts of the world for many years. On the Nile, the Niger, the Irrawaddy, the Meinam, the West River, and the Yangtsze, the aim of France has been and is identical. It is a consistent, preconceived secular determination to block the path of Great Britain by every kind of device. This is what has been euphemistically called in Britain the "policy of pin-pricks," but this is an altogether inadequate description of the process. It is a policy of relentless and ubiquitous opposition, carried out to the utmost limit of endurance. And inasmuch as it costs less in time, in money, and in human resources to throw an obstacle in the way of an assumed rival than to pursue a positive policy of solid self-aggrandizement, the aim of obstructing Great Britain in the present and for the future takes precedence of the advancement of the substantial interests of France. And in the pursuit of this policy France has few more indefatigable pioneers than M. Haas, the consul at Chungking.

Though, therefore, it be the case that Russia is holding the rein on France to prevent her precipitating a crisis which would force Great Britain into action, this, as already explained, means no more than that the time is inconvenient for Russia's support of France to be put to any severe test. Yet France is thereby not hindered from accumulating combustibles against the day when the word can be safely given to apply the torch. Nor is the silent undermining process, in which both powers can without danger unite their forces, retarded.

Besides the protectorate of Christians, the French hold another card in the game they are playing to thwart the development of British interests in China. And they are entitled to hold it as the reward of the foresight of their statesmen. By the instrument known as the Siam Convention of 1896, the British government agreed to a kind of hypothetical *condominium* with France in the Chinese provinces of Yunnan and Szechuan. And, though at the first blush it may appear a square bargain, we know by long experience that it will not be so in practice. The French have their own canons of interpretation to apply to agreements with Great Britain, and it is quite certain that the respective parties to the Siam Convention did not hold identical views as to its working. It puts into the hands of France a weapon by which she can, if so minded, frustrate British enterprise in those provinces, whether it be in the development of minerals or the construction of railways. And, as the persistent object of France, in which she has the covert support of Russia, has been, and is, to cut off communication between India and Central China, it is easy to see what a strong position has been given to her for working towards that end. At the same time she is very energetic in pushing her own schemes in these provinces, with her expeditions of survey in connection with railways and mining, and proofs of "effective occupation"; and there are other evidences of her determination to exploit Southern and Western China and create defensible rights there.

CHAPTER XVI

THE YANGTSZE VALLEY—(*Continued*)

THE British government is not, however, idle, for (although at the eleventh hour) railway surveys are now being conducted on a respectable scale from the Yangtsze as well as from the Burmese side of the frontier. In the dry season of 1898–99 an expedition, headed by several British officers, was organized to work from Szechuan, while at the same time investigations were being made between Hankau and Kweiyang-fu, passing through Yunnan-fu, and extending towards Burma, another party working from the Kunlon Ferry (on the Burmese border) to Tali, and eventually as far as Yunnan-fu, a natural meeting-point for both expeditions. And thus at last the work so frequently urged by the writer in season and out of season for the last sixteen years is put in hand; and as to this newly awakened energy we can only say, "Better late than never." This line of communication between China and India is the one thing most needful to establish British influence and to promote British interests in Central China, and the British government is to be congratulated on this initial step. Let it be clearly understood, however, that it is only a preliminary step, that it has to be vigorously followed up, and that it is prudent to look forward and see the outlines of the problem which lies beyond it. It is as certain as such matters ever can be, that one of these days some power will be called upon, or feel itself called upon, to intervene to preserve order in China, for confidence is gradually being undermined all round, and cannot be restored out of native resources. The high officials are, so to speak, trembling for their heads; the common people are sinking deeper and deeper into poverty; trade and industry are more and more burdened by arbitrary taxation and by the neglect of all public works—such as embankments, roads, and water channels—and the numbers of disbanded soldiers, secret-society men, and thieves keep the law-abiding, industrious people in a state of chronic terror. There is no sense of security anywhere. This condition of things the writer saw for himself in 1899 in the Yangtsze provinces—Britain's boasted "sphere of influence."

Provincial governments have been, and are, afraid to exercise their authority to put down insurrection, for fear of "putting their money on the wrong horse." They left, for instance, the rebel leader Yu Mantze, who had obtained a large following, a free hand in Szechuan to follow his anti-foreign crusade, being unable to divine, in the confusion of affairs at Peking, what the next *mot d'ordre* respecting foreigners might be. At the end of 1898 they had witnessed the degradation of Chen Pao Chen, then the Governor of Hunan, an enlightened and courageous man, who had encouraged the study of English in the schools of Changshah, his provincial capital, introduced machinery into that city, lighted up the great examination-hall with electric light, and endeavored in every possible way to familiarize the Hunanese with the products of Western civilization. When the notorious Chow Han, whose calumnies excited the anti-foreign riots of 1891, ventured in 1898 to recommence the issue of his vile inflammatory literature, Chen Pao Chen had him arrested and imprisoned, and, when the students of the neighborhood threatened to organize a strike in the public examinations and to put a stop to all the business of the province, this vigorous Governor at once laid hold of the ring-leaders and had them punished—an exhibition of high courage rarely met with in any Chinese official. The degradation of this Governor may have had no motive outside the dynastic quarrel then raging at Peking. He had, unfortunately, recommended one of the reformer Kang Yu Wei's disciples, named Tan, to the Emperor. By common consent Tan was the noblest of the whole band of reformers, and was one of the first to be beheaded when the Empress Dowager usurped the throne. Whether Chen's progressive ideas, irrespective of the Peking plot, had anything to do with the vengeance taken on him by the Empress, it is difficult to say; but the fall of such a man at such a moment is, to say the least, little calculated to encourage others. Chen left the city, for which he had done so much, execrated by the lawless mob for his good government, while the more enlightened of the inhabitants were awed into silence. How the new Governor will acquit himself remains to be seen, but those who know Hunan best will not be surprised at a recrudescence of the anti-foreign policy which so long has been characteristic of that province.

Hunan is one of the richest provinces of China, and the opening of a port within its borders has long since been a desideratum of commerce. It is exceptionally well served by waterways, which are capable of accommodating vessels of considerable tonnage and draught. If, therefore, the commerce of the Yangtsze basin is to be exploited at all, Hunan can certainly not be left closed. Of the four trading marts recommended for immediate opening in the Yangtsze basin, three are important centres of trade within the province of Hunan, and the fourth is Laohokeu, situated four hundred miles up the Han, a deep-water affluent of the Yangtsze on its left bank, which gives its name to Hankau. The Hunanese ports are Changshah (the provincial capital), Chang-teh, and Siangtan, all busy marts, as shown in the report of the delegates of the Shanghai chamber of commerce thirty years ago. But we know the value of the nominal opening of new ports of trade. It is a very simple procedure, and what was formerly extorted from the Chinese government as a concession to foreigners has in these later days been almost forced on foreigners by the urgency of the Chinese government. That state of things, however, applied rather to the sea-coast than to any of the inland districts. With regard to these there has always been a reluctance on the part of the British government to seek for any facilities for British subjects to reside or trade in the interior. So far, indeed, has this reluctance been carried, that rights and privileges claimed and exercised by other nationalities have been forbidden to Englishmen, who are denied by their own government the right of residence in the interior. The effect of the voluntary abandonment of this right appears to be that Germans, Belgians, Frenchmen, and Russians are able, where Englishmen are excluded, to acquire land and mining properties in their own names, and to have their titles to the same registered by their consuls. Sometimes it has actually happened that, in places where, for the time being, there was no consul of the particular nationality concerned, the British agent has been asked to render his friendly offices; and a curious result of this situation is that the British consul, when acting for another nation, is able to register properties for non-British subjects which he is forbidden by his own government to do for his countrymen. This will serve to illustrate one of the many disadvantages under which British subjects labor in China. It is obvious, therefore, that the extension of British commerce in the interior will necessitate considerable change in the attitude of the British government and its agents in China. Even so, however, the effective opening of such an important province as Hunan would not be so simple a matter as opening a number of ports on the sea-coast.

The Hunanese as a whole, and on principle, have always been averse to the inroads of foreign men and foreign things. They are proud and conservative, possessing the courage of their opinions in a much stronger degree than is the case with the natives of any other province. There has thus grown up in Hunan a kind of anti-foreign public opinion, which forms a background and a basis for the machinations of fanatics of the literary class and of the lawless ruffians of the streets. These things require to be considered, and it is partly such considerations which have held back the British government from pressing more urgently for freedom of trade within that province, and which induced it to accept as a substitute the port of Yochau, which is not within the province at all, but on the extreme outer margin of it. Probably it was a similar course of reasoning — namely, that the people were not yet ready for it which deterred them for so many years from exercising the treaty right of entering the city of Canton, and more recently induced them to forego another treaty right—that of navigating the Upper Yangtsze by steam. These scruples, in both cases, proved themselves to be unfounded, for there was no difficulty whatever with the people so soon as a resolute stand was made and the authorities forced to show a little strength of purpose; but, in the case of Canton, at least, they cost both British and Chinese a considerable amount of trouble, expense, and bloodshed. The lessons gained from these experiences, and from others which might be instanced, should not be forgotten at the present juncture, for it is precisely the same question which always crops up, and it can only be satisfactorily dealt with in the same way. What is wanted, in order to smooth over all difficulties, is the intervention of the British to strengthen the hands of the native authorities and prove to them that their own safety lies in keeping order by exercising the power they possess.

The problem thus becomes absolutely simple, as, indeed, all Britain's intercourse with China might be; the complications, which are many, have invariably been of her own creation. There is no more reason why she should be afraid of dealing with the Yangtsze basin than the Nile basin; if she has the men for the one, she has also the men for the other —men of sobriety of judgment, force of character, and simplicity of mind; while from the Chinese point of view the advent of such a power would be a godsend. It is the one thing which can preserve many millions of people from the horrors of anarchy. Whatever Great Britain may do for China, to improve the condition of the masses, would promptly be productive, and she would receive back her own with usury; and, as a student of China, writing from the interior of the country, observes, Britain would find it paid her better to have an open door to fifty millions of prosperous people than to four hundred millions of beggars clothed in sackcloth.

To infuse into China a healing and saving influence on a clear financial basis is "the white man's burden" which Britain is called upon to take up. It is no light task, but it is not inglorious if undertaken with honesty. No tinkering or mere opportunism will serve, nor will the fine-spun orations or smart answers which some of the British politicians seem to consider conclusive be of the least service. It is a man's job that has to be done.

The Chinese are not a difficult people to rule; they are, indeed, remarkably docile. As for the authorities, it has been the rule, whether a wise one or not, that no official of rank should hold office within his native province; consequently they are as much birds of passage as British governors of colonies, and are often entire strangers to the people they are set to govern. The officials share with the people the high philosophic quality of cheerful acquiescence in the inevitable. With a clear voice, and a strong hand behind, it would probably be as easy to make friends of the provincial magnates as to make enemies of them. It is a fact not to be forgotten that the appreciation of justice in others is not to be measured by the lack of that quality in one's self. The most corrupt of Chinese understand purity, the most arbitrary understand justice, and the most cowardly respect courage. The key to the whole problem, therefore, of what is to be done in China is to be found in British resolution, in British manhood. Like the conquest of the Soudan, it is as easy under one set of conditions as it was difficult or impossible under another, the difference lying in the nervous constitution or will-power of a few individuals. The key of the Yangtsze basin is in

London, and the practical question to be determined is simply this: Is the game worth the candle?

It was an ominous day for her Asiatic Empire when Britain's statesmen surrendered their initiative in the Far East, because, though the mischief was done in a fit of preoccupation and absence of mind, and in a situation which had been suddenly sprung upon them and in which they were left without any guiding intelligence, yet the step is irretrievable; for the other great powers of Europe, better informed, stepped in without hesitation and occupied the place that Great Britain had vacated. Ever since that fatal day five years ago, British interests in China have been in a derelict condition, like a disabled ship on the ocean, making signals of distress to everything that comes in sight. Where Great Britain had led for two generations, with an undisputed title of priority in all external affairs of China, she has since 1895 been glad to follow the lead of powers over whose interests she aforetime cast the ægis of her protection.

It is this fundamental act which has shifted the centre of gravity, a fact which is not noticed so much in the West as it is in China, for the British government, of course, disguised it, and perhaps not unnaturally so. In the Far East itself, however, it is a bald, staring fact that Britain is the only great power without a definite policy. She has, instead, certain nebulous impracticable aspirations. It has been frankly admitted in the British Parliament that the proceedings in China lacked originality and independence, and that the plan adopted had been to follow—it might have been added, at a very long distance—the action of those powers who had a programme and carried it out. On all sides, and in every department, in fact, the working of this new departure is apparent. It is, of course, a mere *château en Espagne* to place reliance for the promotion of British interests in China upon an alliance, or a working understanding, implicit or explicit, with no fewer than three powers, and these the United States, Japan, and Germany. Before such a conception as this can be reduced to definite action, the interests of the country will have evaporated. In a very vague, general sense the interests of the four countries are no doubt harmonious, but that is a consideration quite in the clouds. When we come down to the region of practical politics we find the interests diverge. Germany in Shantung admits no British partnership, though German financiers are willing to allow a share in a railway from Tientsin to Chinkiang, with a view to getting the full advantage of the greatest money market in the world, it being assumed—though the grounds for this belief are not very clear—that Germany has agreed to abstain from aggression against Britain in the Yangtsze Valley. That the British people have indeed learned to be thankful for small mercies is obvious when it is seen with what delight they regard such a concession from friendly Germany. It is evidently a small matter, in their opinion, that Germany, or at least Germans, actually continue to nibble at concessions within the Yangtsze Valley sphere. This very Chinkiang Railway, for instance, in which they are willing to admit partnership, intersects the Yangtsze Valley in its richest section. Germany, in short, like a wise and eminently practical power, plays her own game in China, and not Britain's in any sense whatever. The United States, too, have with the approval and applause of the British press secured the concession of the Hankau-Canton Railway, which also intersects the Yangtsze Valley through its very centre. The British come in to supply cheap money, but the Americans take, by one means and another, the substantial profits of the concession itself, by means of an intermediate "construction company," out of which and the supply of material certain well-known Chinese also look for remuneration. Japan, wisely, plays a deep and waiting game, and prepares for eventualities.

Alliances on such terms will always be obtainable so long as the great reservoir of Lombard Street holds out, but the conditions require that Great Britain shall politically occupy a back seat, and commercially accept the shell of the oyster for her share. We have seen what the concerted action of the powers in the north of China means; even outrages on British subjects have been referred to this vague cosmopolitan tribunal. It is a pusillanimous policy, wholly unworthy of the prestige and substantial position of Great Britain in the world. It is, moreover, a policy founded on falsehood, and on that account alone must fail; and not only fail, but lead to a mo-

mass of troubles and possibly disputes with those very powers to conciliate whom so much is being sacrificed. What the people of China expect and long for, what the people of Great Britain ought not only to long for but also insist upon, is that Great Britain should no longer wait humbly on the action of the powers, but should resume her former position and lay down her own policy, following it out in her own way. British Imperial interests immeasurably transcend those of all the other Western powers put together, and the only way of securing the concerted action which seems to be so much desired is to act decidedly, clearly, and strongly. Then, and then only, will the other powers fall into line, and then will be revived the good understanding of former times, when British action was recognized by all to be for the equal benefit of all. The cry of Britain's representatives is: "What is to be done?" And the only answer forthcoming from official quarters advocates either this general arrangement with all the world, or some special agreement with Russia. It is a melancholy circumstance that the hope of British statesmen should now rest on an understanding with Russia, for it is the day after the fair. Time was, perhaps, when Russia might have courted a settlement which would have obviated the whole trouble in the Far East, but that time was when Britain had all the cards in her own hands. Neither her government, however, nor her representatives abroad, were able to see the "accepted time," when solid reciprocal arrangements were open to them.

British statesmen constantly deplore their impotence in bargaining with nothing in hand. Everything, they are wont to say, was given away by Cobden and the Cobdenites, and nothing is left to bargain with. In the case of Russia and China, however, everything was in hand, and everything has been given away by successive governments; not, unfortunately, with a good grace, but with a snap and a snarl and a turning of the tail. Had it been Britain's policy to bring Russia into Liaotung, she could at least have obtained solid advantages in return for her acquiescence. Had it been to her interest to allow Russia to occupy the stronghold of Port Arthur, she could, while demanding a substantial *quid pro quo*, have secured the frontiers of her empire for a generation. It is needless to recall her humiliating scuttle from that harbor, except to say that Russia gained that immense prize by most audacious bluff on a very weak hand, for it has been stated, on authority which cannot be contradicted, that at the time when the British ships were withdrawn under the Russian menace the Russian admiral had already received instructions to leave the harbor; a fact of which every one there with whom the writer conversed on the subject was well aware.

As Britain has thus exposed her weakness, or blindness, and allowed Russia to sweep the board and establish herself in virtual control—not of this or that sphere, *but of the cerebral centre of the Chinese government itself*—the arrangement now talked of as so desirable, which, if made, will draw down profuse decorations on the heads of British agents, can only be a ratification of the possession by Russia of all that she desires, in return for which Britain will receive no equivalent except the assurance that Russia will not enter into hostilities with her—a thing which, in any case, that country would not dream of doing.

Among the disturbing elements now at work in furthering the general state of anarchy prevalent in China, the missionary question is not the least important.

It has often been remarked that wherever the viceroy of a Chinese province was resolved to keep the peace with foreigners, orders were given to subordinate officials to avoid quarrels with the Catholic missions or their converts, and, when quarrels did break out, the orders were to patch them up immediately and to cede everything that was required, to prevent the missionaries from making a claim through their consuls. Such was the rule rigorously maintained during the whole of Li Hung Chang's viceroyalty of the province of Chihli, and the consequence was that no outrages were reported from that province between 1870 and the present time (1899). The rule was partly followed and partly disregarded in other provinces, and this has been especially the case in Szechuan, where sometimes the higher authorities, as has been said, have winked at, if not encouraged, the attacks on Christians, while at other times they have repressed these attacks with severity.

Probably it has been always a matter of calculation as to which course would entail the least inconvenience on the high officials themselves. On the one hand, they would make themselves popular by conniving at attacks on foreigners; on the other hand, these attacks might get them into much worse trouble, according to the amount of pressure applied, by the foreign representative concerned, on the Peking government.

It is necessary to bear these facts in mind in order to understand the vacillating conduct of the authorities in Szechuan, and the reason for such vacillation was fairly well illustrated in the history of the particular case of Yu Mantze against the Szechuan missions. He had been at one time arrested by the authorities on account of a quarrel which he had with the Roman Catholics, and he was imprisoned, probably with little regard to his guilt or innocence. The mob thereupon arose, attacked the prison, and released him. The official concerned, either under compulsion or by connivance with the mob, went through the form of a trial and acquitted the prisoner. So far the popular side. But this same official then got into trouble with the higher authorities, was obliged to retire from the public service, and is believed to have committed suicide. The whole incident, of course, greatly enhanced the prestige of Yu Mantze, who set about collecting a large following, and then went into open rebellion, with the secret approval, it is believed, of many of the local officials. The affair of Father Fleury was by no means a sudden outbreak of anti-Christian fanaticism. Yu Mantze had, in fact, been at feud with the Catholic missions for about ten years, and there had been a good deal of trouble between them before the rising which took place in June, 1898.

The story of M. de Fleury presents many features which distinguish it from other outrages which from time to time have been made on missionaries by the Chinese. He was carried off in June, 1898, by Yu Mantze, the rebel leader in Szechuan. He was neither killed, tortured, nor starved, but was carried about in the rebel train, and made an unwilling accomplice in depredations and atrocities. When in Chungking, the writer had an interview with the priest, and found him to be a man of about forty-five years of age, with dark eyes and hair, harmonizing well with the Chinese costume he wore, a sallow complexion, and a broken-down aspect. Were there time to tell his story in full, Father Fleury's experiences would furnish a thrilling record of adventure, including some terrible trials. While he was being dragged about from station to station he was not merely compelled to witness the destruction of property and the expulsion of its occupants, but was forced to look on while his own people, the Roman Catholic converts, were being tortured and killed. He at first refused absolutely to witness these terrible scenes, but his captors were inexorable in their insistence. After remonstrances and arguments had been exhausted, "We will kill you if you do not come with us," they said. To this he replied:

"It is in your power; kill me." Then they carried him along by main force. Apart from these tragic experiences, the father had very little complaint to make of the treatment he received at the hands of the rebels. They supplied him regularly with good and sufficient food, of which there never seemed any lack, and treated him, moreover, as a personage of rank, being careful to show him personal deference. As for the leader of these insurgents, Yu Mantze, he is reported to be a man without education or ability of any kind. What he did, therefore, any common man might have done: the time was ripe, the minds of the people were distracted, the bonds of legality loosened, and he had only to raise his standard to be joined by an imposing number of men, as discontented and weary of the existing *régime* as himself.

So rapid was his progress in the province of Szechuan that the authorities at first were paralyzed, and did nothing to suppress the movement. His extraordinary success accentuated the discontent in neighboring provinces, where more than one Roman Catholic village was destroyed, and where no Catholic priest could be considered safe. No doubt also the troubles which had been for some time brewing in Hunan were partly due to the immunity with which Yu Mantze was allowed to carry on his anti-Roman-Catholic crusade, and what began in the form of outrages on Christians rapidly developed into a general anti-foreign campaign in the Upper and Central Yangtsze Valley. The successful rebel leader was treated by the Chinese authorities in their habitual manner—it is the one piece of strategy that never fails them—that of buying off an enemy. They offered Yu Mantze a government appointment with emoluments, as the readiest and cheapest way of neutralizing his rebellion. It is believed, indeed, that he had actually come to terms with the government, got his button, and become a military officer; but the arrangement, if made, did not last long. The compact was broken, and eventually a state of war existed between the rebel and the provincial authorities. The Chinese troops sent out against Yu Mantze really fought well in some serious encounters they had with him. Father Fleury thought they would be able to break up the rebels' power entirely and would capture and kill Yu Mantze and his lieutenants.

It is an open question, however, whether the local officials had not, in point of fact, been secretly supporting the insurgents in their attack on the Roman Catholic missions, a proceeding with which the mandarins in general are in entire sympathy. But, as has often happened before in the history of foreign relations with the Chinese, the officials, conniving at popular risings which suit their purpose and do their dirty work without compromising them, are in the end unable to put out the fire which they have kindled, and the movement thus spreads farther than they intended; the result being that they become fully compromised with the foreigners, and have then a demon on their hands which they are unable to exorcise. The severe action taken later by the authorities against the rebel leader was no doubt due to stringent instructions from Peking, where strong pressure had been put upon the government, accompanied by unpleasant menaces of ulterior consequences. However that may be, there seems no doubt that the Chinese troops really did some hard fighting, and had honestly determined to put down the rising. Father Fleury himself maintains that this is so, having been a witness of some severe engagements. The father's recital frequently reminded the writer of another Roman Catholic priest's adventures among the Mantzu hill-men, as quoted by Baber. From the priest's narration, as given in *Annales de la Propagation de la Foi*, the Mantzu rebels, like the present band, occupied a mountain fastness protected by inaccessible heights; the difference between the two cases being that Fleury, as has been said, received no personal ill-treatment; in both cases the negotiations for ransom were in much the same terms.

It is not only the Roman Catholics, however, who suffer. Mr. Parsons, of the Church of England mission, early in 1899, was attacked, in his opinion by the local militia. Several of his followers were ill-treated, one having the fingers of his hand chopped off; while Mr. Parsons himself only escaped by jumping into the river, and there clinging to a sedan-chair which had accidentally been pushed into the water, until rescued by a Chinese gunboat or salvage-junk. On board this boat he was compelled to lie as if dead, a crowd hooting on the bank. The master of the boat wisely said: "If you move you are a dead man, for then we cannot save you. Lie still as you are, as if dead." News of the occurrence was telegraphed by the United States consul to Peking and Washington, while, there being no British representative near, the missionaries telegraphed to the consul, Mr. Litton, who was then in the next province, fifteen days' journey away.

The Chinese officials try to make this appear to have been the work of Yu Mantze, but such is not the case. There can be little doubt that the culprits were local militia, precisely as in the case of Mr. Fleming, near Kweiyang-fu, in the next province. In connection with the Fleming murder, it may be noted that Mr. Litton, who was sent from Chungking to investigate the matter, was highly successful in fighting the Chinese authorities at Kweiyáng-fu, securing the punishment of several officers implicated, although the ringleader of all, the head of the local militia there, had evaded arrest at the time the writer was there.

On the road to Kweiyang the writer hoped to have the opportunity of meeting Mr. Litton, then on his way back to Chungking. The general opinion at that place was that he had discharged his mission splendidly at Kweiyang. No man, indeed, is more highly esteemed by the scattered British communities of missionaries and others in the west of China, he being regarded as keen, strong, thoroughly self-reliant and fearless, and one not to be put off with plausible words. He stayed at Kweiyang without any support but his own resolution, and saw the guilty officials punished. A few such men in the interior of China, properly supported, would reawaken hope of the conservation of both British and Chinese interests.* The writer received, during his journey, the greatest kindness and every possible assistance from all the missionaries resident in Chungking, and from the United States consul, in the absence of any British representative.

When the writer was in Peking, the current phrase in diplomatic mouths was, "Everything quiet in the Yangtsze Valley"; but opinions may differ on this point. The truth rather is that there is trouble everywhere, and more always threatening, and the Chinese officials are inclined to take advantage of this state of the country to prevent any foreigners from travelling. The Taotai at Chungking, for instance, tried to prevent the writer from starting for Kweiyang-fu, *en route* to Yunnan-fu and Kunlon Ferry, and endeavored to bring about a delay of a few weeks—delay in Chinese being equivalent to *non possumus.* The authorities, in fact, are much averse to foreigners scouring the country, as they are now doing, spying out the land, as they think. At this time (early in 1899, when the writer passed up the river) there was only one small British gunboat, the *Esk*, on the whole Yangtsze, she being anchored at Ichang, and unable to move either up

* Later reports are to the effect that this meritorious officer has been removed to a subordinate post in the consulate at Canton.

or down until the water should rise. It was expected that the *Woodcock*, a new gunboat, two feet draught and thirteen knots speed, would be soon sent up; but a number of such craft are wanted if any kind of order is to be maintained on the river, and the authorities supported for good and repressed for evil. The provincial rulers being apparently quite powerless, except for evil, it seemed to the writer most lamentable that at such an important crisis all British officers should be absent from the provinces of Szechuan and Yunnan. In any case, there were only three of them, all told—one at Chungking, one at Ssumao, and one at Tengyueh. Mr. Litton was, in fact, as the event proved, the right man to be sent; but it is impossible to understand the policy of denuding the large and important province of Szechuan of its one British representative, to send him on a journey of fifteen ordinary marches, though he actually did it, with immense difficulty, in about ten days. The lack of wisdom in the arrangement is obvious when it is known that Chungking is so situated that, in the event of any emergency, it would have been impossible for any one, either from the coast or elsewhere, to replace Mr. Litton in less than five or six weeks. Surely there were abundance of men at the coast ports available for the mission to Kweiyang-fu; for instance, at Shashi, a small town of no importance in a lower province, the writer found a full-blown consul living, not in the town, but on a pontoon anchored in the river—a useless existence, which might well be called a living death. As has been said, the absence of any British agent at Szechuan was the more to be regretted when it is considered that the French are particularly active both in that province and in Yunnan. Apart from M. Haas, to whom reference has already been made, a staff of French army surgeons have come to Chengtu and Chungking, spreading over Yunnan and Szechuan, to aid the Chinese "to carry civilization into the remote regions of the empire." They are to erect hospitals, *à propos de rien*, in order to create French interests to be attacked, defended, and avenged.

The release of Father Fleury is a great disappointment to the French authorities, who reckoned on vast concessions being obtained by way of revenge for his capture and captivity. There is, in fact, little doubt that the French have been preparing for a big movement in Western China, somewhat on the Russian pattern, and they may still have considerable successes; for though they have lost Father Fleury for the moment as a means of pressure, there is still the destruction of missions and other property, which they will exploit to the utmost. For instance, the Bonin mission, which was at work in Szechuan, came to grief in the Ningyuan district, and, of their Annamite military escort of sixteen men, one, as the French declare, was poisoned. The mission, it may be noted, provoked attack, behaving very brusquely everywhere, and on one occasion even beating a Chinese official. Another French mission, however, has succeeded in surveying as far as Yunnan-fu, and thence to Sui-fu, in Szechuan, examining two routes, it is understood, but they keep their proceedings very secret. There is, in fact, a further development of the French propaganda, which is working like a cancer in the body politic of China, with intent to destroy it.

It is not always remembered that the Roman Catholic missions in China are enormously rich. Especially is this the case in Szechuan, where they have accumulated real estate on a very large scale. This is the practice of the Roman Catholic missions everywhere. The *procureur* is always a very keen man of business, who, through intimacy with family affairs, is able to watch the decay of fortunes, the profligacy of sons, and the other factors which bring about the financial ruin of old families, and the propaganda is always ready in these cases to dispense its help to the needy, irrespective of creed. Property is thus continually passing into their hands, and, in some places, such as Tientsin, for instance, the Church is the principal landlord. It is this funded wealth which enables the Roman Catholic missions to extend themselves over the world without requiring subsidies from Europe.

As is usually the case when an outrage is committed on the Roman Catholic missions, there is more in the affair than meets the eye, and in judging of such one has to contend with the enormous disadvantage of hearing only one side of the alleged persecutions.

The present Taotai at Chungking is very anti-foreign and weak, two characteristics which generally go together. When the writer called on him, in company with a missionary, Mr. Wilson, one of the Taotai's servants was overheard to remark, on their departure, "The dirt has entered and the dirt has gone hence, but it leaves a nasty stain behind." The Taotai was remonstrated with on the subject, but he merely quoted to his followers some ancient maxim concerning the etiquette of hospitality. It was this same official who endeavored, by every argument he could think of—such as the disturbed state of the country, his own responsibility in the matter, etc.—to delay the writer's departure for Kweiyang. His efforts, however, were unavailing, and he was informed that, if he would not provide an efficient escort, the journey would be undertaken without escort, a statement of the case being telegraphed to Peking and to London, and that he would be held responsible for any ill consequences, the writer assuring him that should any outrage take place it would probably not be quite so easily condoned as is usual in the case of British missionaries. Thereupon the Taotai gave way, and ordered an escort of six armed men to go as far as Kweiyang, those from Chungking to be changed on the road.

Both the Protestant and the Catholic missionaries, at the time of the writer's journey through the southwest provinces, considered Szechuan and Hupeh, and the country generally, to be in a very dangerous situation. The empire, in their opinion, was being partitioned by foreigners, the central government having no power; while the authority of the Chinese officials was everywhere weakened, universal unrest and discontent having seized upon the people. The trading and well-to-do classes alone were in favor of order, all others sympathizing with Yu Mantze, and being ready to follow him or any other man who would rise to lead the attack against law and order.

In coming rapidly from the capital to the distant provinces it is impossible to escape certain impressions for which it would not be easy to give categorical reasons. It is by comparing one's experience of one period with that of another, and by contrasting impressions of various localities, that one may reach conclusions which could not perhaps be substantiated by logical demonstration, but which are yet as certain as forecasts of the weather by a gardener or a fisherman, who could not prove them by meteorological data. The first thing that strikes a traveller in these days is the change that seems to be coming over the relations between the supreme government and the provincial authorities. According to Chinese traditions, viceroys and governors have been practically absolute rulers, the court being exceedingly reluctant to interfere. This tradition has been the chief obstacle to foreign powers obtaining redress in the capital for outrages in the provinces. The government would never, except on the most urgent pressure, exercise its authority over provincials, and so crimes against foreigners have too often gone unpunished.

The tendency under the new *régime* is towards

the concentration of power in the Imperial court. This movement has a far greater significance now than it could ever have had before, because in the court itself a similar concentration is taking place. The court and the Imperial Government, boards and councils, now mean one and the same individual—namely, the Empress Regent. "*L'état c'est moi*" is her motto.* But she is invisible, and cannot be approached by the ordinary diplomatic avenue. What passes in the palace and in the inner councils of the Empress is to foreigners generally an unknown quantity—to all, indeed, except to those who have underground intelligence wires to guide them. The various legations do not stand on an equal footing in this matter, and undoubtedly the palm must be given the Russian *chancellerie* for having the completest system both of receiving and imparting intelligence. This is due not merely to the commanding political position of Russia, which naturally presses all sorts and conditions of men into her service, but also to the supreme importance which the Russian government attaches to the functions of the legation in Peking. So many Chinese officials and underlings are now stipendiaries of Russia—Hau, the director of the Newchwang Railway, for example, having been heavily subsidized for the last four years—that it would probably be exceedingly difficult for other legations to place themselves abreast of Russia.

* This was written sometime before the *coup d'état* at Peking, in January, 1900.

So long, however, as the office of minister is maintained in Peking, there seems to be every reason why the British legation should be rendered as efficient as possible. There have been difficulties of very long standing in the organization of the staff which ought to be remedied. One is that the office of first secretary has long been a sinecure. The minister may be worked off his legs and the staff driven to their wits' end to copy all the despatches, while the first secretary is a gentleman at large, who may, if he pleases, volunteer to address envelopes or assist the young *attachés* in their clerical work, but who, for all the aid he renders his chief beyond such trivial services, is little more than a cipher. No blame necessarily attaches to individuals for this state of things, for it has gone on for many years. The names of several able men appear in the list of first secretaries, to mention only Mr. Malet, Mr. Goschen, Mr. Howard, and Mr. Beauclerk, who one and all deplored the necessity of spending their time in idleness, not only doing no good to themselves, but losing their previous experience. Reduced to the organizing of picnics and the arranging of cotillions, some of them driven by *ennui* to the study of Chinese, which would be of no service on their promotion to another post, the secretaries always seem the fifth wheel of the coach so far as the real work of the legation is concerned. One definite function only has always been reserved for them—namely, to make the annual trade report. On this some of the secretaries named established their reputation, but none of them had ever been, what it would seem natural to suppose they would be, understudies for the minister whose place they would be called on to occupy in case of illness or absence. There is no reason to suppose that the present occupant of the office of first secretary is in any way different in these respects from his long line of predecessors.

Why all this should be so has never been explained. The common-sense of the matter would surely be that, instead of being kept idle, between the responsible work of the minister and the mechanical work of the young *attachés*, the first secretary should be called upon to assist the minister, and even in certain cases be consulted by him, as the first officer of a ship is consulted by the captain. In Peking there is an immense amount of work which would, in fact, be far more profitably done by the secretary than by the minister. The diplomatic drudgery, the mere routine work which is undertaken by the minister who attends wearieclly at the Tsungli Yamên day after day, might surely be devolved on his junior. To argue and shout to the board when there is no responsible minister present and no response obtainable, is not dignified work for a high official. It were surely better that this rather humiliating routine should be undertaken by the secretary, while the minister was employing his time and his thoughts on more important questions of policy. By making himself less familiar to the underlings of the Yamên he would be likely to gain respect for his infrequent utterances, and would be able to interfere with greater effect after questions had been threshed out by a subordinate, as in fact is the practice in Europe.

There is one other department of the legation to which a greater importance might be given with advantage. The office of Chinese secretary is a most responsible one, for which the man should be carefully selected. Since the days of Wade and Mayers—that is to say, for the last twenty years or more—it cannot be said that this office has been adequately filled. It has been considered, apparently, that a junior consular officer, without any real experience or weight, or, in fact, any other qualification than a knowledge of the Chinese language, was good enough to fill the post. Matters have, however, come to such a pass now in China that the mere sinalogue, or interpreter, is quite out of place in a position of such importance as that of Chinese secretary; for since it has become the practice in the appointment of ministers to pass over all the men trained in the consular service and having expert knowledge of the country, and to select candidates from the diplomatic service in Europe or from the coast of Africa, the Chinese secretary is practically the man who runs the legation. The demands on the staff are now so great that a new office ought to be created by the elevation of the Chinese secretary to a higher grade. The class of men who have been doing the duties of that functionary would then be admirably qualified for the post of *assistant* Chinese secretary, having charge of the training, examination, etc., of the students, and keeping up the details of the Chinese record. For the Chinese secretaryship the best man in the consular service, of good standing and large experience, ought to be chosen, and such a man would not be overpaid at £1200 or £1500 a year. The days for machine work and accurate clerkship are over. Men of judgment, originality, and receptivity are required to cope with the new situation in China. The additional Chinese secretary, with the qualifications mentioned, would do something to make up for the deplorable want of an intelligence department, but would still leave much to be desired to put the legation on even terms with its rivals. When, however, all has been said and done that is ever likely to be done, it would be too sanguine to expect the British legation to be on the same level of efficiency as the Russian, or even some of the others, and, if that be the case, British interests must always be at a disadvantage in North China, where they will have not only the inherent obstructiveness of Chinese officialdom to contend with, but also the open or secret hostility of Russia. For some reasons it is unfortunate that the first definite creation of a new British interest should happen to be in the very region where our course will be beset by snares and pitfalls.

To a certain extent, no doubt, the disadvantages which face us in Peking and the north will apply generally to the whole empire, for when the Empress succeeds in gathering all the reins into her own hands, and Russia is able to direct those hands, there is no part of the empire where we could be sure of having a fair field. Whatever may obtain in the provinces would be subject to the dual approval of the Dowager Empress and the Russian minister, who would exercise the veto with discretion and always with a careful eye to the circumstances of the time. All these considerations go to show that our safest field of enterprise is at a distance from the capital, and, in fact, in the populous centre of the empire. There we should have to deal with less of mystery, and with men who are more practical, more experienced, and more patriotic than any one connected with the court at Peking. The viceroys, we may be sure, do not relish the curtailment of their authority within the provinces, and would not be likely to resist proposals which would tend to strengthen and confirm them in their position. As for the people, they are easily managed, and their good-will might be counted on so long as the officials gave them the right lead. In the central provinces is concentrated the densest population in China, because it is, taken as a whole, by far the most productive region in the empire, and is so wonderfully provided with waterways that communications are cheap and easy. It is the west and the south with which we have chiefly to do in connection with our railway extension from Burma; so that when the Yangtsze Valley was assigned by the public opinion not of Great Britain only but of the world, long before the government had formulated any views on the subject, as the natural sphere of influence of Great Britain, the idea was simply following the physical configuration of the country. All are agreed that if there is any portion of the Chinese Empire where Great Britain may safely and profitably assert her influence it is that great belt described as the Yangtsze Valley. Whether for mining, railroads, steamboats, or ordinary operations of commerce, it is there that she will find her most promising theatre of action. Seeing, therefore, that her diplomatic operations in Peking are subjected to the serious disadvantages aforesaid, it may appear advisable to cultivate more than she has hitherto done working relations with the various provincial authorities, taking care always to keep the people at her back.

In order to do this, quite as good men are required in the provinces as in the legation itself, and Britain has the men, if her government would use them in a way that would allow free scope to their energies. If a body of such men were employed to advance British interests among the provincial authorities, they would probably do more real good than can nowadays be accomplished by a legation at Peking. Nor would an admiral or two, occasionally, be thrown away on the Yangtsze region. Admiral Seymour made a remarkably good impression on Chang Chih Tung when he visited him at Wuchang. It is a great mistake to suppose that a strong attitude is objectionable among the Chinese officials. On the contrary, it is the only thing they ever appreciate—in which, indeed, they are not very different from the rest of mankind.

M. Pavloff's visit, a short time ago, to the Yangtsze, excited a great deal of interest. The Chinese interpret it to mean that Russia is preparing for a movement in the Yangtsze Valley. The expectation apparently is that Hankau will be made a free port of the type of Port Arthur and Talienwan. It was certainly annoying to hear M. Pavloff constantly commiserating his British colleague in Peking. "Poor Sir Claude, he is so worried!" he was never tired of repeating.

To sum up: Peking and the Tsungli Yamên being Russian, body and soul, Britain's best remaining chance of establishing her influence in the empire is in those provinces which, after all, count for two-thirds of what is known as "China." The provincial authorities are as yet pro-British, because they see that Great Britain, taken at her worst, is a less evil than Russia; but Britain is neglecting these provincials while expending her forces against the blank walls of the imperial palace. In so doing she is assisting to weaken provincial authority, while she is not balancing her action in Peking by adopting such measures in the provinces as are necessary to draw the country to her side. The natural, the inevitable consequence must be that the provincials also will, for their own security, become Russian, as the Dowager Empress, Li Hung Chang, and most of the magnates at Peking have already done. They cannot help themselves, for they must lean on somebody, and must pay the price of their own security, even if that price be the surrender of their country.

CHAPTER XVII

SOUTHWEST CHINA

In endeavoring to trace the early history of the southwest provinces of China—like Indo-China generally, the true land of fable—it is difficult to distinguish between truth and myth.*

It was not till the twelfth century that the Chinese exercised any real authority in Yunnan. Before this period they had, indeed, organized various futile expeditions and made military demonstrations, but were generally defeated and compelled in the end to resort to bribery of the native princes and their ministers. About A.D. 1252 the line of native princes ended, Tali-fu was captured, and the Mongol Emperor assumed sovereignty. Colonization was then attempted. Many Mongols fell during the taking of Tali, and the site of the common grave in which they were interred is still to be seen behind the single pagoda to the west of the town, a Mongol tablet of marble being erected in later years to their memory. In A.D. 1280, the great Mongol Kublai Khan having overthrown the Southern Sung dynasty of China, set up his own under the title of the "Yuen Dynasty," and in this year Yunnan was for-

* See Appendix.

mally annexed to the Chinese Empire, although the province was not effectively subdued till A.D. 1305, a "peace tablet," still in existence, being then erected by the Mongols in commemoration of the event.

The Chinese annals show that about A.D. 1300 a Mohammedan named Prince Hsien-yang, or Sai-tien-ci, commonly known among his co-religionists as Omar, from Hsien-yang, in Central China, was sent to Yunnan-fu, where, seeing the country flooded by the overflow of the lake Er-hai, and the people reduced to poverty, he surveyed the lake and lowered its level by means of a cutting. He also built two mosques, one at the south gate of Yunnan-fu, and one at Yang-pi, on the high-road to Bhamo, some distance west of the Hsia-kwan, near Tali-fu, which, at the end of the great Mohammedan rebellion in 1874, was turned into a Chinese temple. This prince was also the founder at Tali of a society, still in existence, for the relief of the poor. He made roads and bridges, turned waste ground into arable, and did much to improve the social customs and general condition of the people, who held him in great honor. On his death there was general mourning throughout the country, and a statue was subsequently erected to his memory.

The neighboring province of Szechuan was peopled, or rather repeopled, at a no more remote period than the commencement of the present reigning dynasty, the chronology extending not much further back than to the end of the Ming dynasty, about 1645. Even the celebrated emperors Kanghi and Kienlung are referred to by the natives of the province as monarchs of remote antiquity. Before the occupation of Szechuan by the Manchus a certain Chang Hsien-chung gained possession of the province in 1644 and proclaimed himself Emperor of the West. The method of government favored by this singular potentate, which lasted for five years, was the wholesale execution of his subjects, and many are the extraordinary stories current about him.* In alluding to the isolated positions of many of the dwellings in this province, Richthofen attributes the possibility of such a state of things to a feeling of security and an expectation of peace among the inhabitants; "profound peace," he says, "is, indeed, the impression which Szechuan prominently conveys." It cannot be said, however, that such an expectation has always been realized. In comparatively recent times the southwestern provinces have—like other parts of China, the land of revolutions—been frequently devastated by the warfare occasioned by continual risings and rebellions. These outbreaks have caused no little trouble to the Imperial government, whose efforts at restoring order have even at times been retarded by traitors to the "dragon flag," who have been known on oc-

* According to statistics obtained by Baber from De Mailla's *History of China*, the following is his record for five years: "*Massacred:* 32,310 under-graduates, 3000 eunuchs, 2000 of his own troops, 27,000 Buddhist priests, 600,000 inhabitants of Chengtu, 280 of his own concubines, 400,000 wives of his troops, everybody else in the province. *Destroyed:* Every building in the province. *Burnt:* Everything inflammable."

casion to advise the aboriginal tribes, such as the Miaos, to refuse submission and fight the mandarins, who would otherwise oppress them and confiscate their goods—"eat them," as the expressive Eastern phrase goes. The Miao tribes were for many years in a state of warfare against the Chinese government, taking up their position in dangerous fastnesses, and from their ambush firing poisoned arrows upon the Chinese troops, and defying subjection. In 1735 a general rising occurred among the Miao tribes already subdued, towns and villages were besieged, and much fighting took place. At length the Emperor appointed Governor-General Chang, of Hunan, to try to quell the rebellion, and after great difficulties — for the roads were dangerous, mountains had to be climbed, and heavy rains encountered ("the mountains were as if they touched the sun, and the roads as dangerous as if hung on trees," as the official report put it)—he was successful, and was rewarded by being made viceroy of Yunnan and Kweichau, while honors and offices were at the same time granted to his sons and descendants.

In 1874 culminated the eighteen years' rebellion of the Mohammedans. The discontent was at first caused by disputes in the markets between the Mohammedans and the vendors of pork, disputes which were invariably settled by the authorities in favor of the pork-sellers. The discontent thus created gradually increased, and at last the miners, always a turbulent section of the population, and numbering among them many Mohammedans, broke into open revolt. Repressive measures only made matters worse, and resulted in the rising of the entire Mohammedan population and the massacres which ensued. At Tali-fu the rebels were betrayed into the hands of the Imperialists by one Yang-yong, and a massacre, lasting for three days, took place. Large pits were made, into which the dead were thrown; the largest, known as the "Mohammedan myriad grave," being about two miles from the south gate of Tali-fu. Much of the city was reduced to ruins, and the Mohammedans, after this, were not allowed by the *literati* to open shops. It is said that at Yunnan-fu, on the surrender of the rebels, their leader, entering the Imperialist camp, succumbed to some poison which he had taken, saying, as he died: "I have nothing to ask but this—spare the people"—a petition which has often been made on other occasions by Chinese rulers when in extremity. His prayer, however, was disregarded, the garrison and townspeople being slaughtered by the victorious Imperialists. A vivid account of what took place is given by Baber, who says:

"The greater part of the able-bodied men, no doubt retaining some of their arms, succeeded in escaping; but a number of unresisting people, principally old men, women, and children, fled from the city into the rice-fields which border the lake. Hemmed in by the Imperialist pursuers, they entered the water, into which they retreated farther and farther; and, being still pressed, were either forced out of their depth by the crush, or sought a refuge from worse ills in a voluntary death."

The term "Panthay," as applied to this rebellion, among Europeans, is erroneous, being unknown to the rebels themselves, who were always known, both by themselves and by the Imperialists, as Hui-hui or Hui-tzu (*i.e.*, Mohammedans). The word "Panthay," indeed, is merely a Burmese term. It must not be supposed that the discontent among the Mohammedans ended with the massacre of 1874. It still smoulders, and is kept alive by their hatred of the mandarins, and of the Chinese in general, and merely awaits the torch which shall again set it in a blaze.

Among other risings which have devastated the southern and southwestern provinces, that known as the "Taiping" rebellion (in 1852) had far-reaching results. A body of native Christians in Kwangsi, calling themselves "Taipings" (*i.e.*, "perfect peace"), revolted against the oppression of the Manchu rule, proposing to restore the Ming dynasty. They defeated some of the Imperial forces, captured Hankow and neighboring cities, descended the river with many hundred junks of spoil, and took Nanking, slaughtering the Manchu garrison of 25,000 men. A native force was organized at Shanghai against the rebels, and, led by an American adventurer, General Ward, retook the cities, the general perishing under the walls of Tseche. Gordon succeeded to his command, and suppressed the rising by recapturing Suchau, but Nanking was not retaken till 1864. It is said that the town of Wuchang would not have been taken by the rebels, but that the Fu-tai, or officiating mandarin, knew nothing of military matters, being merely, as is so often the case in China, a scholar who had been compelled to leave his books, and, without any preparation whatever, take upon himself the command of an army and the defence of a city. Many of the officials, at this time, committed suicide.

In the southwestern provinces, as in other parts of China, personal investigation is the only means of obtaining a correct idea as to the natural features of the district. To rely on Chinese officials for information is to arrive at absolutely wrong conclusions, for among them the value of accurate surveys, particularly of the river valleys, is not recognized, topographical work being held in but poor esteem; consequently they are as a rule ludicrously ignorant of their own country, the prefect of a town having little or no knowledge of the district outside his sphere. Accurate measurement of distance, also, is unknown in China, as is evidenced by the fact that on a Chinese map a certain iron memorial column, in reality near Tali-fu, has been indicated as being in the southeast of Yunnan, and close to the sea. It is almost impossible to ascertain the exact distance between any two points, even the number of *li* to a mile varying, according to native information, with the gradient of the country; thus, on level ground, two *li* would be about equivalent to a mile, while on steep or hilly roads a mile varies from five to fifteen *li*. Lack of knowledge on the part of the Chinese is not always responsible for the inaccuracies which occur, incorrect information as to names of tribes, places, etc., being sometimes wilfully given, merely to save trouble.*

With certain limitations, it may be said that Yunnan is an uneven table-land, a description applying particularly to the eastern plateau, the hills being apparently of volcanic origin—probably limestone ranges, worn away by rain. The most productive agricultural districts lie in the central, western, and southwestern portions of the province, eastern Yunnan being barren and mountainous, the people poor, and the mineral wealth undeveloped. The mountain ranges are highest in the west and northwest, and near Tali are snow-crested from November till April. It may here be noted that many of the beautiful and extensive though poorly timbered valleys of Yunnan appear to be the bottoms of dried lakes.

The southwest provinces generally are well watered by the many rivers which traverse this part of the country, the most important being the Upper Yangtsze, otherwise known as the Kinshakiang, or "River of Golden Sand"—the local name being "Gold River," † and the picturesque

* Baber, in his interesting account of western Yunnan, says that "if a Chinese of average intelligence and education be asked what he knows of Yunnan, he will reply that it is rich in gold, silver, white copper, and precious stones; that it is a long way off; that travelling is very difficult throughout the province, as shown by the proverb 'Chih Yunnan-ku' (To eat the bitterness of Yunnan); that it is a very unhealthy country; that the inhabitants speak a very intelligible tongue; and that it is cool in summer."

† Said by Marco Polo to contain much gold-dust.

Red River or Papien, also known as the Yuan-kiang (or as Song-ka by the French), whose course is in some parts through a country rich in abundance of roses, azaleas, and other flowers, in others past ruined and deserted villages whose once busy streets were depopulated by the Taiping and Mohammedan rebellions, or whose flourishing trade with Canton was gradually diverted to the route by the Yangtsze. In many parts of the Canton and Red River valleys, especially at Pêse and Manhao, unhealthy vapors rise from the water itself and from the neighboring land, causing malarial fever, which is very prevalent. Other important rivers are the Salween or Lukiang, and the Mekong, Cambodia or Lantsan. The Red River and the upper portion of the Canton River, or Si-kiang, provide the best water communication between the sea and Yunnan. The value of these to Yunnan, and to the southwest provinces generally, would be greater if they were easier of navigation. During the rainy season they are almost entirely unnavigable, owing to the increased volume and violence of the waters, while in dry weather navigation is rendered difficult, even for shallow craft, by the numerous rapids which occur. Even the mighty Mekong is only navigable by canoes, in the neighborhood of Kiang-hung, and not even by these above that town.

The chief lakes are the Kwen-min or Tien-chih, south of Yunnan-fu, forty miles in length, and from five to eight in width; the beautiful Er-hai, at Tali-fu, thirty-five miles long and about six broad, whose waters, which sometimes inundate the country farther west, empty themselves into the Mekong by way of the Hsiakwan; and the Ilong, in the midst of a land of plenty, where fruit and flowers abound on every side, its shores dotted with prosperous villages, surrounded by well-cultivated fields and acres of poppy-land.

Yunnan, like Kweichau, is often called the "Switzerland of China," and, in some parts of the province, the description is more than justified, the scenery on the road from Pêse to Kwangnan, for instance, having a remarkable similarity. The climate is, on the whole, a healthy one, being cold and bracing in the north, while, for about nine months of the year, from September onward, sunshine and a clear sky predominate, reminding one of Italy. It must be admitted, however, that, among the Chinese, both Yunnan and Laos bear an evil reputation as regards climate and security of life. In the south and southwest the bubonic plague (Chang-chih) is prevalent, being caused by a poisonous vapor which arises from the ground during the rainy season, giving rise to high fever. As has been said, the Red River valley is noted for these malarial vapors, while at Kinung, in the west of the province, the beautiful and fertile plain is almost entirely deserted, owing to the prevalence of the Yunnan plague. The reputation borne by both Pêse and Manhao for unhealthiness may probably in part be attributed to the fact that the people from the more hilly districts, used to a drier climate, descend into the valleys during the

CHIN FO SHAN ("GOLDEN BUDDHA") MOUNTAIN, ON THE BORDERS OF YUNNAN AND SZECHUAN

unhealthy season, when the atmosphere is hot and moist, thus getting chills and fevers. The unhealthiness of Pêse, however, so fatal to strangers, is also attributed to the badness of the water, which is obtained from one of the streams forming the West River, and passes through limestone ranges. The aboriginal hill people are more affected by it than the Chinese natives of the place, or even the Cantonese settlers. In almost all parts of Yunnan, but especially in the southwest, between Puerh-fu and Tali-fu, it is dangerous for strangers to use the water for drinking purposes, and at one point, at least, in the Red River valley a tablet has been erected to give warning to the traveller.

At certain seasons of the year, generally between January and April, strong winds are prevalent, the province being often spoken of as "Windy Yunnan" —"Szechuan's sun, Kweichau's rain, Yunnan's wind," says the proverb—while the word Yunnan itself is sometimes interpreted as meaning "the cloudy south," though there is some doubt as to the correctness of this interpretation. At times the winds on the Kwen-min Lake (which only occur during the daytime), although not cold, are so strong that, in order to avoid them, the boats actually ply at night. The four seasons are practically indistinguishable:

> "When the clouds gather it is winter,
> When the clouds scatter it is summer."

The rainy season, however, may be said to commence towards the end of May, the rains, though not heavy, continuing for about a hundred days, during which time communication becomes very difficult, and sometimes ceases almost entirely.

Southwest China is rich in mineral resources, the natives of Kweichau and Yunnan boasting of the mineral products of the "wu-pao," or five precious metals—gold, silver, copper, iron, and lead. The mines, properly developed, and with better means of communication, might be made very profitable, but, as at present worked by the government, they do not yield much profit to the Imperial exchequer. Even of the mineral extracted, a large proportion never reaches the Imperial government, it being admitted by those concerned in the mining that, as regards the copper, for instance, only from three to five tenths can be truly said to reach headquarters. The manner of working, too, is primitive, the Chinese being averse to foreign help, although themselves incompetent. They never attempt to overcome any obstacle, such as the flooding of the mine by foul air or water, but invariably take refuge in their respect for the "fengshui," or wind and water, attributing the calamity to the geomantic influence governing the place. Confronted by a flooded mine, a Chinese will say it is "Heaven's decree" (the usual Chinese solution of a difficulty), and the mine must be abandoned. In his opinion, a flood denotes that the "dragon's pulse" is affected. This belief in supernatural powers has been proved, however, to be no longer an all-powerful objection to the construction of railways or to the further development of mines;

the prejudice was for long years kept up by *literati* and officials, but signs are not wanting that it is gradually yielding to the spread of Western ideas. Before the mines can really be worked with profit, many things remain to be done; chief among these may be placed the construction of roads and improved navigation of the Yangtsze. The general state of disorder, prevalent to such an extent in Yunnan, would need to be remedied, and the Lo-los conciliated, measures which are hopeless of accomplishment under the present *régime* of chaos prevailing in China.

It is curious to note the influence exercised by the "fengshui," even in agricultural matters. There is a prevalent superstition that demons can only travel in a straight line. Therefore, to baffle them, the paths between the fields (as in the terraces on the shores of a lake) are curved and twisted, lest pestilence and famine should find their way into the land, while throughout southwestern China "weikans," or sandstone slabs dedicated to the tutelary genius of a spot, are common. The manner in which foreigners, and especially missionaries, have from time to time run counter to such superstitious prejudices —as, for instance, in erecting churches with steeples, which are supposed to take away good fortune from the surrounding country—has done much to keep alive the ill-feeling between them and the natives, an animosity often culminating in such tragedies as the murder of Margary at Manwyne (on February 20, 1875), said to have been ordered from Yunnan-fu, the capital, although actually carried out by the brigand Lisitai. This ill-feeling is especially noticeable at Chenyuan, near to which city Fleming, the missionary, was murdered.* After Margary had left this place, his boat was destroyed, the people threatening to demolish any other boat that should thereafter convey foreigners to the town.

So far as agriculture is concerned, the richest portions of Yunnan, as has been said, are the central, southwestern, and western districts, but there is room for increased cultivation, especially on the mountain-sides, which, although both soil and climate are favorable, are almost entirely neglected, while no attention whatever is paid to the development of forest land. Much more might be done, both here and in southern China generally, in the way of terracing the hill-sides.

The agricultural population in the southwest have a novel method of disposing of their produce. At intervals on the high-roads groups of shops, known as "chang," or markets, occur, these being the property of the farmers, who let them to traders on certain days set apart for the holding of a market,

* According to the account of a Chinese general, Margary's death was brought about by the outlaws (train-bands) of Teng-yueh, a set of ruffians who kept the border districts in a continual state of disturbance and disorder. It is worthy of note that the prefect of Chenyuan, in whose district the Fleming murder took place, is the man who was secretary to the governor of Yunnan at the time of the Margary murder. The governor of Kwei-chau was treasurer in Chengtu at the time of serious anti-foreign riots which occurred some years back.

and on these days most transactions of importance are carried out, such as negotiations for the sale of land, arrangements for weddings, festivals of all kinds, and other matters of interest. The number of traders and the amount of merchandise gathered together would lead a traveller to suppose that these "markets" were in reality small villages, were it not that he occasionally comes across some which are entirely deserted, owing to the fact that it is not market-day.

The trade of the southwest provinces was formerly in a much more flourishing condition than it is at present. At one time the greater quantity of the cotton exported from Burma passed through Yunnan, on its way to Kwangsi, Kweichau, and Szechuan; but since lower Burma came into the hands of the British, this trade has been diverted to the sea-route, the cotton being sent by steamer to Canton, and thence inland, little of it passing through Yunnan. It is found that, sent by the circuitous route from Burma to Canton and thence to Yunnan-fu by way of Pêse, it will reach its destination more quickly, and at a lower cost, than if sent by caravan from Mandalay *via* the overland route through Bhamo. The brigand Lisitai did much to drive the trade from the Bhamo route, by gaining a monopoly for his own cotton-caravans, thus compelling merchants, who did not approve of the "only-door" system, to trade by way of Shanghai and Canton. A further cause for the declining prosperity of this route was that for many years the Chinese authorities exaggerated the dangers to be encountered from the Kachyen and other tribes. The trade of the province generally is injured by the distance from open ports and the difficulty experienced in navigating the rivers, and also by the number of *likin* and other taxes imposed. For instance, goods for Tali by way of Hunan and Kweichau pay, or till lately paid, no less than nine *shui* or prefectural taxes, in addition to two *likin* taxes; and so numerous are the *likin* or customs stations on the Chinese rivers that goods rapidly increase in price the farther they are carried. At these stations, also, in addition to the regular heavy charges, a sum has to be deposited for the "mandarin's purse."

Under a Western power, the road between Yunnan-fu and Pêse (eighteen days) could be improved and shortened, and the navigation of the river improved. This done, and security to life and property guaranteed, traffic would naturally increase. At present the return journey for travellers between Tali and Shanghai occupies eleven months, the expenses being enormous and the risk great.

The principal export is opium, the poppy thriving in Yunnan at a level which is five thousand or six thousand feet higher than the poppy-fields of the West River, and yielding a good quality of the drug, not so strong in flavor nor possessing so great a narcotic power as the foreign article, it is true, but having the much-appreciated advantage of being cheaper.* There is no doubt that, should any-

* Ninety taels per thousand ounces is the usual price.

thing occur to suppress or diminish the import of foreign opium into China, Yunnan and other provinces would supply sufficient to meet the increased demand. Large quantities of the "black smoke," as the Chinese call the drug, are exported from Yunnan to Nanning, the carriage being by porterage through wild and mountainous country, and involving some risk and much difficulty. It is, however, preferred locally to foreign opium, which is much more expensive, and which, when used at all, is generally smuggled. The boatmen on the West River take every opportunity to smuggle both opium and salt into the interior, and as, when they have a mandarin on board, the *hotau* is subjected to a less careful inspection on the part of the customs authorities, it is often found expedient to carry one at a low rate, the mandarins themselves being quite willing, if occasion offers, to carry away a portion in their own baggage in order to avoid paying duty. Traders and peddlers bringing wares to Yunnan very often carry back with them quantities of the drug, chiefly for mixing with the foreign opium.

Another product is salt, wells being found in some fifty places throughout the province. The working of these salt-wells is certainly an industry in which steam-power would be an advantage. At present the salt water is drawn up in a species of bamboo bucket, to which several hundred feet of bamboo, lashed together, are attached. The motive power is supplied by buffaloes; the animals, owing to the hot atmosphere and the speed at which they are driven, dying off rapidly. On reaching the surface, the salt water is run off into pans and the salt obtained by evaporation over coal or wood fires, or by means of gas, wood being used in Yunnan, while in Szechuan gas obtained from wells is employed. The town of Mohe is largely engaged in the trade, the mines here yielding nearly all that is required by Southern Yunnan.

Large quantities of the so-called "Puerh" tea are imported into Yunnan from the districts of Ibang and Iwu, a considerable proportion being sent on by caravan to the Yangtsze and thence to Peking, Shanghai, and other northern towns. In the southern and southwestern districts of China this tea is drank by all the peasantry, but, owing to the heavy carriage charged, by the time it reaches Shanghai it is too costly to export to Siberia or to Europe. Tea extract is also imported, a small piece placed in boiling water being equal to the ordinary leaf-tea. This extract comes from the tea-mountains of Ibang, the leaf being made up into round cakes, ten of which are placed in a packet. Of these, one is extracted at Ibang for *likin* duty, one at Ssumao, and one at Puerh-fu for *shui*, so that only seven cakes are eventually sold in Yunnan. Once in five years a tribute of "Puerh" tea is sent to Peking. A cake of inferior tea, principally made at Shwenning-fu, and an imitation of the genuine article, is frequently substituted by dealers when selling a packet of Puerh-fu tea.

Tändstikkor matches form another article of import, but imitations of these, also, are sometimes placed on the market and sold to the unsuspecting aborigines. These imitations are of Japanese origin, and are greatly inferior in quality. The Mohammedan traders in tea and cotton frequently take with them, when journeying into Burma, odds and ends of all kinds, such as straw hats, buffalo-horns, raw silk and drugs. It is worthy of note that thousands of artisans annually leave the districts to the north-east of Tali, in the eighth and ninth moons (Novemember), and proceed to Burma and the Shan states, returning in the fourth and fifth moons (May).

The price of coal, which is transported from place to place by coolies on their backs, the charge for such porterage being high, varies considerably in different parts of the province; at Pingihsien it is sold at 1 cash for ten catties, while in other parts 4 cash will purchase seventy catties.* Another important industry in the southwest, as in other parts of China, is the keeping of ducks, the duck-feeder of the Yangtsze frequently having considerably more than six hundred birds in his flock.

The most common medium of exchange, when brick-tea is not used, is silver, which is carried in bars, portions being cut off as wanted. At one time 1 tael of silver would buy 1300 good cash, 3000 base brass cash, or 4500 iron cash. At the present time, however, the base is often mixed with the good cash.

Many and various are the caravan routes by which

* With the development of Southwestern China, it is possible that coal-mining may become an important industry.

traders can find entrance to Yunnan. Among these may be mentioned two *via* the Yangtsze, from Hankow, by way of Chenyuen-fu, in Kweichau; and from Chungking, in Szechuan. The Chungking route to Yunnan-fu has two branches, one of which passes through a part of Kweichau, and the other through Sui-fu in Szechuan. From Canton and Pakhoi, also, there is a road *via* Pêse and Kwangsi, while on the Tibetan side a road runs direct from Batang to Tali. From Burma there is a route, formerly much used by traders, *via* Ssumao, and through the Shan states, but the chief western approach is by way of Bhamo, another being from Hwenting-pa, on the Burmese frontier, to Yongchang-fu. During the Ming dynasty there were three routes into Burma, one from Tengyueh, one from Monglai, and one from Kingtong. From Tongking the approach to the province is by way of the Red River, from Hanoi to Laokai. Of the river routes before referred to, perhaps the most important in the south is that by way of the West River, a route which in reality divides into two branches—the chief one by the main stream through Pêse, and the other by the Namhou or South River. As Pêse commands better water communication than the southern stream, and lies on the borders of Yunnan, the Pêse route naturally takes all trade, and is the one adopted by mandarins and merchants. The most important commercial cities on this route are Nanning and Wuchau.

CHAPTER XVIII

SOUTHWEST CHINA—(Continued)

ALTHOUGH travelling in the southwest provinces has, during the last eighteen or twenty years, been greatly facilitated, by reason of the ever-increasing number of missionary stations (of which there are many more now than when the writer visited that district in 1882), there is still room for improvement in the matter of roads, the dilapidated condition of which is a serious hinderance both to travellers and traders. In most of the provinces are to be found traces of what were once magnificent roads, paved with flag-stones and bordered with trees. But the Tartar-Manchu dynasty, on their advent to power, allowed these works, and also the marvellous system of canals introduced by the Yuen dynasty, to fall into disrepair, even helping in the work of destruction by cutting down the trees, tearing up the flag-stones, and altering the frontier lines of districts. At the present time nothing is repaired or renewed in Yunnan. Here, as in other provinces, the utmost that is ever done is to partially repair a road when a viceroy is expected to make a progress. Yamêns and temples, ruined and abandoned, are met with on all sides, testifying to the weakness and want of enterprise of the present ruling powers. The comparison of a Chinese highway to "a London street with the pavement up" is well exemplified in the Kwangnan-fu road, that from Yunnan-fu to Sui-fu, and, perhaps worst of all, the road from Tali to Tengyueh, in which district an improvement might easily be effected by the construction of a good cart roadway up the Papien valley as far as Tali. Another very bad road is that from Yunnan-fu to Bhamo.

The bridges are in no better state than the roads. Many excellent specimens are to be found in Southern Yunnan—as, for instance, in Ssumao—constructed of slabs of fine white limestone. But they are in a neglected and ruined condition, never being repaired from year's end to year's end. Perhaps one of the finest is the iron chain bridge at Kingtong, over the Papien River; the first structure is said to have been built in A.D. 50. The first bridge across the Upper Yangtsze was constructed in A.D. 785.

The most convenient starting-place, in commencing a journey into the western or southwestern districts, is Chungking, where facilities are offered in banking matters, or for arranging transport, while for the central provinces Hankow forms a convenient station of departure. Once on the road, however, the traveller must rest content with whatever accommodation presents itself, and must reconcile himself to occasionally putting up at one of the dirty *matiens*, or stable-inns, which abound in Southern Yunnan, and which consist of a yard with a low-

BRIDGE AT LAN-CHUAN, SZECHUAN

roofed building, round which guests, baggage, and animals are indiscriminately housed.

In journeying in the southwest one is struck by the number of *pai-fangs*, or stone portals, generally of marble more or less richly carved, and sometimes, as in Yunnan-fu, ornamented with pottery-work. They are usually erected to commemorate widowhood (that is to say, in honor of a woman who abjures a second marriage), length of years, or official virtues, the spontaneity of the memorial being in the latter case somewhat open to question; indeed, it is said that the official himself usually defrays the cost. Pagodas, also, are continually met with, and these, like the *pai-fangs*, vary greatly in style and material, being generally of stone. In Szechuan, notwithstanding that stone is much used for other purposes, the pagodas are constructed of brick, covered with a white plaster as *chunam.* They are sometimes used for the preservation of relics; one of them is even said to contain a particle of the ashes of Buddha. In Szechuan the upper stories of the pagodas are as broad as the lower, sometimes broader, differing in this particular from those farther east.

Among the interesting features are the mysterious caves carved out of the sandstone, of which there are probably several hundreds, of all shapes and sizes, sometimes containing many apartments and generally decorated with carving and sculpture. At present their origin and the purposes for which they were used is unknown, and there is here a wide field awaiting exploration.

Tali-fu, one of the most important strongholds of Western Yunnan, and thirteen stages from the capital, was built in A.D. 746, and from that time till 1260 was the residence of the Nan-choa, or Southern princes. It is supposed by Marco Polo, who visited Yunnan in 1295, to be identical with the ancient

TIBETAN WOMAN ON THE FRONTIER, NORTHWEST SZECHUAN

"Yachi" or Kin Yachi—*i. e.* "Golden Teeth." The name probably owes its origin to the practice, common in this region, as in Burma, the Shan country, and Western Yunnan, of chewing betel mixed with lime, causing discoloration of the teeth and gums, to both of which is given a bright-red hue. Tali is described by Baber as being "as unpicturesque a city as any in China," but from this description the writer ventures to differ. The Mohammedan pagodas or minarets, to be seen on the Tali hill, are in themselves imposing and picturesque; but the finest building is undoubtedly the palace built by Yang-yu-ko, the late Mussulman ruler of Western Yunnan, now used as a college. The ancient palace was destroyed in 1874, on the capitulation of the Mohammedans, by the Chinese governor Tsen Yu Ying. The large tower, which is a noteworthy feature, was built by Prince Fong, between 825 and 860 A.D.

The temperature around Tali is very even; poppy, wheat, and rice being largely cultivated. Hot and boiling springs, some composed of hot sulphur water, and much resorted to by the sick and maimed, are numerous. This town is famed for its marble quarries, high on the mountain-sides, producing a white variety used for tombstones, and a colored or variegated kind, much prized for the designs in the grain of the stone, resembling mountain scenery and cloud effects. An annual fair, which attracts traders and travellers from long distances, is one of the great sources of prosperity of the town, a prosperity which is further aided by the regular immigration of Kutsong or Eastern Tibetans, a sociable people, fond of singing and dancing, and very unlike the Chinese. These Kutsong come annually at the beginning of the cold weather, and leave at the end, invariably taking back with them quantities of pounded rice, which they beg as a present. Large numbers of Cantonese also annually leave Canton to spread themselves over Northern Tongking and Yunnan, working as a guild—each party of twelve or twenty having a head man, and generally regarding Tali or Teng-yueh as their terminal markets. Tali is a great *entrepôt* for medicines.

GROUP ON THE BORDER OF TIBET AND SOUTHWESTERN CHINA

Yunnan-fu, the capital of the province, whose first walls were built in 765—the present one, which is substantial and well-kept, dating only from 1383—is a town of temples and yamêns, fully one-half being occupied by these structures. Some distance outside the eastern gate, and standing on a hill, is the "Kintongsi," or chief temple. One of its rooms is entirely of copper, and on the ascent to the temple are three large arches, known as "Heaven's Gates." The town is a station of the China Inland Mission, and contains native post-offices, banks, and other public buildings, but on the whole it is dirty and crowded beyond description. A large trade is carried on in jade-stone, brought from Burma, and here cut and polished and made into jewelry; while many of the inhabitants make a good living by retailing fish, meat, and vegetables, which are remarkably plentiful. Two mails a month are sent to Chungking, and two to Kwei-yang-fu and Chenyuan-fu. The town passed out of the hands of its Mongol princes in 1382, when, as Prince Rantsima refused to submit, the Chinese took possession.

An important market for South Yunnan is Talan, possessing a magnificent and costly temple—the Wu-miao or Wu temple; but of still greater importance is Ssumao, the last administrative town on the southwestern frontier of Yunnan. Situated in the midst of a plain, it has a large market, where a considerable trade is done in Shan tea and cotton and in Szechuan silk; piece-goods, tobacco, and matches from Canton, by way of Pêse, and from Tongking, by way of Manhao. Iron comes from Chingtung, and copper from Yunnan-fu. There are many fine temples in the town, often left without even a single priest in charge, a practice common in Yunnanese temples. Another important town in the south is Kaihua, situated in a valley on the river Tsin-ho, the Rivière Claire of French maps. It is a prosperous town, with wall-paved streets and houses of Chinese pattern, constructed of sun-dried bricks. Its people, a mixture of Chinese and aborigines, have a much franker appearance than the Chinese proper. Many of them are descendants of Mohammedans, the town having been a rebel camp during the Mohammedan rebellion. South of Kaihua are some silver mines, which have been closed since the Mohammedan rebellion, as permission to reopen them cannot be obtained. A considerable import trade is carried on in tobacco from the West River. Kwangnan is an important market town, but Linan, visited by the French commission of 1867–68, is not so wealthy and prosperous as is generally supposed. Mentzu, where the French troubles recently occurred, a town well situated as a distributive centre, is the *entrepôt* for a considerable trade between Manhao and the Shan country and different parts of the province.

Excepting in the valleys along the highways, the inhabitants of Yunnan are all aborigines, who still constitute about half the entire population of the province. The Chinese element is the result of intermarriage of the soldiery (who came during the wars waged by various dynasties) with aboriginal women, the soldiers, when disbanded, settling on confiscated and vacant lands. At the present time the population of the province is being continually augmented by immigrants from Szechuan, who compose nine-tenths of all the artisans, tradesmen, and coolies to be met with and present a marked contrast to the Yunnanese themselves. The latter are erect, independent, agile, hardy, and only moderately addicted to opium-smoking, while the Szechuanese are suave and cunning, and are confirmed smokers, although it must be said in their favor that they are hospitable to strangers when once assured that these are not officials, who are held in great dread. Education in Yunnan, and indeed in the southwest generally, is backward, owing to the continually recurring rebellions which have kept the country in a state of ferment, and also to remoteness from Peking and general lack of communications by which to reach the civilized world. The inhabitants, unlike the majority of their countrymen, are generally lazy; in the towns many of the shops do not open till late in the day.

The ancient Chinese* made their entry from the northwest, and, following the course of the Hoang-ho, gradually introduced their civilization and subdued the aborigines, who were driven farther and farther south; the valley of the Yangtsze, and regions even south of this, being, till the Christian era, inhabited almost entirely by savage tribes, who became gradu-

* The Chinese are of mixed blood. During the early Chinese incursions they absorbed some of the aborigines, pressing always farther south and west, and, later, the Tibetans, Huns, and Mongols; and, lastly, the Manchu Tartars became fused into the present Chinese people. The difference between the inhabitants of north, west, and south is remarkable, especially those of north and south, who have been well described as respectively "tall, strong, slow," and "short, small, cute."

ally absorbed and assimilated. The aborigines are now mostly found in Formosa, Hainan, Kweichau, Szechuan, Yunnan, Kwangtung, and Kwangsi, numbering among them many tribes of warlike character, who still hold their own against the Chinese. Altogether they amount to some millions in number, and occupy an area equal in total size to that of France. In Southwestern China the Mantzu share with the Miaotzu and the Lo-los the unique distinction of not having entirely submitted to the Chinese yoke, a considerable number in Szechuan still remaining independent.

The Miaotzu and Lo-los are contemptuously looked upon as barbarians by the Chinese, who are, however, themselves despised by the inhabitants of Eastern Kwangtung, and these again by the people of the more northern provinces. Although the term "Mantzu"* is used by the Chinese in the sense of "barbarian" or "savage," it now really denotes an aboriginal race found in the mountainous parts of South Szechuan, North Yunnan, and West Kweichau, who merit the name of "savage" more than the other tribes. When the Chinese conquered Yunnan, these Mantzu, together with the Lo-los, took refuge in the snow-covered mountains of Szechuan, and have ever since defied the Imperial troops. Expeditions have from time to time been sent against them, but without result. They are a hardy race, fearing neither cold nor hunger,

* The word "Mantzu" is said to mean "sons of barbarians," but this is doubtful.

and possessing great powers of endurance. Frequently they make raids into the neighboring Chinese villages, bribing the mandarins, it is said, to shut their eyes to these attacks; in consideration of an arranged sum which yearly changes hands. The Miaos, who are found mainly in East Yunnan and in Kweichau, may be roughly divided into three tribes, the Hei, Pei, and Hong—or black, white, and red Miaos—these names probably originating from the color of their clothes. They are a pleasure-loving people, among whom courtship occupies a prominent position, and who indulge to a large extent in waltzing and other amusements, much to the disgust of the Chinese, who regard them as "immoral" savages. Their theory as to the origin of the rainbow is rather poetic. The legend runs that two young Miaos fell in love, but their parents disapproved and forbade them to marry. Being parted, both lost their joy of life, and eventually death came to their relief. Their graves were placed on either side of a stream, and from each arose one day a column of vapor, which met above the water, forming a bow; and thus the lovers, though parted in life, were joined in death. A curious custom practised among this tribe is that known as the *convade*—on the birth of a child the husband does not leave the house for a month, the wife having, meanwhile, to procure food and carry on the affairs of the household. The Chinese never tire of saying that the Miao women are immoral, and in this view they are supported by some of the missionaries, but it cannot be denied that in many respects they are superior to the Chinese women, being simple, honest, hospitable, frank, generous, and brave.

The Lo-los are divided into two clans, the Hei and Pei, and are mostly found in the hilly districts to the south and southwest of Tali; the Hwa Lo-los, inhabiting the district near Chang-na-hsien, are a particularly handsome race and much superior to the Chinese. Almost without exception the border Lo-los are extremely tall, muscular, and well-built, with a tawny skin; they have somewhat high cheek-bones and low foreheads, the latter characteristic being perhaps accentuated by their style of hair-dressing, all the male Lo-los having their hair gathered together over the forehead and twisted in a cloth to resemble a horn, sometimes nearly a quarter of a yard in length, a style of head-dress which is looked upon as sacred. Their principal article of clothing is a mantle, reaching from the neck almost to the ground, generally gray or black in color, the material in winter being felt and in summer cotton. A conical hat of felt-covered bamboo serves as a protection from the rain. The women of the tribe are treated with great consideration, and the rejoicings are great when a *girl* is born, in which particular the Lo-los differ considerably from the Chinese. The term "Lo-lo," like "Mantzu," is one of contempt; they are sometimes called "I-chia" or "I" families; among themselves they have different names for the different tribes. The total area inhabited by the various tribes extends to many thousands of square miles. They will have nothing whatever to do with Buddhism, but have deities of their own, and the medicine-man is in high repute among them, presiding over the frequent trials by ordeal that take place.

The Lo-los have from early times had a writing of their own, and in Tating-fu is to be seen a tablet with an inscription half in Chinese characters and half in Lo-lo. As Chinese civilization advanced, however, this writing gradually died out, and at the present time is almost unknown, except in Western Yunnan, where it is said that the tribe still read books and preserve their own system of writing. The tribe known as Minkia, or Minchia (*i.e.*, "native families"), who are mostly found on the shores of the Tali Lake and in certain western districts, say that their forefathers came from Nanking during the Ming dynasty. The Hanjen and Oni tribes, inhabiting the Papien valley, are, on the whole, peaceful and industrious, but fierce when aroused. The Oni have some taste for music, and have a certain reed instrument known as *ho-lu-shen*, in which they take great pride. Another tribe, found in large numbers in Northwestern Yunnan, Northwestern Szechuan, and Tibet, is that of the Si-fans. Throughout Yunnan the "mandarin" dialect is spoken, the people having been forced, on pain of death, to learn the official language. Each district, however, has its own local *patois*, called *hiang-tan*, a village brogue for the understanding of which interpreters are needed, especially when a case has to go before the local courts. So greatly do the provincial dialects differ one from another that they are practically distinct languages. The aborigines are rapidly adopting Chinese customs, even to the introduction of "lily-feet" among their women. A peculiarly local custom, however, is that known as *shangmen*, or "entering the family," whereby, on marriage, a man adopts his father-in-law's name.

Here, as in other parts of China, the New-Year's festival is the only time when there is a cessation of labor among all classes. At this period it is usual to have a number of proverbs—such as "Better not do kindnesses at all than do them in the hope of recompense;" "Kindness is greater than law;" "Do good regardless of consequences;" "It is a little thing to starve to death, it is a serious matter to lose one's virtue," and others of similarly exalted sentiment—written on strips of differently colored paper, these strips being then affixed to doors and windows, to masts of ships, or wherever possible. Whether the advice contained in these sage maxims is followed in every-day life is another matter. The Feast of Lanterns is held at the time of the first full moon of the new year. The Yunnanese are fond of music, and it has been said that the mandolin is their typical instrument; there is, however, some doubt as to whether its use is so general as to warrant this statement.

In Yunnan and Kweichau coolies are generally employed by travellers, the best being obtained through the *hongs*.* These *hongs*, or coolie establishments, do not seem to be existent in the south of Yunnan — as in the north and in other parts of China—horse or mule being the usual means of conveyance in the south. One of the most original types of coolie met with is the palanquin-bearer, who is always alert and good-tempered, even amid the greatest difficulties. His needs are small, "Three meals per day, one sleep per night," being the extent of his ambition. The marvellous endurance of these coolies when on the march is an admirable example of the mobility and vitality of the Chinese race. The peasantry in some parts, especially in the eastern districts, are extremely poor, being able to obtain very little for their support from the stony and barren soil, and dwelling in mud huts affording small protection against wind and rain. Luckily these people are content with the merest necessaries of life. As one of their proverbs says:

> "That man is well-to-do in whose house we see
> Fuel, rice, oil, salt, sauce, vinegar, and tea."

In their opinion, according to another proverb, "He is equal to any task who can subsist on cabbage-stalks."

Buddhism was introduced into Yunnan by the

* The usual load carried is seventy catties, the charge being from eighteen to twenty tael cents per stage. A horse-load is one hundred and twenty catties, at fifteen tael cents per stage, and the *ma-hongs* do not care about providing less than ten horses, a *futau* or head man being always in charge.

original Hindu settlers in A.D. 61, but is now enfeebled and corrupt, having reached its prime in the eleventh century. At the present time the temples often serve as resting-places for travellers, the bonzes themselves sometimes serving out tea to the weary wayfarer—provided he does not come with empty purse. The Roman Catholics have for the past hundred years been working hard to introduce their religion, and have now many converts. At Kwei-yang-fu, the capital of Kweichau, they have a Kiao-an-chu, or "office for foreign affairs," managed by mandarins, of whom one is Romanist, its object being to arrange Roman Catholic litigation. In the newer part of the town is the Roman Catholic cathedral, built in great part from money paid at different times in compensation by the Imperial government. It is evident that missionary work among the aborigines of the southwest, to be effective, must not be delayed, since the natives are so rapidly assimilating Chinese ideas and customs. Missionaries themselves admit that it is almost impossible to make any impression on the Chinese, involved as they are in such a maze of superstition. To obtain real converts it is necessary to begin with the children.

In passing through the various provinces it is possible to gain some insight into the characteristics of the Chinese. Perhaps their prevailing weakness, at least where foreigners are concerned, is inquisitiveness, which in time becomes extremely monotonous to the traveller, who, on taking up his residence in town or village, is invariably besieged by a curious crowd, not only looking in at the windows, but even forcing an entrance, in order to pursue their investigations. They have a great contempt for exercise in any shape or form, and when they see an Englishman walking for exercise they assume that he must be carrying out some religious observance. The upper classes themselves never take exercise; they lead a sedentary life, and in consequence suffer horribly from dyspepsia and stomachic ailments, which are also common among the poor, who "bolt" their food, swallowing their rice or beans at a rapid rate. It may be said that lung complaints, on the other hand, are uncommon, and the average Chinese can stand any amount of cold, fatigue, or pain; and, so far as noise is concerned, would seem to have no nerves at all. One of their strongest points is cookery, in which they one and all excel, most of them being able at the shortest notice, under most unfavorable circumstances and with few appliances, to produce a highly satisfactory meal.

It must be admitted that they are dirty, and their ignorance, especially of foreign inventions and discoveries, is profound. Travellers are frequently asked how many feet into the earth they can see, and the ideas generally entertained as to the characteristics of "the foreign devils" are fearful and wonderful. On the other hand, many Chinese are not at all disagreeable companions. They have the gift of humor, and are exceedingly good-tempered, even settling most of their disputes by argument.

They are capable of gratitude and of strong attachments, but are lacking in philanthropy, being able to perpetrate the greatest cruelties unmoved, and even laughing heartily when relating tales of misfortune or cruelty. It is generally supposed that they are of a stolid disposition; the lower classes, however, are far from unemotional, displaying great feeling when listening to a pathetic tale, while at the theatre groans are not unusual, even the coolies having been known to weep at some more than usually tragic situation.

As regards the relations subsisting between the Chinese generally, particularly the mandarins,* and the aboriginal people, these cannot be considered entirely satisfactory. The "science of officialdom" has come to be expressed in the formula, "Big fish eat little fish, little fish eat shrimps, shrimps eat mud," and certain it is that while the mandarins enrich themselves, justice is often denied and the people oppressed. The general opinion entertained by the peasantry of the "lying machine," as they designate an official, is evidenced by the popular proverbs. "Yamêns," they say, "are deep as the sea," and their corruptions "lofty as heaven." "Quand les mandarins sont très polis, gardez-vous!" said an astute Frenchman. "Our time has come," was openly said by the Kansuh officials when the late rebellion broke out. "I have been in office twenty years," said one, "and never had a chance!" the

* The term "mandarin," so commonly in use among Europeans, as denoting an official, is unknown to the Chinese themselves.

"chance" referred to, of course, being the opportunity of making a large coup. And while the mandarins act in this way, the official underlings also "see money as a fly sees blood."

> "As sheep drop into a tiger's jaw,
> Cash drops into the underling's paw"

is another saying, and the excuse made in reply by the Yamên runner is, "What paddy-fields and corn-fields belong to the Yamên?" The people at large are *their* paddy-field. So corrupt, indeed, has become the system of government that it is a generally recognized fact that an honest magistrate cannot maintain his position.

"Even an honest *Chih-fu* (magistrate) may, during a three years' term of office, save ten myriad snow-white taels of silver!" runs a popular saying. All officials are surrounded by a crowd of servants and unpaid hangers-on ("rats under the altar," according to a Chinese proverb), and it is difficult for a mandarin or his subordinates to act independently of them. An audience with the mandarin himself is impossible unless bribery is resorted to, and, even if the officials should by chance be honest themselves, the people have to suffer from the impositions of the crowds who surround them. As a rule, however, the officials make no attempt to gain the good-will of the people, some of the country districts, in fact, never seeing them except when the time of taxation comes round, when rulers and underlings alike expect to make a harvest, thus being always associated in the public mind with extortion. The miscellaneous horde composing a mandarin's escort are known among the country people as "locusts," because they eat up the villages. When they arrive they are generally carrying guns, but after a very short time these are transferred to passing coolies, whose labor they enforce, the "locusts" contenting themselves with carrying their pipes and umbrellas. The soldiers and police are great opium-smokers, and, being of a predatory disposition, are much dreaded by the country people; the pestilential nature of the climate is their invariable excuse for indulgence in opium.

Mention has already been made of railway surveys recently begun by the British government between the Upper Yangtsze and Burma. It does not, however, appear probable that the government of India is at all alive to the necessity for the overland connection of India and China, the two most populous empires of the world. They are inclined still to bring such consideration as, by pressure of public opinion, they are compelled to give to the question of whether such a railway will prove commercially remunerative or not. It is no difficult matter to demonstrate that such a line, as a purely commercial undertaking, cannot at once, or indeed for some years to come, prove a paying concern; but the time has passed for viewing the question from any such narrow standpoint. The line can only be carried through either as a government undertaking or under government guarantee; it is one of those railways whose future prospects cannot be estimated; and it is imperative that it should be made, if the influence of Britain is ever to become a reality in the Yangtsze basin, and politically and strategically for the security of the Indian Empire.

The view adopted by the government of India, and those in sympathy with their attitude of *non possumus*, is that Britain should confine her attention to extending and developing the internal railways of Burma, and not incur the heavy expenditure necessary for the construction of a line to the Yangtsze, still less commit itself in any way to the extension to Szechuan, a line of which the financial success is altogether problematical. The general line of argument is that, apart from purely political and strategical considerations, the improvement of existing communications converging on important points on river or railway within Burma affords more promising commercial opportunities than the construction of a railway into and across Yunnan. It is contended, too, that the natural chief outlet for the trade of Southwest China is the Yangtsze River (navigable, with its affluents, for some 3000 miles), and that any important deflection of trade from this natural outlet towards Shanghai is altogether improbable. Yunnan, it is said, is not so rich a region as has been supposed. An abnormally expensive line to tap the trade of Southwestern Yunnan by means of a railway will not be remunerative, for the simple reason that this lofty plateau produces nothing in the nature of a trade capable of great expansion. The returns would not be adequate to the outlay. To be profitable trade must be reciprocal; and there seem to be no products in Yunnan which can be utilized in exchange for goods of British manufacture to a sufficient extent to make the railway in question remunerative. Such trade as there is on the Yunnan plateau probably already finds its way into Burma, without any expensive railway. Unless the expense of construction can be shown to be less than has been anticipated, and the probable returns greater, it would be better not to extend beyond the Burman frontier. Such are the arguments employed. But, as already said, the question of its financial prospects as a purely commercial line, or whether the bulk of traffic will flow to Shanghai or Rangoon, is not the one which has *now* to be decided.

There are undoubtedly good reasons for believing that British commercial interests, merely in the narrow sense, would be better served by devoting the money which would be spent in railway extension beyond the frontier of Burma to linking together the Burma and Assam railway systems, to the construction of branch railways as feeders of the existing Burmese trunk lines, and to the creation of short new ones falling entirely within British Indian territory. There exist favorable openings in Burma for profitable investment of capital, and it is desirable that more British money should be invested in the fertile but only partially developed province of Burma. But the whole question must be considered and dealt with on the ground whether, as a political, strategic, and commercial line, it is or is not the duty of the British government to see that this line is made. It seems clear, in view of the Russian advance southward, that, if British influence is to be asserted in the Yangtsze region, the connection of the Upper Yangtsze by rail with Burma must be undertaken and carried through without delay. And the assertion of British influence in the Upper Yangtsze is a vital necessity for the preservation of India. To allow Russian, or Franco-Russian, or German-Russian influence to grow up in the Upper Yangtsze would add another and infinitely more serious frontier question and endanger the stability of the Indian Empire.

It is rightly urged that, if for political purposes it be decided to make a railway to Yunnan and Szechuan, the necessary guarantees must in equity be provided by the British government, for to saddle the government of India with such a responsibility would be adding yet another to the many financial wrongs already done to India in the name of Imperial requirements. The government of India should construct the railway to the limits of Burma; but any extension beyond that should rest entirely with the home government on its own financial responsibility.

The management of the Burman railways was some years ago intrusted by the government of

India to a private company, which, it was believed, would understand commercial needs and prove the means of more rapidly introducing European capital. It cannot be said that the progress made so far has been satisfactory. The Mandalay-Kunlon line is proceeding at a veritable snail's pace. Some fifteen miles only—*i. e.*, from Myohaung to the foot of the Shan Hills—were open last autumn. The ascent of the Shan Hills, from a level of about 500 feet on the plain to 3000 feet on the edge of the plateau, within a distance of less than 10 miles, involves, with two reversing stations, a gradient of the unusual steepness of 1 in 25, which will probably have to be reduced at great expense to 1 in 40. The line should shortly be opened as far as Maymyo (over 35 miles). The alignment follows a zigzag course across the face of a precipitous hill, rounding sharp curves, passing through heavy cuttings and rocky galleries. When once this short section is opened and rails can reach the plateau, the laying of the permanent track can follow rapidly up to about the eightieth mile. Here the formidable Gokteik gorge offers a natural obstruction that will probably take the best part of two years to overcome. Earthwork and bridging are completed thus far, ballast has been collected, and only the rails are wanted to enable the permanent way to be laid.

Such is the condition of the 230 miles of the Kunlon ferry line six years after it was begun. Compare this with the Russian rate of progress—500 miles a year, or some 3000 miles in the same six years! And, with a Russian railway traversing Siberia and Manchuria, connecting the Baltic with Port Arthur, and joining the Russian territory with Peking—which line will be completed by 1902—what is Britain doing to counterbalance this Russian advance?

CHAPTER XIX

TONGKING

At the time of the Franco-Chinese War of 1883, when the writer first visited Tongking, that country was practically a *terra incognita*, and that not only in England, but, in even greater degree, in Hong-Kong and other neighboring districts. Nothing was really known of any part of the country except the delta and a small portion immediately bordering it on the north and northeast. Matters have, of course, improved in this respect, but even now information regarding this important possession, which the French term "colony," is singularly meagre, notwithstanding the numerous official missions despatched from Paris, missions which provide snug berths for friends of the ministers in power for the moment, and which constitute one of the scandalous abuses under which the country suffers so seriously.

On former occasions Tongking had been always reached by the writer from the seaboard, but on the journey furnishing matter for the present work it was entered from Yunnan, the Chinese province bordering it on the northwest, which had been traversed on the way southward from the Upper Yangtsze. The precise route followed was that from the capital Yunnan-fu, *via* Mengtzu, the last town before reaching the Songkoi or Red River, at Manhao, whence shallow native boats suitable for passing the rapids are used to Laokai, where usually a passage on a light-draught steamer can be secured. The writer's journey, like that across Southwest China, was entirely uneventful. But for a certain novelty attaching to the province of Yunnan, the fine scenery on the Red River, and more especially the fact that this is practically the future French railway route through Tongking to Yunnan-fu, *en route* to Szechuan, it would have been uninteresting, almost monotonous.

On the route between Yunnan-fu and Hanoi, the capital of Tongking, there are no serious difficulties in the way of railway construction except the ascent from the Red River, at Manhao, to the plateau, some five thousand feet, whence a descent, rather steep in places, lands one on the plain on which stands Mengtzu. Thence to the provincial capital is plain sailing for the French engineers. The railway, and in connection with that undertaking the proposed visit of M. Doumer, the governor-general of Tongking, to Yunnan-fu, were the chief topics of conversation among the Europeans (all missionaries, excepting an employé in the telegraph department of the Chinese government, a Dane), encountered in Yunnan province. Great preparations had been made to receive with all due pomp and ceremony the governor-general and a numerous suite, who were to accompany him. The object of the journey was ostensibly to pay a visit of courtesy to a neighboring magnate. But Frenchmen — officials of high rank especially — are not given to undertaking for such a purpose a journey which involves a considerable amount of discomfort and an absence of several weeks from the *cafés* and *coiffeurs* to be found in profusion at Hanoi. The real object was believed to be closely connected with French aims at obtaining a predominating influence in the provinces of Yunnan and Szechuan, and, at any rate, of being first in the field in the railway race to Szechuan, the premier province of China, known to be the British objective, as the undoubted key to the Yangtsze valley, the much-talked-of British sphere. The scenery on the Red River is in places fine, and generally extremely picturesque, closely resembling that of many of the rivers in Burma and Siam, a dense tropical foliage usually reaching down to the river bank from the slopes of the hill ranges on either side. The valley has the reputation among the French and Chinese of being extremely unhealthy. "Beautiful, but fever-stricken," was a French officer's description.

It would be out of place here to enter at any great length on the early history of Tongking, but it may be briefly chronicled that till the beginning of the nineteenth century that country was a powerful and independent kingdom. In 1802, however, it was conquered by the King of Annam, with the aid of some French officers despatched by Louis XVI., and thenceforward became part of the kingdom of

Cochin China, being designated by the Annamese "the Kingdom of the North," while to the Southern Chinese generally it was known as Yuan. The word "Tongking," which is not in use among the Annamese, is derived from the surname of the former principal capital Kesho, close by which stands at the present day Hanoi, which was called "Capital of the East," namely Tongking, in opposition to Taykinh (Capital of the West). Annam, Tongking, and Cochin China now form one united empire—French Indo-China nominally still recognizing the authority of the Emperor of Annam—the native customs, language, religion, and social organization being practically the same in all three countries. The administrative system is, of course, that created by the French.

The facts regarding the occupation of Cochin China by the French in 1862, the Garnier and Dupuis expeditions to Tongking in 1868–9, the episode of 1873 which cost the gallant Garnier his life, and the treaty of 1874 are well known. A vagueness of policy, and an absence of any settled programme, similar to that which brought about the sad occurrences of 1873, were again in evidence some years later, precipitating events beyond the anticipation and control of the central government. In 1881, two and a half millions were voted for a "flotilla of observation" on the Songkoi, and, as was natural, events moved rapidly under this quickening influence. A year later the Hanoi citadel was bombarded, and the governor of Saigon sent seven gun-vessels, with a small but fully equipped force to Tongking. Haiphong and Hanoi were occupied, the intention being to free the Red River from the banditti known as the Black Flags, and to occupy Laokai as an *entrepôt* for trade with Yunnan. These steps were the beginning of the end. The difficulties had not been recognized, the troops were insufficient, and the French commander could get no definite instructions. Indecision was the order of the day. To revive confidence among the troops, he executed a sortie and lost his life. A vote was then passed by the French Chamber for an expedition, and troops were despatched by instalments as rapidly as possible, the result being that, in 1883, the main towns of the delta had been occupied, Hué had submitted, and the King of Annam executed a treaty with the French. The bombardment of Hué, it may be mentioned, was hurriedly effected in order to blind the public with a show of victory and announce the termination of the difficulty. But matters were in reality far from settled. The lower portion of the delta, even, was still not subjugated, some of the strongest positions remaining in the hands of the Black Flags, reinforced by Chinese. The Annamese, as was anticipated, when encountered alone, never showed fight, but the French found that they had to meet enemies who were more formidable than the timid, unarmed Annamese, who had nothing better than pikes, tridents, shod bamboos, or matchlocks with which to encounter them. The Black Flags were well armed and fought well. To make matters worse, an exceptional inundation of the country took place that year, while the malarious climate affected the French troops, sickness attacking large numbers—a serious calamity, for the hospital accommodation was anything but sufficient, while provisions, stores, and medicines were far from plentiful. The troops thus becoming inadequate, large reinforcements were ordered, but, under such conditions, the subjugation even of the delta was impossible, and operations were for a time abandoned. The military men who took part in this campaign expressed great dissatisfaction at the institution of a civil supreme command, and the introduction of a body of civil officials before the country was conquered: and, as a consequence, great diversity of opinion arose between the civil, military, and naval commanders, giving evidence of a dangerous indecision in the councils.

This unfortunate state of affairs led to the active intervention of China, with a view to defending her right of suzerainty, which resulted in the Franco-Chinese war. The French took Sontay, Bacninh, and eventually Langson, after a disastrous contretemps which necessitated the retreat in great disorder of a French column. The French commanders were changed so frequently—Admiral Courbet, Generals Brière de l'Isle and Négrier succeeding each other, each after a few months' command—that no one knew who was master, and confusion reigned supreme. The French troops behaved with great gallantry, but under such a chaotic direction of the operations it took a long time before the original resistance was crushed, and for many years, until recently, in fact, the Black Flags and other Chinese irregulars were succeeded by the "pirates" of Tongking, the equivalent of the dacoits of Upper Burma. For some years past resistance has ceased, but it has cost France the expenditure of an immense amount of blood and treasure to pacify the country. Little wonder, then, that under such circumstances Tongking acquired a degree of unpopularity in France which ruined Jules Ferry—*l'homme de Tongking*—one of the ablest of latterday French statesmen, and that the colony is anathema with the French electorate and the despair of French governments, as it has been fatal to the reputation of so many French administrators.

During the earliest days of the pacification (the term employed for the conquest of Tongking) no French newspaper correspondent was in the field, several Englishmen and one American being the only representatives of the press following the operations, among these Cameron, who lost his life in the Soudan, acting for the *Standard*, Colonel Gilder for the New York *Herald*, and the writer for the London *Times*. But the early intelligence and unfavorable criticisms appearing in the English journals, anticipating in many instances even the first official French news, induced the leading papers of Paris to at last despatch representatives to the seat of war. The appearance of these gentlemen, when they made their *début* in the field, was in striking contrast with that of the English and American correspondents. Their get-up—impossible helmets and gorgeous pugrees, bright binoculars and new revolvers, dainty footgear and delicate-colored gloves—was rather that of *boulevardiers* proceeding in correct racing attire to Longchamps and Chantilly than of men who were to follow the fortunes of war in a tropical country and under conditions involving many hardships. The rough-and-ready Englishman, with his battered topee and flannel shirt, old belt and revolver, and trousers encased in leggings, both much the worse for wear, looked much more like business. This contrast, denoting a radical difference in the two races, was also noticeable in the conduct of the campaign.

The English and American correspondents were not in favor with the troops, and still less so with their French comrades of the pen. Many adventures were experienced, all sorts of obstacles being thrown in their way, which had to be overcome by *finesse* and the gentle art of stratagem. Such an episode was recalled to the writer's memory in passing down the Red River on his recent journey. It had been necessary to leave the headquarters of General Négrier, then commander-in-chief, and proceed to Haiphong with a steam-launch, the only one then available in Tongking for hire, and on returning the writer was stopped at a post and told he could not proceed without a *visé* from the commander-in-chief. An attempt to interview the commandant having at first failed, it became necessary at all hazards to see him, and when, after considerable difficulty, this had been accomplished, it was to be told the same story. It was useless to explain that no *visé* was necessary to proceed to the front, as the writer was merely returning to rejoin the commander-in-chief. "No *visé* no journey" was the verdict. Ruefully returning to the launch, it seemed impossible to overcome the difficulty. An attempt to negotiate with the Annamite commander of a tug-steamer about to leave for the front with a number of barges had ended in failure, when it occurred to the writer that it might be possible to slip into a covered canoe lying alongside and tie on to the steamer when it got under way. The commander was ready, for a consideration, to notice nothing, and eventually away we went, towed off under the very eyes of a number of officers standing on the bank. On arrival at "les Sept Pagodes," the temporary base for operations, the *capitaine du port* came off to demand explanation of the writer's scandalous conduct, and there was, of course, a serious contretemps, which, however, ended happily, owing to the benevolent intervention of an Irishman, a captain in the *Légion Étrangère*, in whose hut we all dined merrily later on.

The primary object of France in obtaining possession of Tongking, now one of her most costly colonies, was, it may fairly be assumed, chiefly to secure ready access to the markets of China, a secondary inducement being the general resources of the country, especially the value of the coal mines. It has been said that the unsatisfactory results obtained in the colony prove the worthlessness of the acquisition, but this is a mistake. The country is rich, if properly administered, and the position of neighboring China is unique. The true cause of the slow internal progress made in Tongking is to be found, as in other French colonies, in the maladministration. To this must also be partly attributed the still undeveloped condition of the trade with China, the prohibitory customs duties tending to retard all commercial enterprise.* The French themselves do not deny that the English and Dutch are more successful in their colonies, and more than one of their own writers even admits that, after many years of French occupation of the country, the Red River is in much the same condition as regards the development of trade as when the colony was first acquired, next to nothing having been done to overcome existing difficulties. Tongking is, in fact, regarded by the French government merely as an overflow place, whose principal object of existence is the creation of officials, posts being literally invented for the sole purpose of providing for the *protégés* of influential personages. Wherever one goes the same tale is heard, especially from the few French traders. Nothing

* Owing to these heavy customs duties, and dread of the French colonial officials, the Chinese have preferred to continue their trading ventures by the longer Yangtsze route, or by way of the Canton River. The remedy of free trade proposed by several distinguished Frenchmen seems as far off as ever.

is done to encourage colonists, rather are difficulties thrown in their way, and the disastrous results of favoritism and constant change of officials are intensified by the ludicrous attempts of government to turn everything to financial account, at all hazards, and altogether regardless of the methods employed. Thus obstacles are placed in the way of the few applicants for concessions who happen to be men of substance and enterprise, who have to deposit a sum of money with the administration on opening a negotiation; while, on the other hand, mischievous monopolies are granted, no matter what the injury to trade, to those willing in return to pay a sufficient sum to the treasury. To this same miserly and avaricious policy is attributable the fact that necessary expenditure is by small outlays capriciously dealt out, instead of fixed large sums distributed over a term of years. The evil consequences of this policy may be seen, to give one instance, in the unsatisfactory condition of the troops, to whose lodging, food, and clothing scandalously little attention is paid, the smallest possible sum being devoted to this branch of the service. Justice, too, is not always administered in a satisfactory manner, as has been exemplified in a case recently under investigation by the home government. A general readjustment of local taxation having taken place, the leading men of a certain village felt deep dissatisfaction with regard to the new assessment, and placed the matter in the hands of a Hanoi advocate, with the object of obtaining redress from the local authorities.

These authorities, however, having compelled the advocate to divulge the names of the malecontents, immediately issued a proclamation of a most extraordinary character, to the effect that, in employing the services of the advocate the moving spirits had offended against the administration. The mayor of the village was sentenced to a month's imprisonment and fifty strokes with the rattan, and his supporters to twenty-five days and forty strokes. Such a state of things can hardly be said to advance the welfare of the colony.

The general natural features of the country can be described in a few words. The country naturally falls into four divisions. The delta land forms an isosceles triangle, with the base lying along the sea from Kwangyen to Ninhbinh and the summit at Sontay, the delta being in a measure protected from inundations by the embankments of the innumerable channels connecting the different mouths of the Songkoi. The plateau country in the north rises in steppes from the Songkoi and its affluents near Hanoi, and attains its greatest heights north of Kwangyen. A mountain belt, traversed by various rivers, lies south of the delta. The hill region in which Sontay is situated stretches westward to the Mekong River — the Laos country — a region of dense forest, inhabited by various native tribes and fugitive Chinese.

The Songkoi — known to the Tongkingese by many other names—the Red River of the French (so called because of the red-colored clay carried along by its waters), dominates the whole fluvial system of the delta, and at present most of the trade which exists in Tongking is by way of this river, "the great navigable artery of the colony," of which, according to Prince Henri d'Orleans, so high an opinion has been formed by travellers. Even Frenchmen, however, do not all adopt this view. The river, which takes its rise in the mountains of Yunnan, in which province the writer crossed it in 1882, is navigable for small boats throughout its whole length, although between Laokai and Manhao in Tongking, and higher in its course, some rapids occur. Laokai was always talked of by Jules Ferry and others, in the days of the French colonial boom, as being admirably situated for becoming an important *entrepôt* for the Red River trade, and for the exchange of European and Yunnanese merchandise, but the place has not justified these expectations.* On the banks of the Nam Ou, which from the west joins the Songkoi, is the celebrated grotto known as Tham Pa Kouan, or "Grotto of the Great Stag." †

* The French consider that Manhao, close by the navigation limit of the Red River, would be a favorable town for the purpose. At present some foreign goods are actually brought from Hankow to Kaihua, in South Yunnan, by way of the Yangtsze, Szechuan, and Yunnan-fu, one thousand miles by river and five hundred by land caravan—a very roundabout and expensive route.

† The entrance to this grotto is through a fissure between vertical strata, in a calcareous cliff. Inside is a large hall, with a ceiling of stalactite, the walls covered with moss. In every part of this hall, on the floor and in niches of the rocks, are statuettes of gods and figures of animals of various sizes, made of all kinds of material—wood, marble, and bronze. Within are endless corridors and galleries.

The main affluents of the Songkoi are the Black River and the Rivière Claire, which join right and left above Sontay. The former, nearly as considerable as the Songkoi, but still more impracticable, takes its rise in Yunnan, where it is known in different parts of its course as the Papien and Lysien. Navigation is only possible for light-draught steamers as far as a point thirty miles south of Honghoa, where there is a barrier of rocks and a cataract. Here the river, after traversing the Laos Plateau on its way eastward, turns dead north and enters the Songkoi. The region of the Black River, particularly in its upper portion, was, during the occupation of Tongking, practically under the domination of Deo Van Tri, a powerful chief and supporter of the French, whose ancestors were Cantonese. On the fall of the Ming dynasty, his ancestor, a Chinese general, marched southward to Tongking with some of his supporters and settled at Bacninh. Later on he was given a military command and was sent by the King of Annam to the Black River, to wage war against the pirates, and became the paramount power in that region. The Claire, also rising in Yunnan, on leaving that province passes through a subterranean passage, and is navigable no greater distance than forty miles from its junction with the Songkoi, and that with difficulty. Its character is that of a torrent, absolutely valueless for the purposes of navigation.

The delta-lands, notwithstanding the admirable natural channels and artificial dikes, are exposed to severe periodical inundations. In August and September, indeed, the lower delta often presents the appearance of an enormous lake, as the writer has seen it, with here and there clumps of trees, villages, pagodas, and occasional needled rocks standing isolated from the water surface. The floods, carrying clay and red mud, are very irregular and sudden in their rise, commencing at the end of April or early in May, and ending in October. A flood has been known to rise thirteen feet in one night at Hanoi, where the river is half a mile wide. The Tongkingese are necessarily experts in the construction of embankments, canals, dams, and similar works. Another factor of importance throughout the delta is the tide, the influence of which is felt a few miles above Hanoi, there being only one ebb tide daily. The land in the gulf is being rapidly reclaimed from the sea, owing to the alluvial soil carried down by the rivers, as is proved by the interesting fact that in the eighth century, when Hanoi was built by the Chinese, the city was on the seaboard. In the seventeenth century half the extent between the present coast and Hanoi was covered by the ocean, while at the present time populous districts flourish where within living memory there was sea.

In order to understand Tongking it is necessary to have some knowledge of its fluvial system, for the marvellous fertility of the soil is due to the sediment deposited by the rivers on a clay foundation. Once the seaboard is left behind the

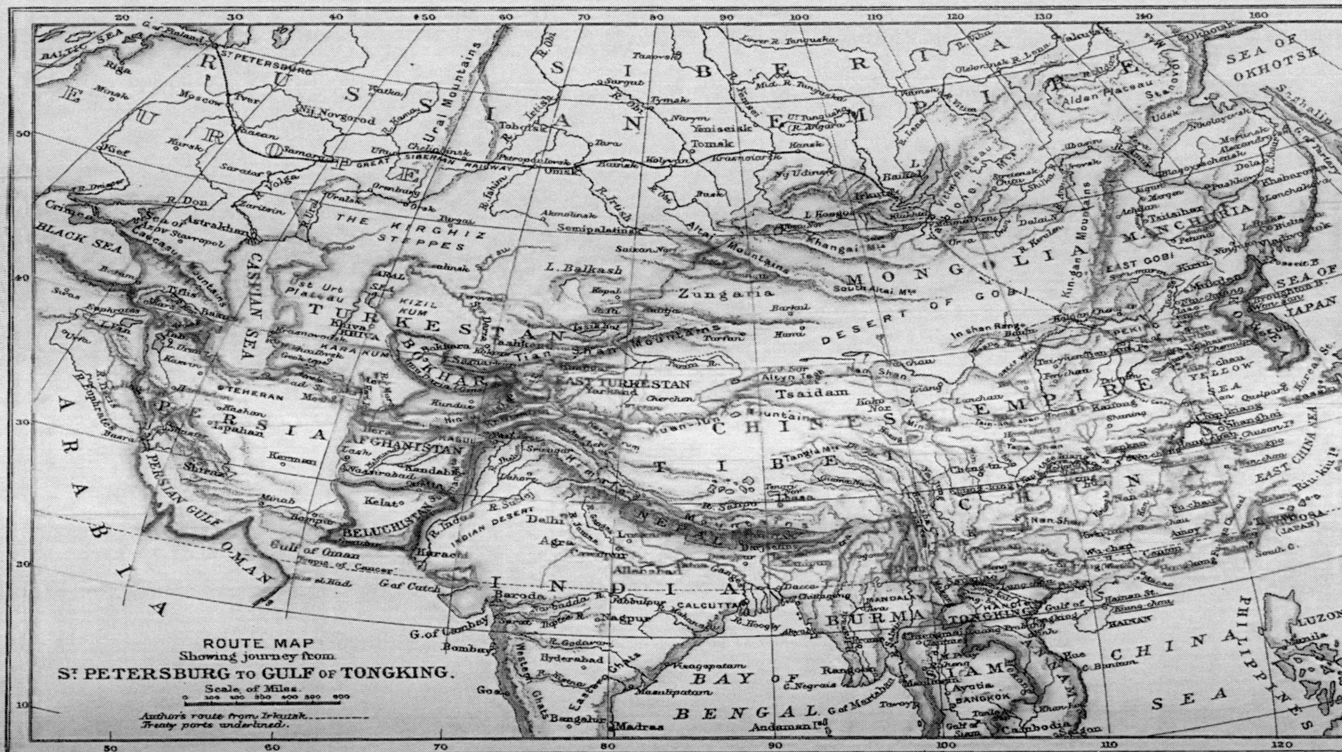

London & New York, Harper & Brothers, 45 Albemarle Street, W.

F.S. Weller, F.R.G.S. lith.

country improves rapidly, and is capable of a further and, indeed, indefinite development, being rich in mineral wealth, exceedingly productive—especially along the whole course of the Black River—and well watered. The coal-working industry is already one of the most important in the colony, the coal produced at Hong-Hai and Kébao enjoying the monopoly of the market in several of the neighboring large ports. The total extent of the carboniferous strata is unknown, but it is supposed that they traverse the whole country, while the fact that they run parallel with the river in its upper portion should be of advantage in the development of steam-navigation, as the fuel would be ready to hand. The total area at Hong-Hai is about seventy-five thousand acres, and extends twenty miles along the coast, the laborers employed here being mostly Annamites, as they are found to be more tractable, though less clever and persevering, than the Chinese, who are given the preference at Kébao. The pay of the Annamite laborers is only a franc per day, out of which food (rice) has to be paid for, the gangers getting about a shilling for ten hours' labor. Cheap as this seems, it must be admitted that an Annamite will do only about a quarter as much work in a given time as a European. At some of the mines the coal is obtained almost at the surface, being extracted "like stones from a quarry." Gold is found on the Red River, and is bartered chiefly in exchange for opium with the Chinese, who take advantage of the Tongkingese, as they do of the Mongols in the north, inducing them to take more goods than they can pay for, and then lending them money at a heavy rate of interest. Thus the whole of the native produce and labor, year after year, serves to further enrich the crafty Chinese trader. One of the products for which the country is noted is a beautiful variety of marble, known in Tongking as "*pierre à fleurs.*" Amber and precious stones abound, the most common being the carnelian. Tin, lead, zinc, bismuth, and arsenic are found in sufficient quantities to justify further development, and the copper mines are plentiful and productive; the cost of transport, however, is so great that little profit is to be had from the working of the mines. In the upper portions of the Black River the mineral wealth has been almost entirely neglected, owing to the oppression of the natives and the dread in which the pirates are held.

On the whole, the people prefer to devote their energies to agriculture, navigation, and trading. The fertile soil certainly is marvellously adapted for agricultural pursuits. At harvest-time the country has the appearance of an inexhaustible fertility and richness, much like Lower Burma. As there is practically no fixed dry season, cultivation on a large scale is rendered practicable, without heavy expense in the way of irrigation. One of the principal products, of course, is rice, of which there are two crops annually. In the delta, of which absolutely every inch is under cultivation, the rice-fields are protected by dikes or embankments from the overflow of the Red River, which occurs during July and August. The river on receding after the floods leaves immense fertilized tracts which are immediately sown with seed, the harvest being gathered in only a day or two before the next encroachment of the waters. Cotton also, for the cultivation of which the climate is exceedingly favorable, is largely grown. It requires little attention, and on the high table-lands, indeed, the Muongs merely sow the seed, and four months later, when it has attained full growth, gather what they require. The building of cotton factories in parts where coal abounds would probably lead to an extension of the trade. Silk is another thriving industry open to further development, while tobacco and opium are cultivated to a large extent. The export of opium into China, however, like that of salt, which was at one time a flourishing industry (being largely exported to Yunnan and Kwangsi), is forbidden by treaty. Other natural products, cultivated with more or less success, are sugar-cane and maize (abundant in the north), tea (especially on the hills at Sontay), coffee, badiane (aniseed), mulberry, cinnamon, betel-nut, indigo, the areca-nut and cocoanut trees, and bamboo ; also the castor-bean, haricots, pease, vegetables and fruits of all descriptions. The Chinese nettle abounds, and would yield good results as a textile plant. An important manufacture is that of rice-brandy, or *tchoum-tchoum*, which is popular with the natives. Such improvement in cultivation as has been made may be attributed to the existence at Hanoi of a garden maintained by the government solely for the purpose of agricultural experiments. One of the productions in which the Tongkingese excel is a fast black dye for cotton goods, obtained from leaves of two varieties, but of which the secret is carefully kept. Among the Annamites are many clever workers in stone and marble, and expert jewellers are to be found in every important town; but, on the whole, arts and industries are not yet properly developed, the demand being small, because of the comparative poverty of the people. Annam and Tongking both produce for themselves the greater part of what they require in the way of clothing, food, and furniture. The native houses, particularly of the richer class, are mostly of brick and native-made tiles, occasionally, however, being made of iron. One of the industries in which a considerable number of the people engage is cattle-breeding; poultry also are plentiful. The mountain and forest regions, five times greater in extent than the delta, are full of big game, the elephant, rhinoceros, and monkey being especially plentiful in the forests, the mountains abounding in tigers, bears, the roebuck, otter, and other wild animals. In some districts also are found "wild cattle, with short yellow hair," civet cats, peacocks, silver pheasants, and other species of animals and birds. Fish of many kinds abound in the rivers, and fishermen and boatmen form a considerable portion of the population. In fact, the Tongkingese live either on the water or in the paddy-fields. As might be expected in so fertile a country, an impression of luxuriant vegetation is made on the traveller, the flora being remarkably rich and varied, and including many medicinal herbs and plants. Among these are the *ydzi* and the *hoangnan*, the former being a valuable tonic and the latter a powerful poison, reported to be a sovereign remedy for plague, paralysis, leprosy, and snake-bite.

The towns which, under French rule, are of the most importance are Haiphong and Hanoi. Haiphong, the seaport town from which trade permeates by means of channels throughout Tongking, stands in an important position commercially speaking, and also from a military point of view. It has two disadvantages, however—standing on land flooded by the highest tides, and having no good water supply in the neighborhood. The town is regarded by the French as "a beautiful town which in time will have nothing to envy Saigon." It cannot be said that the scenery surrounding the place is attractive, for at the mouth of the Cua-Cam, on which branch of the Songkoi it is situated, the coast is little above the level of the sea. Here vegetation is far from luxuriant, trees being entirely absent, and rice-fields the principal feature. The plain is broken only by the Dong-Trieu, a mountain chain which is a continuation of the cliffs at Halong, whose jagged points and contorted shapes make a striking impression upon any one visiting Tongking for the first time. The entrance to the port of Haiphong is rapidly becoming silted up with accumulations of sand, notwithstanding much discussion, but nothing has been done by the French to remove this. Large vessels being unable to reach Haiphong, it has been proposed again and again to create a port at some other point on the coast, and one of the natural harbors formed by the rocks in the Halong bay might perhaps provide a better position. Such a port, closed in by islands, would be easy to defend in time of war, and coal would be close at hand; Haiphong would retain its trade in rice and native products, and still be the centre for river traffic. The town is now a very different place from what it was in 1885, when it consisted of mud-cabins and a few European buildings placed on a marshy plain. It now has thriving ship-building yards and docks, fine streets, well-built houses, trees and shrubs, hotels, boulevards, and a canal, and is lighted by electricity. There is, however, little European trade, not one-fiftieth of that of Hong-Kong. Whatever the commercial future of Tongking may be, a deep-water port is a necessity, if trade is to be increased to any extent, and Haiphong will always remain the principal centre for general imports and exports.

Between Haiphong and Hanoi the delta scenery is monotonous, consisting of long reaches of water with occasionally a few palm-trees or bamboos. On the left, and beyond the plain, can be seen the Elephant Mountain, so named because of its shape. Hanoi was founded in the eighth century by a Chinese mandarin, and its official name was "the City of the Red Dragon." It is also called Kecho (the Great Market), Bac-Thanh (Citadel of the North), and Dong-kink (Capital of the East). The French think a great deal of Hanoi, and are never tired of telling you it is one of the most beautiful places in the Far East. The town is certainly more picturesquely, or rather less hideously, situated than Haiphong, and has fine streets, good houses, plenty of building-land, and beautiful gardens. It is lighted by electricity, and here, as at Saigon, the *café* and the *coiffeur* are well in evidence. Hanoi may, in fact, be regarded as the centre of Tongkingese civilization. One of the principal vehicles in use here is the *mababar*, which resembles "a coffin on four wheels." The *pousse-pousse* (jinrikisha) is also a common form of locomotion. The native, or Annamite, part of the town lies between the citadel and the Red River.

The only water supply for the sixty thousand inhabitants of Hanoi is that obtained from the Red River, which is muddy and unwholesome, and has to go through a process of filtration by means of alum. One of the most picturesque portions of the country is the Bay of Halong, with its hundreds of islets, overhanging cliffs, creeks and natural caverns, and general air of solitude and calm. Towards the north the country is picturesque, being covered with brush, while the summits of the hills are thickly wooded, the forests offering a rich field for the naturalist and sportsman.

Although the delta is covered with embankments which serve as roads, there is practically only one road, the old imperial highway from Hué to Hanoi. Thence to China there are two routes, one by way of Langson, the other through Kwangyen, which are impassable during half the year. No wheel carriage exists throughout the country, except an occasional wheelbarrow near the towns. The main roads, formerly intended merely to facilitate the passage of mandarins in chairs, and the "trams," or official post, have been but little improved, except in the neighborhood of Hanoi. The minor roads of the delta serve for native foot-passengers and horsemen, while outside the delta nothing but footpaths are found. Improvement and extension of roads and railways is still much needed, and it is surprising how very little has been accomplished by the French, who acknowledge that the English have set them a good example in this respect, especially in Burma. After nearly ten years of occupation, in 1893, communication by steamboat was begun between Hanoi and Laokai, but the service is still very imperfect, and the railway now under construction from Hanoi, *via* the Red River to Yunnan-fu, is an absolute necessity, for the river varies considerably with the seasons. A railway has been already constructed to Langson, and from Hanoi to Lungchow in Kwangsi, but these lines are unimportant.

The population of Tongking cannot be given with any degree of accuracy, but is now probably about ten millions. Here, as in the river valleys of China, the delta is densely populated, and probably the exaggerated estimates of the French have been based on the population of the waterways, for away from the delta the population is sparse, and markedly so in the north and northwest. The dominant race, the Annamite, is in greater proportion than the Chinese, occupying a great part of the delta. Originally sprung from the union of the aborigines of the hills with the seaboard people, they have been intermixed with the Chinese, and have to a large extent adopted Chinese literature, administration, and religion; and this domination for eleven centuries, and union with the inhabitants of the low delta-land, have conspired to produce the mixed race as it is. They have a nose less flattened than the Chinese, and cheek-bones more projecting, and, though stout, are bigger and better proportioned than the Annamese farther south. Their principal characteristic is slimness in contrast to the Chinese. They have black eyes, less oblique, a fine skin, a good presence, and beautiful black hair, which is never cut, but worn chignon fashion with the aid of a pin. They are much addicted to the practice of betel chewing. Effeminate, sober, indolent, intelligent, and of a pleasure-loving nature, docile, and submissive when led, they can on occasions become extremely vindictive. They have a reputation for amiability, which, however, has been crushed by despotic rule, and an air of apathy and of quiet defiance is now usually their aspect. Enforced submission has led to a strongly developed trait in their character—namely, trickery. They are, however, generous and good-hearted, possessing much wit, of which they are able to make good use. The Annamite woman takes a leading part in the household, and in many ways is superior to the man. Many of the women also work in the fields, while the men are engaged in militia duty—in past days in the service of the King or mandarins—while others take goods to market and dispose of them, thus acquiring a noticeable independence and force of character. They are, as a rule, exceedingly kind-hearted, and in many cases the home depends almost entirely upon them. It will be seen that the position they occupy is very different from that held by the Chinese women, and rather resembles that of her Burmese sisters, who enjoy so much liberty.

It may be added that among the Tongkingese is a freedom from fanaticism, due to the absence of religion. The only creed is the welfare of the family. They honor their ancestors and respect old age, believing in a future life for wise and good men, who after death rejoice at the honors paid them by the survivors. Misfortune is calmly endured by this people, who are also noted for their sobriety, although they are beginning to indulge greatly in opium. The moral influence of the Chinese, to a great extent, is felt throughout Annam. The Annamite language, it may be noted, is as complicated as the Chinese, and is extremely difficult for Europeans to learn.

The aborigines number among them the Khamouks, who are numerous, the Miaos (the Méos of the French), and the Muongs. The Khamouks have no knowledge of writing, but communicate with each other and keep accounts by means of small pieces of bamboo, in which notches are cut to express different meanings. They are great opium smokers. The Méos, found chiefly in the mountainous regions of North Tongking, are a handsome race, tall and strong, the women small and pleasing. The men are more industrious than the Muongs, and from the method in which they dress their hair in front are called "Unicorns" by the French missionaries. The inhabitants of the mountainous regions generally differ greatly from those of the delta, and particularly so the Muongs, the aboriginal race conquered by the Annamites, whose women do not blacken their teeth. These Muongs are probably in great part of mixed Chinese and Malay descent. They are taller and stronger than the Annamites, and, having a more open expression of countenance, make a better impression on Europeans, but are neither so intelligent nor eager for work or gain. Their social and administrative organization is primitive, the only authority they recognize being that of their hereditary chiefs, and they absolutely decline to submit to taxation. In their small and isolated villages in the mountains they have been exposed on the one hand to the attacks of Chinese malefactors, and on the other to those of the pirates and bandits, to whom they have been forced to give asylum and food. They thus brought themselves under the displeasure of the French, who, to vindicate their authority, have destroyed the Muong villages, previously sacked by the Chinese outlaws. The delta is still largely infested by pirates, notwithstanding many years of operations against them. Although now comparatively quiet, the country, and especially the delta, was, till quite recent years, in a most unsettled condition, the pirates being much dreaded, and the French troops almost powerless against them. To restore order, the French had recourse to the help of the *linh-co*, a kind of militia, the members of which are provided by the different villages, on certain conditions, and are placed at the disposal of the mandarins, from among whom the officers are selected. In 1895 the number of *linh-co* had been greatly reduced, but even now the pirates still give a considerable amount of trouble. The government officials, too, are continually changed, and the general policy pursued with regard to *les pirates* is vacillating in the extreme. It is necessary that France should have a vigorous policy, an organized administration, and be feared by her neighbors, Siam and China. It seems, indeed, impossible to crush the pirates. It has been said by Frenchmen who know the country that to subdue them one must go to Peking, or at any rate to Canton. The meaning of this is obvious, when it is explained that the pirates sometimes employ regular Chinese troops, and this with the knowledge of the neighboring Chinese authorities, as the French are well aware. In the delta all the villages are protected from attack by thick bamboo hedges and trenches, access being thus rendered difficult. In the mountainous regions, also, the hamlets are similarly fortified, entrance being only by a few doors, closed at night.

The climate of Tongking, like the people, varies greatly, the summer being too hot for Europeans. In the delta in summer the heat and the rain give rise to dysentery and sun-stroke, especially among the troops. In the hill country dangerous fevers are common, while the more southern provinces are said to be extremely unhealthy. The seasons may be divided into "rainy" and "dry." During the former the atmosphere is hot and humid, being the warmer period; the immense heat is occasionally tempered by monsoons. The dry season (from October till the end of March) is the Tongkingese "winter."

The trade of the country, as has been said, is very far from having reached its fullest development. The internal trade, indeed, is almost entirely in the hands of the Chinese, the external trade centring in Hong-Kong.*

* *Imports*—Opium (from Yunnan), tea (also greatly from Yunnan), Chinese pottery, Chinese and Japanese paper, Japanese matches, tobacco, sugar, flour (from America and Australia), coal, wine and beer (from England), textile fabrics, jewelry, furniture, arms and ammunition, toys, timber (from America and the Philippines), salted meats, tinned beef and mutton, tinned milk, cotton and woollen goods, iron, copper, and other metals, etc.

Exports—The greater part of the produce is bought by the Chinese and exported to Hong-Kong, the exports chiefly consisting of rice paddy, haricots, raw and floss silk and silk fabrics, horns, gum-lake, fish, cotton, etc., and timber (including bamboo) to some extent. The export of oil might be further developed.

The French have evidently not utilized the admirable position occupied by them in Tongking, nor the advantages as regards China from a commercial point of view. The gifted Louis de Carné wrote in 1878, shortly before his death: "The force of circumstances, and the weakness of the Chinese themselves" (this was during the Mussulman rebellion in Yunnan), "enable us to foresee the dismemberment of that ancient empire. In the presence of such an eventuality France should be prepared. Her part is traced out by the position which she already holds on the Annamite Peninsula. It is absolutely necessary that she should exercise a paramount influence at Tongking, which is for her *the key of China*, and that, without hurrying by any impatience the course of events, she should show her flag to the people whose protectorate may some day fall into her hands. . . . Perspectives full of the deepest interest and attraction open from Saigon, beyond the mountains of Tongking, over the fertile and healthy countries of Western China and Tibet. Fortune, which has so often made us pay for her favors of a day by lasting betrayal, appears to have become less cruel." Many distinguished Frenchmen have since urged that steps should be taken to take advantage of the position, but in vain.

The issues involved by the expedition to Tongking were absolutely uncomprehended by the French public. Blinded by the dream of the easy creation of a vast Indo-Chinese empire, the moment was thought to be opportune for the birth of a *France Nouvelle*. The annexation was regarded as a mere *bagatelle*, not involving the discharge of a single musket, and the idea of anything more than a mere armed expedition—a campaign, an adventure—was ridiculed. The French have had the Chinese and then the Tongkingese and Annamites to deal with, and between them and China the hardy and resolute hill tribes, who have to this day remained unsubdued before the most absorbing nation in the world—the Chinese.

Notwithstanding these difficulties, a general survey of the position of Tongking at the present day compels the conclusion that the progress made is altogether incommensurate with the opportunities afforded to France by the exceptional natural resources of Tongking and its admirable situation, which amply justified De Carné in calling it the "Key of China."

CHAPTER XX

CONCLUSIONS

BEFORE stating the conclusions arrived at, it may be well here to briefly recall the general course of the writer's travels, as dealt with in the present volume.

Having traversed Siberia as far as the present railway terminus, China was entered from Russian territory; Peking was revisited; coming south, the Yangtsze was ascended to the navigation limit in Szechuan, whence the provinces of Kweichau and Yunnan were crossed, and the journey completed by a march through Tongking. Unusual opportunities were afforded the writer of judging of the conditions of these countries, more especially of the state of China, with the normal conditions of which he was already familiar. Everything observed during the whole course of the journey confirmed the belief that China is breaking up at lightning speed.

In contact with foreign powers by land and sea the Chinese government has lost its supremacy, its vitality, the ability to defend its possessions. Abandoning bit by bit the territory on its land frontiers north and south, and on its seaboard, internal China is rapidly passing into anarchy.

CONCLUSIONS

When, in 1895, Japan shattered the naval and military defences of the empire, the extremity of China was the opportunity for certain foreign powers, and was promptly utilized. Russia appropriated the great territory of Manchuria with its hundreds of miles of seaboard and its ice-free ports, magnificent resources, and fine hardy population. Germany took Kiao Chau and assumed an exclusive control of the province of Shantung with its valuable minerals and fine people. Russia then acquired the Liao Tung peninsula, with Port Arthur, Talienwan, and other ports; Great Britain obtained Wei-Hai-Wei, and Kaulung; France acquired important territorial and economic rights in the south, with permission to penetrate Southwest China by a railway, which is to effect junction on the Upper Yangtsze with railways advancing from the Russian territory in the north; Japan has her eye on Fukien province, facing Formosa; even Italy attempted to seize a slice of territory. Meanwhile entire provinces, especially in the Yangtsze region, are seething with revolt, which meets with hardly any opposition. Nominally still alive and in full operation, the organism of the Chinese government is hardly perceptible, and is unable to cope with foreign aggressions, barely sufficing to keep in restraint the three hundred and fifty millions of its own people. The most cursory glance at any map, showing the railway schemes and spheres of interest or influence, or whatever they may be called, of foreign powers, must shatter any belief in a responsible or organic government in China. The trail of the foreigner is on the land from north to south. The Western powers have come to stay, and the extension of the present spheres is merely a matter of time. Internally, the forces making for rebellion on a grand scale are daily gaining strength, and once they realize that no power exists to suppress them, will usurp in vast regions the office of government. In a word, China is being dismembered and broken up.

Since the close of the Chino-Japanese war there has been a succession of varying and at times opposite policies on the part of Great Britain, the spirit of resistance having alternated with the spirit of benevolence. First came the suggestion to Russia that she should take an "ice-free port." Then on Russia's approach to Port Arthur there was something like an ultimatum accompanied by the presence at Port Arthur of British men-of-war. This was succeeded by a fresh fit of compromise. The ships departed, and the Russians occupied Port Arthur. Once more the government became bold, and insisted on China ceding Wei-Hai-Wei and Kaulung. Afterwards came various questions of concessions; at one time the British government was firm and the Russians conciliatory; then the attitudes seemed to be reversed. Finally there was a compromise, which apparently is an agreement to let things continue as hitherto. There is no trace throughout the whole course of events of the past few years of any indication of a plan thought out to meet the exigencies of the case. No such plan has been announced; none can be detected either in the official papers or in what has actually occurred. A policy was indeed announced, based on the idea of preventing annexations by other powers, of abstention from British annexations, and of free trade for all. But the other powers had begun to annex, and could not be stopped; Great Britain shortly found herself following their example; and the "open door" was manifestly a doctrine that could not be enforced except as far as the other powers might please. This visionary scheme has been abandoned, but has not been succeeded by any comprehensive plan. Meanwhile, in the Yangtsze Valley, the so-called British sphere, disorder is rife, and no step has been announced which looks like part of a plan for protecting British interests. Important railway and mining concessions both in Northern and in Central China have been obtained for British syndicates, but the value of these concessions is extremely doubtful. The position appears to be that Great Britain has obtained from the Chinese government, in the form of treaty rights and of concessions to British subjects, a number of legal or legitimate bases for claims in China—claims to build and manage railways, to open and work mines, to navigate rivers, to trade at certain ports, etc.—but that nearly all these claims will prove to be of no practical value unless they are made good by actual enforcement. They are legal titles against all the world, but in order to be effective must be made good by action—perhaps by force.

The interests of the United States and Britain, and to a large extent Japan, are mainly identical: to keep as much as possible of what remains of China as an open market. The active diplomatic co-operation of the United States with Britain is a matter of direct and vital interest to both, in case of war Britain merely requiring the benevolent neutrality of the States. But the support of British policy by either the States or Japan depends upon the strength and determination of Britain herself, who has eight-tenths of the interests in the Far East. To be strong, Britain, sea-girt like Japan, must alter her military system to proportions commensurate with her scattered world-wide empire. Strong and determined, Britain will have friends and allies; irresolute and weak, she will have none. Strong and determined—only then can she come to an arrangement with Russia.

The policy of Germany in the Far East is and must be, dependent on the basis of her world-policy—a good understanding with Russia—and it is idle for the British to expect Germany, now the neighbor of Russia in Asia, as in Europe, to depart from that programme. Her policy, like that of Japan, is opportunist, but, unlike Japan, she is committed, by force of circumstances, to Russia.

As for the present attitude of Japan, it may be defined as one of masterly preparation. The disposition of Japanese of all classes is to avoid foreign alliances as entangling and unreliable, and to depend upon themselves, utilizing the opportunities which are likely to occur through the dissensions of foreign Western powers. The party in Japan, once influential, favoring co-operation with Britain is now dwindling. Bent on having, as a *quid pro quo*, a binding guarantee against the risks attending an alliance with Britain, they observed that, while there was plenty of loose talk in England about such an understanding, the government evinced a dread of committing itself in the matter. They noted the irresolution and want of a determined line of action, and they entertained grave doubts as to whether the British government, swayed by a fickle democracy, could be counted on in case of her commerce suffering severely through the strain of war. There is also a growing belief that Britain is irresolute because she herself feels doubtful as to her power to defend her interests in Asia. Britain's power at sea they acknowledge, but that they believe to be *relatively* declining, for Russia and Germany, already the most powerful military nations in the world, are now making abnormal efforts to also become sea-powers on a grand scale, and Japan herself is making the greatest sacrifices to equip herself as a maritime power. And while these military nations are trying to turn themselves into sea-powers, Britain is doing nothing to build up an efficient army, as a counter-balance, or even to increase her naval strength on a commensurate scale. The land forces of Britain the Japanese look upon with disdain. Compared with the German military engine of war, admirably devised and in perfect working order, the military system of Britain, with its small paid force broken up for service in many quarters of the world, seems hardly worth consideration, and as a nation, of which every man bears arms, they are not greatly impressed by the patriotism of Britain. Encouraged by Russians, Germans, and French—and even by Americans—in their growing disbelief as to the fighting power and will of Britain, the drifting and irresolute policy of the past few years confirmed them in the opinion that she could not be counted on to undertake and prosecute a war against Russia, still less against Russia and France; that her wars, with their cheap glory, were only with hill tribes or Soudanese, and that she was unable to stand against a power like Russia. The moral drawn from the events in South Africa is not likely to lessen the growing want of confidence felt by the Japanese in Britain. If, they say, Britain finds such difficulty in dealing with some sixty thousand peasant farmers, what stand can she be expected to make against, say, the Franco-Russian forces by land and sea?

The year 1902, or 1903 at latest, will see European Russia connected by the iron road with Vladivostok and Port Arthur; and the New Siberia, which must be held to include Manchuria, will have fully entered on its great career as the coming country of the twentieth century. Russia will be enabled to prosecute her plan; Corea and Northern

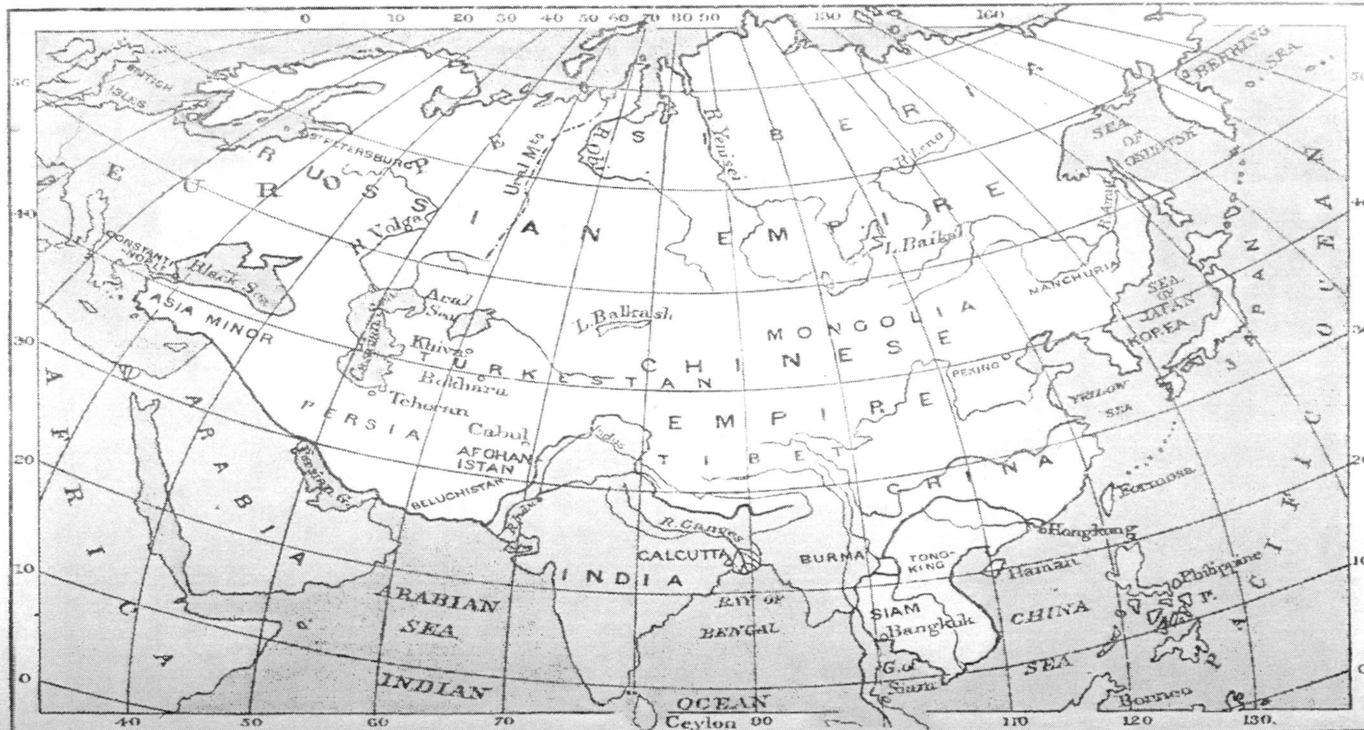

RUSSIAN ASIA.

To face page 112.

China will be acquired, and gradually, step by step, by means of railways (favored always by France in the south, and probably covertly, if not openly, by Germany in the north), she will extend her influence southward until the Yangtsze is reached, and there a connection made with the sphere of French influence.

Russia, whose strength has hitherto been entirely on land, now aspires to be a sea-power. And in Manchuria she has got coast, coal, and a maritime population—excellent material for making sailors—and her presence on the Pacific Ocean and the Chinese Sea must give a great impetus to the aspiration for a navy. It may be taken for granted that, having got so much, she will want more—ports in other quarters, in many quarters, of the globe.

Russia once on the Upper Yangtsze would involve a second, an eastern, Indian frontier problem for Britain of an infinitely more serious character than the western, for the utilization of the greater part of the resources of China would mean Russia hanging over India on the northeast, as she is now on the northwest, by sheer weight able to shake to its foundations the British rule in India. And in the Far East she would be supported by European allies.

Orientals instinctively divine weakness, and the Chinese already turn to Russia, the rising power. In their view Russia moves steadily forward, never turning aside, always keeps her promises and fulfils her threats; devotes her energies to a steady advance, and does not waste time in talking. Britain, they say, talks loudly of her rights, but is unable to enforce them; and, while showing keen displeasure at Russia's advance, has been unable to check it in the least degree, and is not prepared to stand to her word where her Northern rival is concerned. In diplomatic matters Russia lays down the law which England submissively accepts, and the Celestial looks upon Talienwan, Port Arthur, the Newchwang Railway loan, and the Peking-Hankau Railway as eloquent examples of the way in which Britain constantly challenges Russia and then gives way. Finally, they consider that Russia, because of her superior knowledge of facts and circumstances, and her singleness of purpose, is better equipped for the contest than Britain, who is conscious of her inferiority.

If such be the rapidly growing opinion throughout China, who shall venture to say that this belief is not already taking hold, imperceptibly as yet, of the subject races in India? And what will be the effect if this process be continued until one day Russia is mistress of China, as well as paramount in Afghanistan and Persia? On the northeastern frontier Britain can only defend India by introducing a counterbalance in China itself, by developing the Yangtsze basin, which contains the greater part of the resources of the empire and half its population, and by controlling Southwest China, where lies the access to Burma, and, through Burma, to India. This would afford Britain a proper base and line of defence on the Upper Yangtsze, which, combined with her sea-power and the control of the great Chinese waterway, would enable her to hold her own.

How to oppose by means of diplomacy, and if necessary by force of arms, the policy of Russia and France, not improbably supported covertly by Germany—that is the problem which faces Britain and must be of immense consequence to the United States. Both countries are not only behindhand in all special, essential information, but they have been indifferent where interest and enthusiasm alone can move their governments, which are still without any consistent plan. Such a plan must take into consideration the condition of China, the action of foreign powers, and the entirely new conditions arising in Asia—chief of these being the New Siberia.

There is no disguising the fact that a period of intense and increasing energy is about to begin and must be met by preparedness, to be ready for a conflict which is more than probable. It is time, therefore, that Britain and the United States should interest themselves and decide on some common plan.

INDEX

INDEX

INDEX

INDEX

THE END